The Comedy of Menander

The Comedy of Menander

Convention, Variation and Originality

Netta Zagagi

Indiana University Press

Bloomington and Indianapolis

Manufactured in Great Britain

Library of Congress Cataloging-in-Publication Data

Zagagi, Netta.
   The comedy of Menander : convention, variation, and originality /
Netta Zagagi.
     p. cm.
   Includes bibliographical references (p.   ).
   ISBN 0-253-36851-0
   1. Menander, of Athens–Criticism and interpretation. 2. Greek
drama (Comedy)–History and criticism. I. Title.
   PA4247.Z19 1995
   882'.01–dc20   94-30098

Contents

To the memory of my father,

the biblical scholar

PERETZ SANDLER

Preface

Until the beginning of this century Menander was one of the majority of classical authors known to us, who have survived only in a few fragments and testimonia. Classical scholars were reduced to studying the Latin adaptations of Plautus and Terence in order to obtain some picture of what might have been his dramatic technique. The discovery in papyri, between 1908 and 1992, of whole scenes and parts of scenes from a number of his plays, and especially the discovery in 1959 of an almost complete play – *Dyskolos* – have changed the picture beyond recognition. We can now investigate much of Menander's manner of composing a comedy on the basis of first-hand Menandrian materials, and compare him more properly with his Latin adapters.

This book is based almost entirely on the new Menandrian texts discovered in the papyri. It deals with Plautus and Terence only occasionally, and mainly for the sake of comparison and contrast with Menander himself. It is understandable that, as long as we had virtually no writings of Menander in Greek, Menandrian scholars concentrated on the second best, the Latin adaptations. Out of sheer inertia, a number of Menandrian scholars have continued to treat Plautus and Terence as if they were almost first-hand evidence, even during and after the discoveries of extensive new materials in Greek. In this book, I have followed a tendency in some recent works of scholarship, attempting to interpret Menander out of Menander, and using the Latin adaptations mainly for filling gaps and for highlighting differences.

The discussion combines a literary analysis of the Menandrian texts with comparisons between Menander and other Greek authors – mainly dramatists like himself – who influenced or may have influenced him. I have also used materials known to us of the laws, customs and social life in Menander's Athens, in order to bring out the social aspects of Menander's characters and their behaviour in the dramatic context of each of his plays, an issue which has not generally attracted the attention it deserves. This way of studying the social background to Menander's plays has helped me to view the problem of realism or the lack of it in the best-preserved comedies – a cardinal issue in Menandrian scholarship – in a new light. Much of the book concentrates on the analysis of individual plays and on the relation between the divine speaker of the prologue and the plot of the play itself as part of the more general discussion of Menander's realism.

This book is not meant to be a general survey of all aspects of Menandrian comedy. One major aspect of Menandrian comedy which I have treated as subsidiary to my main discussion is the stage production of the plays, although I do refer constantly to Menander's audience and its expectations of his dramas, and devote a whole chapter to the question of the dramatic behaviour of the chorus.

Since the book is meant to be read not only by experts on the Greek text, my discussion of linguistic and textual issues is restricted to passages in which such issues are essential for the understanding of literary and dramatic problems. For the sake of readers who are not experts on the Greek (and the Latin) text, translations of all passages are provided.

Chapter I (pp. 35-8) includes an abridged, revised version of my paper '*Exilium amoris* in New Comedy' published in *Hermes* 116 (1988) 193-209. My discussion of *Dyskolos* in Chapter V is a revised version of a paper first published in a volume of studies in Hebrew in honour of Prof. S. Perlman, formerly Head of the Department of Classics, Tel-Aviv University (*Commentationes ad antiquitatem classicam eiusque hereditatem pertinentes docto viro emerito Shalom Perlman Seminarii Philologici Praesidi ab amicis, collegis discipulisque cura W.Z. Rubinsohn – H. Roisman dedicatae* (Tel-Aviv, 1989) 163-79. Chapter VI is a revised version of my paper 'Divine Interventions and Human Agents in Menander', published in *Relire Ménandre* (ed. E.W. Handley and A. Hurst; Genève, 1990) 63-91.

*

It gives me great pleasure to be able to record my gratitude to scholars and friends who have helped me in various ways in the writing of this book. First and foremost, my thanks are due to Sir Hugh Lloyd-Jones for encouraging me to embark on this voyage round Menander as well as for his constant stimulation and support. His pertinent criticisms of successive drafts have saved me from many errors. I am deeply grateful to Mr P.G. McC. Brown for reading and commenting on an earlier version and for generously allowing me to make use of his unpublished translations of Terence as well as other materials. He offered many valuable suggestions from which I profited a great deal. Special thanks are due to my colleague Prof. John Glucker, who took a lively interest in my work and spent many hours on the text. He has drawn my attention to points of both form and content, given all possible help in correcting language and style and done much in general to improve the book. I am indebted to my colleagues in Tel-Aviv University: Dr Shlomo Biderman, Head of the Shirley and Leslie Porter School of Cultural Studies, for assisting with incredible kindness in the successive printings of the entire manuscript and for patiently guiding me through the technicalities of using the computer; Prof. Benjamin Isaac, Head of the Aranne School of History, for facilitating the typing and xeroxing of an earlier draft; Prof. Zeev Rubin, Prof. Miriam Eliav-Feldon of the Department of History, and my friend Mrs Elisheva Steckel for sparing the time and effort needed to help me at the early stages of my work.

I gratefully acknowledge awards from the Faculty of Humanities, Tel-Aviv University, including a publishing grant from the Ruth Sheffy (Shafrir) Fund. Acknowledgments are also due to Wolfson College, Oxford, La Fondation Hardt pour l'Étude de l'Antiquité Classique for their hospitality; and to the staff of the Ashmolean Museum Library for their never-failing assistance.

Lastly, I would like to express my deep sense of gratitude to my family, and especially to my husband Gadi, for bearing with me so gracefully during the long and difficult period of writing. To his love, constant help and support this book ultimately owes its existence.

My father, who initiated me into the mysteries of the classical world and took an exceptionally lively interest in my work, died shortly after I became seriously involved in Menandrian studies. In dedicating this book to his memory I sadly acknowledge an enormous debt – as a daughter as well as a scholar.

Tel-Aviv, 1994   N.Z.

References and Abbreviations

The names of ancient writers and the titles of their works are abbreviated generally as in *L&S* and *LSJ* (for Menander, Plautus and Terence, see below). Periodicals are abbreviated generally as in *L'Année Philologique*.

Modern works listed in the bibliography are cited in the notes by author and dates only.

Unless otherwise indicated, all translations are my own. The following translators of the comic texts are cited by name only:

Arnott (= W.G. Arnott 1979*b*)
Bain (= D.M. Bain 1983*b*)
Barsby (= J.A. Barsby 1986)
Brothers (= A.J. Brothers 1988)
Brown (= P.G. McC. Brown, unpublished translations)
Hunter (= R.L. Hunter 1985)
Miller (= N. Miller 1987)
Nixon (= P. Nixon 1916-38)

Where no indication is given, references to Menander follow the Oxford text, and its numeration, of F.H. Sandbach (*Menandri Reliquiae Selectae* (2nd edn, 1990). Other Menandrian fragments and testimonia are quoted from Körte's *Menandri quae supersunt, pars altera* (2nd edn, rev. by A. Thierfelder; Leipzig, 1959). The edition of Körte and Thierfelder is indicated by 'K.-T.'. References to the surviving plays of Aristophanes follow the numeration of the Budé edition of V. Coulon and H. Van Daele (*Aristophane* [Paris, 1923-30; corrected reprints of individual volumes, Paris, 1963-]). References of the form '[author] fr. [ ] K.-A.' are to R. Kassel's and C. Austin's *Poetae Comici Graeci* (Berlin & New York, 1983-). Other fragments of Greek comedy are cited from C. Austin's *Comicorum Graecorum Fragmenta in Papyris Reperta* (Berlin & New York, 1973), indicated by 'Austin, *CGFPR*'. The plays of Plautus are cited generally from the Oxford Classical Text of W.M. Lindsay (*T. Macci Plauti comoediae*), those of Terence, from the Oxford Classical Text of R. Kauer and W.M. Lindsay (*P. Terenti Afri comoediae*).

The following abbreviations are used for Menander's plays and the Latin adaptations of Plautus and Terence:

Menander
> *Asp.* = *Aspis*
> *Dis Ex.* = *Dis Exapaton*
> *Dysk.* = *Dyskolos*
> *Epitr.* = *Epitrepontes*
> *Mis.* = *Misoumenos*
> *Perik.* = *Perikeiromene*
> *Sam.* = *Samia*
> *Sik.* = *Sikyonios*

Plautus
> *Asin.* = *Asinaria*
> *Aul.* = *Aulularia*
> *Bacch.* = *Bacchides*
> *Capt.* = *Captivi*
> *Cas.* = *Casina*
> *Cist.* = *Cistellaria*
> *Curc.* = *Curculio*
> *Men.* = *Menaechmi*
> *Merc.* = *Mercator*
> *Mil.* = *Miles Gloriosus*
> *Most.* = *Mostellaria*
> *Pers.* = *Persa*
> *Poen.* = *Poenulus*
> *Pseud.* = *Pseudolus*
> *Rud.* = *Rudens*
> *Stich.* = *Stichus*
> *Trin.* = *Trinummus*
> *Truc.* = *Truculentus*

Terence
> *Ad.* = *Adelphoe*
> *And.* = *Andria*
> *Eun.* = *Eunuchus*
> *Heaut.* = *Heautontimoroumenos*
> *Hec.* = *Hecyra*
> *Phorm.* = *Phormio*

I

Convention and Variation

Any attempt to characterize Menander's approach to the literary traditions he inherited from his predecessors and from his contemporaries would require us first to throw off the modern tendency to attach too much importance to originality in evaluating the artistic achievements of a specific writer or poet. This tendency was never an important component of the ancient conception of the nature of the literary work. On the contrary, variations on a given theme were far more likely to stimulate the imagination, and the more complex and comprehensive the link between the individual work and the literary tradition from which it sprang, the greater were the prospects of the writer winning praise and recognition for his work.[1]

This applies in particular to the genre of New Comedy, in which convention in plot, characters, situations, performance and costumes is of the essence. Satyros, the Peripatetic biographer, discussing the special contribution of Euripides to the formation of the tradition of New Comedy, stresses the conservative nature of that genre, which was at the height of its popularity in his day:

> ... confrontations between husband and wife, father and son, slave and master; unexpected changes of circumstances, rape of virgins, exposure of children, recognition through rings and necklaces – these are, no doubt, the main components of New Comedy, and it was Euripides who had brought them to perfection.
>
> (*Vita Euripidis, P.Oxy*. 1176, fr. 39 [col. vii])

The little which has reached us of the huge body of creative works of New Comedy supports this assumption concerning the special role played by convention[2] in the theatrical experience of Menander's audience – a fact which the modern reader at times finds hard to accept. 'The ultimate impression of the New Comedy,' writes Post, 'despite Antiphanes's exaltation of its invention above that of tragedy, which draws upon the store of mythology (fr. 191K = fr. 189K.-A.), is even more unrelieved than that of classic Italian opera, although, fortunately, the similarity of plot does not result in so ludicrously small a vocabulary.'[3]

Nothing could have been further removed from the attitude of the contemporary Athenian spectator to this dramatic genre than this description of the hypothetical response of the modern theatre-goer. The ancient spectator – like the viewers of twentieth-century Westerns – preferred to build up his expectations upon familiar territory, rather than grope in the dark in the mysterious world of a writer who is cut off from traditional patterns of thought, and creates his situations from scratch.

It was this special relationship between the writer and his audience – the result of a literary tradition developed over many years – that Menander had to take into consideration in his competitive struggle for success. He did not belong to that small group of creative thinkers and writers who left their mark on the collective memory of the Greeks as *heuretai*, inventors, and there are no indications in his works that he ever attempted to be creative in this fashion. On the contrary, the ancient sources treat him as a conventional writer not afraid to repeat formulae over and over again – formulae which had proved their potential for success. Thus Plutarch, discussing the moral aspect of his work, comments on the stereotyped endings of his plays:

> … the deflowerings of virgins end decently in marriage. As for the prostitutes, if they are audacious and bold, the affairs are cut short by punishments of some kind or by repentance on the part of the young man; but if they are good and return a man's love, either a father is discovered for them who is a citizen or some extra time is allowed for their affair, which brings a humane relationship of respect.
>
> (*Mor.* 712C = K.-T., *Testimonia* 42)[4]

Terence notes the almost total similarity between the plays *Andria* and *Perinthia*:

> Menander wrote two plays, *The Girl from Andros* and *The Girl from Perinthos*. The man who knows either of them properly

will know both of them; they are not so very different in plot, but they are written in different words and style.

(*And.* 9-12 Brown)

On the other hand, Menander apparently went so far in relying on earlier traditions that this in itself was perceived as plagiarism. Aristophanes of Byzantium, a great admirer of Menander, wrote a book called *Parallels to Menander and a selection of the sources from which he stole*. This would appear to have been a naive attempt to pinpoint the sources of the admired writer's inspiration, which 'inadvertently exposed his weakness for theft'.[5] A less innocent attempt may be found in the six volumes Latinus wrote on the *Non-Menandrian Elements in Menander* – in which he revealed 'the full extent of his lifting'.[6]

Then there is the evidence of the Roman comic playwright Caecilius – himself an adapter of Menander's plays – who maintained that Menander's play *Deisidaimon* was in fact nothing but a transcription of Antiphanes' play *Oionistes* from beginning to end.[7]

Even the little we have of Menander's comedy contains ample evidence that he, while pursuing the only certain path open to a dramatist of New Comedy to prove his superiority over his rivals – i.e. to make varied attempts to introduce new elements into the framework of the comic tradition – did not hesitate to make purely conventional use of certain familiar and tried-and-true elements, both from his own previous works and from the works of others, if they served his artistic purposes. Thus, for example, the end of the prologue to the play *Sikyonios* – 'The details / you'll see, if you like; but do like!' (23-4) – is virtually identical with the end of Pan's narrative in the prologue to the play *Dyskolos* (45-6).[8] Undoubtedly these lines are a standard formula, as are the lines with which these two plays end:

May laughter-loving Victory, daughter of a noble line,
attend us with her favour all our days!

(*Dysk.* 968-9; cf. *Sik.* 422-3)[9]

Let us have a few other examples. The comic moment resulting from the complaint of the slave Getas upon his entrance on stage in Act III of *Dyskolos*, about the heavy load he was forced to carry – 'Damn the women!/ They fastened up four donkey-loads for me/ to carry!' (402-4 Arnott) – is as old as the opening scene of Aristophanes' *Frogs*, and in the form in which it appears in Menander, it bear no marks of innovation.[10]

The two soldiers Thrasonides and Polemon appear in Act V of *Misoumenos* and *Perikeiromene* respectively, each anxious about the outcome of his love affair (*Perik*. 976ff.; *Mis*. 259ff.). Both these scenes take place after the beloved, in each play, has unexpectedly discovered or identified her father, and from then on, the main issue, in both plays, is how to bring about the reconciliation between the lovers, to be followed by marriage. Despite the different causes of the lovers' quarrels – in *Perikeiromene* it is Polemon's violent jealousy of his beloved, and in *Misoumenos* it appears to be Krateia's suspicion that Thrasonides is responsible for the death of her brother – Menander chooses to show the response of the soldiers to the new situation in virtually identical terms. The gradual way in which each of them is informed that his deepest wish is to be realized – first, by a secondary character (the slave Getas in *Misoumenos*, and the maid Doris in *Perikeiromene*), and then by the girl's father himself – shows a preference for the conventional solution, once the elements of tension and the emotional potential of the plot have been exhausted by the end of the previous act.

The same applies to the hasty decision of Pataikos in *Perikeiromene* to marry off his son Moschion, shortly after the reunion of his family (1025f.). There is nothing in the earlier part of the plot that would lead up to this decision, which comes towards the end of the play. Nor is there any justification for regarding it as an artificial attempt by Menander to do 'poetic justice' to his reckless hero, whom he has earlier presented as having fallen in love with Glykera, unaware that she is his sister. What we have here is a conventional expression of the restored authority of Pataikos, the father, over his son, whom he has just discovered. In accordance with the authentic norms of Athenian life, Moschion is forced into one of the traditional endings to New Comedy – i.e. *gamos*, marriage.

Another conventional scene of this nature, which is more justified in dramatic terms, may be found in the decision of Chremes to force marriage upon his son Clitipho at the end of Terence's play *Heautontimoroumenos* (1056ff.), an adaptation of Menander's play of the same title.

This conventional aspect of Menander, which might be designated as non-creative, should be regarded as an essential constituent in the works of a playwright striving to reach out to the taste of his audience. He does it within the limitations of a specific genre, and he is fully aware of the scope of action allowed him within these limits, from a mere repetition of familiar elements in various combinations to original variations which breathe new life into a hackneyed tradition. In this chapter I shall try to examine some of the more significant ways in which Menander's creativity found an outlet for itself, within the limitations imposed on him by tradition. This will enable the reader to form a balanced evaluation of the nature of Menander's works before we examine them in detail.[11]

Let us begin by considering the placing of parallel situations in the different plays. We have seen that Menander does not hesitate to use the same elements repeatedly in order to build up his plot. This use of repetition,[12] which is in itself conventional, can become a powerful and versatile dramatic tool, if these similar elements are placed differently in each play, thus determining their relative importance in the general pattern of the respective plots.

Let us take as an example a situation which seems to be one of Menander's favourites, that of the false suspicion of a love affair, or of some erotic intentions. At the end of Act I in *Dyskolos*, the slave Daos witnesses a brief and innocent encounter between Sostratos and Knemon's daughter. Since this encounter does not fit in with accepted social norms,[13] it is only natural that suspicions are aroused in Daos as to the purity of Sostratos' intentions, and he hurries to report to his master Gorgias, the girl's step-brother, on the threat to her honour.

That encounter and its social implications become the subject of dialogue between Daos and Gorgias at the opening of Act II, and, later on, between Gorgias and Sostratos himself, who returns to the scene after a brief absence. Sostratos is thus given a chance to clear himself of the suspicion of evil intentions and, already at this point, in the early stages of the second act (which could be regarded as belonging to the exposition),[14] we come to the end of this particular plot line, which had begun towards the end of Act I. The momentary suspicion of a love affair is used by Menander to establish a link between Sostratos and Gorgias, whose friendship is to be one of the most important elements in the major plot. Here Menander has managed to make use of the brief misunderstanding that has arisen, by solving it in such a way as to lead to the development of a significant relationship between two of the major protagonists.[15]

In *Misoumenos*, the same situation is secondary both in significance and in its timing in the play. Here, the character suspected of undesirable erotic intentions is Demeas, father of Krateia, who is prisoner and mistress of the soldier Thrasonides. Getas, Thrasonides' slave, spots Demeas embracing his daughter, whom he has just found after a separation forced upon them by war. At the same time Getas is unaware of the paternal relationship and does just what would be expected of him to protect his master's interests:

> Hey, what's this? This woman – what's she got to do with you,
> sir? You there, what are you doing? *(aside)* Didn't I say so?
> I have caught this man red-handed – the very man I was
> looking for. He looks old and grey, about sixty,
> but all the same he'll live to regret the day.
> You there – who do you think you are hugging and kissing?
>
> (216-21)[16]

Krateia is quick to point out his error, telling him that the old man is none other than her own father. This brief exchange between Getas and Demeas is enough to remove the last remaining vestiges of misunderstanding, and the slave, now equipped with this fresh information, goes off to brief his master, this time with the true facts, namely that Krateia has found her father.

This scene takes place in Act III, *after* the central dramatic event (the hoped-for encounter between Demeas and his daughter) has already occurred. Since we are dealing here with two characters, both of whom are aware of their family relationship (Demeas-Krateia) and a third one (Getas) who has a direct link with one of them (Krateia) – as distinct from the position of Daos in *Dyskolos*, who has no such links – any attempt to develop the element of suspicion beyond that single scene would have been superfluous, and dubious in terms of its dramatic value. Furthermore, such an attempt would have unnecessarily diverted the plot from its intended course – namely the reunion of Demeas and Krateia with the lost son and brother (Kleinias?). Within these limitations, the unfounded suspicion assumes its proper place – as an *ad hoc* comic means to soften the emotional impact of the encounter between father and daughter.

In contrast to the two plays discussed, in *Perikeiromene* the same element may be found in the initial situation of the play as presented by the goddess *Agnoia* in the prologue. Sosias, slave to the soldier Polemon – or perhaps Polemon himself – has spotted Moschion, son of their neighbour Myrrhine, kissing Glykera, Polemon's mistress.[17] Since neither Sosias nor Polemon know that Moschion is the girl's brother, they reach the erroneous conclusion that an affair is going on behind Polemon's back. This erroneous assumption – and the violence it brings out in Polemon (a violence inspired by the goddess *Agnoia*)[18] – are the main motifs of the plot and run through it from beginning to end.

Our final example comes from *Samia*. At the start of Act III, Demeas tells the audience that he has seen Chrysis breast-feeding what appears to be Moschion's baby. He suspects that his adopted son is having an affair behind his back with his own concubine. Though in this case what Demeas is witnessing is not an encounter between Moschion and Chrysis, the situation presented to us is of the same type as those we have described in the earlier plays. As in *Perikeiromene*, we are dealing here with an event of decisive importance to the plot development, indeed a direct result of the opening situation as described in Moschion's introductory monologue (21ff.).[19] This time, Menander places the event at the very centre of the play – the opening of Act III, a juncture in the play from which it becomes the starting-point for the comic misunderstandings that are about to unfold between Demeas and Moschion, and Demeas and Chrysis, as well as a significant and surprising turning-point *vis-à-vis* the preceding chain of events.[20] This dual function of the element of suspicion in *Samia*, resulting from its central placing in the play, provides clear evidence of Menander's conscious approach to the conventions which form the basis of his work.

From the above examples,[21] it is clear that the intrinsic dramatic value of the familiar scene is determined largely by the nature of the protagonists in any particular play. You do not get the same theatrical comic effect from an unknown young man being mistakenly suspected of intending to seduce a girl, as you do from a father or brother being suspected of such intentions towards their own kin, or from a son believed to have such intentions towards the mistress of his adoptive father. Realizing this simple fact, Menander uses the

technique of depicting the familiar scene with different protagonists[22] – unless plot considerations oblige him to do otherwise.[23]
Thus, in a series of radically different plays, he makes the most of
the potential inherent in this basic formula.

An impressive example of the successful use of a conventional
element, involving an intermingling of protagonists from different
social backgrounds, in order to achieve a particular dramatic effect,
may be found in the above-mentioned encounter between Sostratos
and Knemon's daughter.

In form and theme, this encounter could be compared to the
meeting of Ampelisca with Sceparnio in Plautus' play *Rudens*
(414ff.), which in itself is an adaptation of a lost play by Menander's
older contemporary Diphilos.[24] In both cases, a girl trying to fill her
pitcher of water gets help from a young stranger who is bowled over
by her beauty. But whereas in Plautus, the protagonists are slaves,
Menander has the scene involve Athenian citizens of free origin.

This distinction is important: the Diphilian version does not
involve any stage situation that would not correspond to the Athenian norms of everyday life. Since the protagonists are slaves, there
is nothing wrong, from the point of view of accepted conventions,
with their behaving freely with each other. That allows for the
vulgar merriment of this scene, which Plautus uses for his own
purposes by exaggerating various elements in it.[25] But in *Dyskolos*,
Menander attempts to present a situation which is a departure from
everyday norms, as part of the general atmosphere of the play,
particularly of the first act, of which this scene is one component.[26]

Knemon's daughter, as a free citizen whose duty it is to preserve
her virginity, is *not* free to make any contact, however limited, with
strangers. One might have expected both her and Sostratos to
honour this severe restriction on contacts between the sexes, but
Menander has chosen to present them in a different way.[27] It is
important to note how careful Menander is to show his characters
behaving with the utmost discretion in this innovative situation
(which, surely enough, comes in for criticism from Daos!),[28] as a
concession to the moral attitudes of his audience:

Girl: *(coming from Knemon's house, carrying a pitcher. She is
        unaware of Sostratos' presence at first.)*
      Oh, wretched me, what an ill fortune is mine!
      What would I do now? Nurse has dropped the bucket

down the well when she was drawing water.

So.: *(aside)* Oh, Father Zeus and Healer Apollo,
Oh, dear Dioscuri!
What irresistible beauty!

Girl: And Dad, on his way out, ordered me to heat some water.

So.: What a marvel, folks!

Girl: If he should learn about this, he'll beat her to death.
There's no time for useless chatter!
Dearest Nymphs, from *you* our water must be fetched.
I'd be ashamed, though, if there're people
sacrificing in there, to be a nuisance –

So.: *(coming forward)* But if you give the pitcher to me,
I'll dip it in water for you and bring it back straightway.

Girl: Oh, yes, by the gods, but do hurry!

So.: *(aside)* Country girl though she is, she has
the manners of a lady.[29] Oh, revered gods,
what divine power can save me now?
                    (goes into shrine)

Girl: Oh, wretched me, what was that noise? Is Dad coming?
I'll get a beating, if he catches me outside.
                    [Daos' part omitted]

So.: *(emerging from shrine with the pitcher full of water)*
Here, take it.

Girl: *(from her doorway)* Bring it over here.
                    (goes into house.)
                    [Daos' part omitted]

So.: Goodbye, and take care of your father.

                                        (189-213)[30]

New Comedy offers innumerable variations of the *anagnorisis* situation, of blood relations finding and recognizing each other after a separation forced upon then by circumstances.[31] Menander himself had a particular penchant for using this element in the solution to his plots.[32] The banality of this basic dramatic situation, which so fascinated many generations of Athenians, both in epic poetry, tragedy and comedy, forced the dramatist to reconsider every time the nature and the role of this scene in the context of each individual play. The following examples will suffice to demonstrate Menander's manifold approach to the problem, as further illustration of his inventiveness as playwright within a given genre.

The play *Sikyonios* contains two *anagnorisis* scenes. The first (280ff.) occurs in Act IV, between the soldier Stratophanes and his parents. Because of the fragmentary state of the extant text, it is not possible to determine precisely the content and form of the scene. It does, however, seem certain that at some stage, Stratophanes examines his tokens of recognition together with Smikrines and his wife – who later turn out to be his own parents.

Since we know from earlier parts of the play that the tokens were left to Stratophanes by his presumed mother before her death, together with a letter stating that he was not her real son, it was only logical to assume that the *anagnorisis* here was an event planned by Stratophanes who in some way had recognized Smikrines as his father, perhaps from the letter left by his presumed mother.[33] If that is so, then what we have here is the only known case in New Comedy, in which *all* the facts necessary for family reunion are known in advance and the *anagnorisis* comes about by the conscious choice of one of the parties. If indeed, as Webster suggests,[34] Stratophanes and his newly discovered parents now all go home to inform Moschion that Stratophanes, his rival for the hand of Philoumene, is actually his own brother – then this is the only case of an *anagnorisis* planned right through, from beginning to end.[35]

Of an entirely different nature is the second scene of *anagnorisis* in the same play – a scene which occurs in the next act (361ff.). This is how Webster sums up the events leading up to it:

> *Sc. 1.* Theron enters with a reluctant old man, whom he is trying to bribe into saying that he is the father of the girl. In his fury the old man gives his name and deme, Kichesias of Skambonidai. As Theron goes on with his coaching it becomes clear that the old man is in fact the father of the girl.
>
> *Sc. 2.* Dromon enters (361), saying 'My mistress is safe', and he is going on, 'Now I must find her father', when he recognises the old man as Kichesias. Kichesias faints, and Theron rushes into House B to fetch water and Stratophanes ...[36]

Everything here is ruled by coincidence. Furthermore, information about the background to the separation of father from daughter is not, as in other instances, provided in the form of facts which could help with the recognition,[37] but as a figment of the imagination of the parasite Theron which, by a rare combination of circumstances, tallies with the actual facts. Most important of all, the emotional effect of the situation is created not through a direct recognition between father and daughter (as we find, for example, in *Misoumenos* (210ff.)) but indirectly, between the father and the family slave Dromon – an unexpected twist which heightens interest in the *topos* while diminishing the opportunities for the sentimentality which is latent in the scene. Only after the identity of Kichesias is determined does Menander turn his attention to the main issue:

Dr.: Your daughter has been found,
      she has been saved from death.
Ki.: And is she safe with honour, Dromon,
      or is she simply safe?[38]
Dr.: She is still a virgin;
      she hasn't known a man.
Ki.: Good!

                                          (370-3)

We have mentioned the scene of recognition between Krateia and her father Demeas in *Misoumenos* (210ff.). This recognition too is the result of pure coincidence. Demeas asks the elderly maidservant of Kleinias (at whose house he is staying) to knock at the door of their neighbour Thrasonides, and inquire about a certain sword which had aroused his interest. The old woman refuses, and Demeas has to do the job himself. When the door opens, Krateia and her nurse come out. Father and daughter immediately recognize each other and, of course, give due expression to their feelings.

This emotional scene, together with the comic element of Getas' suspicion of Demeas' intentions towards Krateia, provides the kind of complex dramatic experience characteristic of Menander.[39] In terms of the dramatic technique applied, there is a fundamental difference between this recognition scene and that which takes place between Kichesias and Dromon in *Sikyonios*.

In the latter play, the *anagnorisis* – always a moving event – comes *after* the comic potential of Theron's intrigue has been exhausted. Here, the comic element of Getas' interference is introduced in order to nip the sentimental moment of recognition in the bud.[40] As in *Perikeiromene*, this recognition scene is virtually a prologue to the second scene of the finding of long-lost kin – that between the long-lost brother (Kleinias?) and his sister and father. But whereas in *Perikeiromene*, this second recognition scene comes immediately after the first, in *Misoumenos* it is put off to a later phase of the play, probably Act IV. Instead of the feeling of relief and infinite joy which generally go with such a recognition, in *Misoumenos*, when father and daughter rediscover each other, it is an event that arouses mixed feelings in the *dramatis personae*: the joy of meeting again after so long an interval is overshadowed by grief over the bitter fate of the missing brother, believed to be dead. It is on a tone of sadness (after the brief comic interlude of Getas' interference) that the scene concludes:

De.: I am done for.
Kr.: Woe is me, how wretched am I, for
    ill fortune is mine! What a bitter fate
    has befallen us, father dear. He has been killed.
De.: By one who had the least cause.
Kr.: You know him?
De.: Indeed I do ...
    Oh what an unexpected and wretched life!

(247-58)

Whereas in the above examples, the moment of recognition is presented with the utmost economy,[41] in *Perikeiromene*, by way of contrast, it is dealt with at great length and in full detail by the dramatist (742ff.).[42] Once again we have the familiar elements of coincidence[43] and the alternation of the serious and the comic.[44] But this time, language and style are noticeably influenced by tragedy.[45] This fact, combined with the 'epic' sweep of the situation, highlights this incident as the climax of the entire plot.

Intrigue is another familiar area in which Menander's creativity finds a characterisic outlet.

In Euripidean tragedy,[46] in Old Comedy and in the Latin adaptations of New Comedy by Plautus and Terence, we are accustomed to finding the protagonist's plans, designed to help him achieve his aims by sophisticated means, crowned with success.[47] Menander's plays *Aspis* and *Dis Exapaton* (the latter is extant in Plautus' Latin version *Bacchides* and only partly in the original), were written in this spirit of conventional expectations.[48] That is not the case with *Dyskolos*. Here we have a protagonist – Sostratos – failing all along the line to attain the purpose of his machinations. Both this failure, and the solution to his problem – obtaining the consent of the misanthrope Knemon for him to marry his daughter – could be interpreted as the result of intervention by the god Pan, who is speaker of the prologue to the play.[49]

The basically ironic quality of the situation is enhanced by the emphasis put by Menander on Sostratos' erotic impatience.[50] Irony is also to be found in the manner in which Menander deals with Simo's intrigue in the play *Andria* – which is extant for us in Terence's adaptation, and apparently also in *Perinthia* (if we accept Terence's own assertion that the plot of this play is identical with that of *Andria*).[51]

Menander's unconventional approach to the element of intrigue is also evident in the improvisatory character of his intrigues. In remarkable contrast to the well-planned intrigues of Euripides, Aristophanes and Plautus,[52] Menander's intrigues tend to appear as the result of a sudden inspiration stemming from an inadvertent remark dropped by one of the characters, or from the stage situation itself.[53]

In *Dyskolos*, Sostratos insists on accompanying Gorgias and Daos to their work in the fields, close to the field of Knemon, in the hope of a chance encounter with him – perhaps through Gorgias – in order to persuade him to give him his daughter's hand. It had been Sostratos' original intention to join the two as an onlooker in his usual garb – i.e. in refined city clothes, evidently without any intentions of intrigue. But the situation changes because of the chance intervention of Daos, and Sostratos, the city-dweller, puts on peasant's clothes and joins them as a fellow farm worker:

So.: I'm ready to go where you say.
    But please do help me!
Go.: How?
So.: How? Let's go ahead where you say.
Da.: What's the idea?
    Are you going to stand by us at work,
    wearing your best?
So.: Why ever not?
Da.: He'll throw his clods at you right away, and call

> you a lazy pest. But you must dig with us. If he saw
> that, he might, just, might suffer you to say a word,
> assuming that you live as a poor peasant.
> So.: I'm ready to obey all orders. Lead on.[54]
> Go.: Why force yourself to suffer?
> Da.: *(aside)* I want *us* to get loads of work done
> today, and *him* to break his back
> at the same time. *Then* he'll stop bothering us
> and coming here.
> So.: Bring out a mattock.
> Da.: Take mine and go ahead. Meanwhile,
> I'll be building the wall up. That needs doing too.
> So.: Give it to me. You've saved my life!
>
> (361-78)

In *Aspis*, the improvisatory nature of the intrigue is even more emphasized, since we are dealing with a moment of genuine crisis. Chairestratos is in deep melancholy because of his failure to dissuade his brother Smikrines from marrying his niece, the intended bride of Chaireas, his adopted son. Daos the slave tries to comfort him, but to no avail. 'By the gods, I'll be dead, if I see it happen!' (314-15), he declares in desparation.

This banal declaration gives Daos the key to a solution: Chairestratos must pretend to be dead, and then the avaricious Smikrines will be tempted to marry the wealthy man's daughter – whose financial worth is four times that of his niece. Daos himself tells Chairestratos the source of his inspiration:

> You must put on a tragic act
> of an unpleasant sort:[55] what you've just said
> is what you must now appear to be.
>
> (329-31)

The very same technique is used to introduce intrigue into Terence's play *Eunuchus*, an adaptation of Menander's play of the same title. The only difference is that in the latter play, it all starts off with a *joke* which inadvertently becomes a reality (something similar to the situation in *Dyskolos*):

Ch.: Oh that lucky eunuch, to be a present for that household!

Pa.: Why so?

Ch.: How can you ask? His fellow slave, the height of beauty, he
will see all the time indoors; he'll talk to her, he'll be
together with her in one and the same house; sometimes
he'll take his food with her, and from time to time he'll sleep
next to her!

Pa.: What if *you* were now to become the lucky one?

Ch.: What do you mean, Parmeno? Tell me!

Pa.: You could put his clothes on.

Ch.: His clothes? What next?

Pa.: I could take you over instead of him.

Ch.: I'm listening.

Pa.: I could say you're him.

Ch.: I'm with you.

Pa.: You could enjoy those advantages which you said just now
that he would enjoy: you could take your food with her, be
together with her, touch her, play with her, sleep next to her
– after all, none of them knows you or has any idea who you
are. Besides, you look just right, and you're the right age;
you can easily pass yourself off as a eunuch.

Ch.: Well said! I've never seen better advice given. Come on, let's
go inside right now. Dress me up, take me over, take me as
quickly as possible!

Pa.: What are you up to? I was only joking.

Ch.: Rubbish!

Pa.: I've had it! What have I done? Help!

(365-78 Brown)

It has long been recognized that in Menander 'the type figure
tends to disappear, because he has been given individual traits that
cut across typological boundaries'.[56] Impressive examples of this are
the soldiers Polemon and Thrasonides in the plays *Perikeiromene*
and *Misoumenos* respectively.

In most of the texts relating to the soldier in Greek comedy, the
character-type presented is boastful, stupid, coarse and lustful – in
other words, an easy target for satire.[57] The traditional image of the
soldier is replaced, in both these plays, by a humane, likeable and
sensitive character, deeply and sincerely involved with the object of
his desire. Even here, however, Menander does not lose contact with
traditional expectations, which have their place in the general

framework of the plot – though not, it should be stressed, in their own right, but rather as a contrast to Menander's revised interpretation of the character, which is thus given the greatest prominence.

In *Perikeiromene*, these expectations are taken into consideration by Menander when, in the introduction to his play, he makes his hero commit an act of violence against his mistress Glykera, perpetrated in a sudden outburst of passionate jealousy. It is only when *Agnoia*, the goddess who speaks the prologue, says in her speech *following* the opening scene, that it was *her* intervention which brought the violent rage on Polemon (162ff.), that the spectator is made aware of the gap between his own expectations and the present Menandrian version.[58] The characters on stage do not share this awareness, and accordingly they can judge Polemon's behaviour only on the basis of surface appearances or in the context of purely traditional expectations.

This limitation is reflected in an extremely lively fashion in the way Polemon is described as 'true to type' by Sosias and Doris:

So.:   Our swaggering soldier of a moment ago, our war-hero, the
       one who won't let women keep their hair, is lying down in
       tears.

                                               (172-4 Hunter)

Do.:   Miserable
       the woman who takes a soldier for a lover. They're
       all thugs; you can't trust them an inch.

                                               (185-7)

The siege which Polemon lays to Myrrhine's house in Act III, in order to force his beloved to return to him, is another traditional element used by Menander in order to highlight the originality of *Perikeiromene* (see below). One point is evident from this stock scene (which has been preserved only fragmentarily) and is of particular importance for a study of the Menandrian art of characterization: the military operation is directed less by Polemon himself than by his personal attendant Sosias. This, then, is a case of transfer of functions (as well as personality traits) from the character to whom they would traditionally pertain. In the present case, this is perfectly logical, for what could be more natural than for a soldier's servant to assume the norms of behaviour of his military environment?

This technique is even more impressive when applied to a character in the play who is remote from the world of the soldier, as in the case of the young lover Moschion. As MacCary points out:

> Polemon is ... not a *miles gloriosus*, but rather a soldier who is favorably contrasted to a young man in the *Perikeiromene* who has more attributes of the *miles gloriosus* than does Polemon himself.[59]

It is quite possible that a similar technique of playing on the traditional anticipations from the character of the soldier was applied by Menander in *Misoumenos* as well. In the text, which has reached us only in a fragmentary state, there is no evidence to show that soldierly bragging and the other unpleasant attributes which generally belong to the *miles* were an integral part of the character of Thrasonides. On the contrary, his character, as it emerges from the few extant fragments, is that of a lover who shows consideration for the feelings of his captive Krateia, far beyond the norms of behaviour current in ancient society.[60] Nevertheless, for some reason, she bears him a grudge. Yet we have the following external evidence, from Choricius:

> You can take examples from comedy of the pomposity, conceit and excessive boastfulness of the soldier. Any of you who envisages Menander's Thrasonides knows what I mean. The poet tells us that the fellow's excess of soldierly unpleasantness causes him to become antipathetic to the girl he loves and the hate felt against Thrasonides has naturally given the play its name.
>
> (Choric. XLII, *decl.* 12, p. 509 = *Mis.* fr. 1 Sandbach)

On the face of it, this does not fit what we know of the play. But if we assume that it relates to the way Thrasonides *appears* in certain stages of the plot to the other characters, above all to Krateia, rather than to his *real* personality in the play, we may conclude that here we have a similar ambivalent approach to the character of the soldier as we had in *Perikeiromene*.

The opening scene (see mainly A36-A40) and lines 305ff. lead one to the certain conclusion that Krateia's hatred for Thrasonides marks a turning-point in their relationship: previously they had been cohabiting.[61] If that is the case, then it is not reasonable to suppose that basic character traits of Thrasonides, such as the bragging described by Choricius, were the cause of the couple's separation. Yet it would appear more probable that Krateia's sudden detestation was brought about by some specific event which *might* have involved bragging on Thrasonides' part, but – and this too is a distinct possibility – might also be due to something he said that she *interpreted* as boastful self-aggrandizement. Here again, let us see how Webster reconstructs the background events of the play from the point at which the question of the fate of Krateia's brother arises:

> ... the brother fought, was wounded, and ultimately escaped; in the confusion he had exchanged swords with a comrade, who was killed by Thrasonides (this theme we now know from the *Aspis*). The sword was inscribed, and Thrasonides therefore listed the brother among his casualties, whom he recounted to Krateia (cf. fr. 1). This caused her hatred, which gives the play its name, a hatred based on misunderstanding, like the fury of Polemon described by the prologue figure of the *Perikeiromene*.[62]

In any case, we are dealing here with someone who most definitely is not a negative character, ludicrous or repulsive – as the *miles gloriosus*, the bragging soldier, was generally presented.[63] If this were not so, then there would be no way of explaining the fact that eventually Thrasonides, like Polemon, wins his beloved – in itself a significant departure from the conventional handling of the soldier character. The same favourable treatment of the soldier figure is adopted by Menander in *Sikyonios*.[64]

We have noted the flexible use Menander makes of traditional elements in building up a character. This enabled him to create colourful variations on the gallery of characters – limited in itself – which was at his disposal. Thus, adding the element of arrogance to the character of the young lover (Moschion in *Perikeiromene* and *Sikyonios*) was a refreshing departure from the usually pale and hesitant portrayal of the young lover in comedy (such as Moschion in *Samia*).[65] Another case is that of the soldier portrayed without the traditional bragging, and whose character is redeemed through love and understanding.[66] The role that he is destined to play generally corresponds to that of the young lover of civilian status, whose intentions towards his beloved are honourable (Thrasonides in *Misoumenos*; Polemon in *Perikeiromene*; Stratophanes in *Sikyonios*).[67] Or let us consider another outstanding example, the *hetaira*, the professional courtesan, who is traditionally portrayed as selfish, calculating and avaricious,[68] but whom Menander, by various means and in different plays, portrays as a sympathetic character (Habrotonon in *Epitrepontes*; Thais in *Eunuchus*), who genuinely shares the concerns of the family in whose household she lives (Chrysis in *Samia*) – again, in contravention of traditional expectations.[69] Habrotonon in *Epitrepontes* has the role of the scheming slave, whereas Chrysis in *Samia*, who plots with Moschion against his father, represents a pattern of behaviour traditionally reserved for the character of the *mother* in comedy.[70]

The fact that this technique can be applied by Menander even to minor characters in the plot, indicates his particular interest in 'character experiments' in general. In *Dyskolos*, presenting the parasite without the quality most obviously attached to this traditional character (concern for food), and transferring this trait from Chaireas to Kallippides, Sostratos' father,[71] is a particularly bold experiment along these lines.[72]

The redeeming process undergone in Menander's comedies by professional characters such as the soldier and the *hetaira* draws our attention to an important aspect of what might, with due caution, be defined as Menander's moralistic approach to the comic conventions or, in other words, his tendency to add an *ethical dimension* to conventional situations and motifs. We can demonstrate this approach by comparing the siege scene in *Perikeiromene* (467ff.) with that in Terence's *Eunuchus* (771ff.), both Menandrian variations on a traditional theme.[73]

The scene in *Eunuchus* lacks all dimensions of moral evaluation. Insofar as the *legal* implications of the attempt of the soldier Thraso to win back Pamphila by force are mentioned, this is done through vulgar exchanges between the soldier, his accompanying parasite, and Pamphila's brother, with brutal threats on both sides. Undoubtedly, Terence has added a number of comic effects to this scene; yet we have no reason to believe that his Greek original departed in any way from traditional expectations regarding a siege by a lover-soldier.

In *Perikeiromene* we have an entirely different approach. The siege, imposed by Polemon on Myrrhine's house so as to force his beloved Glykera to return to him is lifted when Pataikos intervenes, not long after it has begun. Thus the way is paved to a logical discussion of the moral and legal implications of the path of violence chosen by Polemon.[74] By means of this discussion, Menander takes the banal situation out of its traditional, vulgar context and transfers it to another, higher plane – that of serious consideration of human relationships:

Pa.: If what has happened, Polemon,
    had been the way you say it was,
    and to do with your wedded wife –
Po.: What are you saying, Pataikos!
Pa.: But there's a difference.
Po.: I have regarded her as my wedded wife.
Pa.: Don't shout! And who gave her away?
Po.: Who? To me? She herself.
Pa.: Fine. Perhaps she liked you then, but now no more.
    She has gone away because you were treating her
    incorrectly.
Po.: What are you saying? Incorrectly?
    Of all you've said that
    has upset me most.
Pa.: You are in love.
    I know that for sure. So what you are
    doing now is lunacy. Where are you
    rushing off to? Who are you trying to drag back?
    She is her own mistress. What's left for a lover in a
    bad state is persuasion.
Po.: And the man who has seduced her in my absence –
    hasn't he done me any wrong?
Pa.: He has wronged you enough for you to
    talk prosecution –
    if you ever have a chance to speak to him.
    But if you use force, you'll be convicted in court.
    This sort of wrong doesn't call for vendetta
    but for prosecution.

Po.: Not even now?
Pa.: Not even now.
Po.: I don't know what to say, by Demeter –
only that I am ready to choke.
Glykera has abandoned me, abandoned me
Glykera has, Pataikos. But if that seems to you to be
what I should do – you who were a
close friend of hers, and who often talked to her
before – go and talk to her now, be my ambassador,
I beg you.
Pa.: That, you see, should be done, I think.

(486-511)

We can discern the same differences of approach to traditional comic values, i.e. a preference for ethical as against non-ethical considerations on Menander's part, in the following group of examples which are related to another stock feature of New Comedy, the threat of the lover to go into exile (*Sam.* 616ff. and Plaut. *Cist.* 284ff.). Here we are given an opportunity to extend the comparison to another poet, Menander's acknowledged rival, Philemon, whose play *Emporos*, adapted by Plautus as *Mercator*, contains a development of the motif under discussion (644ff.; 830ff.).[75]

Moschion's exile scene in *Samia* is the earliest example we have of this motif. It occurs at the beginning of the fifth act, at a point in the action where one would have expected Menander to proceed with the traditional wedding feast, after all the unnecessary obstacles to the marriage of Moschion and Plangon – the professed aim of the play – had been removed in the course of the previous act. But the chief interest of the playwright lies not in the union of Moschion and Plangon, but in the relationship between father and adopted son.[76] Menander therefore postpones the solution of the filial conflict to the last act, thus laying the strongest stress on the problematic nature of the father-son relationship.

However, since Moschion was not present at the confrontation between Demeas and Nikeratos at the end of the previous act, one may suppose he had no knowledge of the new understanding between his adoptive father and his future father-in-law. The audience thus expects him to deliver either the traditional monologue of the desperate lover (threatening suicide or exile), or the speech of the lover impatiently looking forward to the consummation of his courtship.[77] Surprisingly enough, he does neither. Instead, he reveals that he is aware of the impending marriage, but states his intention to postpone the fulfilment of his expectations in order to avenge the unjust accusations of his suspicious father (633-8). Thus the focus of interest shifts from the expected marriage to the ethical problem which has presented itself regarding the relationship between the two major figures – a turn of events that is contrary to traditional expectations.

The manner in which Moschion intends to carry out his revenge contains an additional surprise for the audience. The threat of exile is usually made because of frustrated love. Moschion, however, makes the threat for other reasons. In fact, rather than treating Love as the prime motive for carrying out the threat, Moschion now presents it as the major factor preventing it:

> So if only everything to do with the girl were all right, and there were not so many obstacles – my oath, my desire, the length and intimacy of our relationship, factors by which I have become enslaved – he wouldn't accuse me of that kind of thing a second time in person to my face, but I'd clear off out of the city and out of his way, to somewhere like Bactria or Caria, and spend my time there spear in hand. But as it is, because of you, darling Plangon, I shan't do anything manly; I can't – Love, which is now master of my mind, doesn't let me.
>
> (623-32 Brown)

By sharing his secrets with the audience (683), Moschion puts it in a position where it is able to pass objective judgement on both him and the other characters in the scene. The audience's superior knowledge enables it to differentiate between the exile-motif and the traditional love-despair context. Thus, in the following scene, we find the slave Parmenon strongly adhering to the traditional motives for exile, while the audience is capable of seeing it in its new ethical context. It can be concluded, therefore, that Menander's treatment of the exile-motif displays an innovative originality in both form and substance.

Menander's originality in *Samia* becomes even more pronounced when compared with his own treatment of the self-exile-motif in *Synaristosai* and with that of Philemon in *Emporos*, as represented in the Plautine *Cistellaria* and *Mercator* respectively. In both plays, the exile-motif is seen only in its connection with the traditional erotic context. Thus in *Cistellaria*, the exile-scene serves to highlight Alcesimarchus' mental condition after he has been separated from Selenium against his will, whereas in *Mercator* it serves to stress Charinus' determination to do everything in his power to find Pasicompsa. Indeed, the passage in *Samia* is the only example known to us of the exile-motif being used not for the stock portrayal of a *fervidus amator*, a passionate lover, but for the delineation of a particularized, individual lover – in an essentially *non*-erotic context.[78]

As I have shown in detail elsewhere,[79] the comic elements which Plautus introduced into his adaptation of the scene from Philemon, even if they were introduced at the expense of a more credible portrayal of the characters, did not in essence alter the general dramatic structure.

The scene involves two rapid mood changes. The first occurs in line 910. Hearing from his friend Eutychus that his beloved has been found, Charinus takes off his military cloak, thus illustrating his willingness to give up his former plan. Had it been a simple variation of the exile-threat, the scene would have ended here. But Philemon chooses to elaborate the theme by introducing a complex pretence of both exile and madness, involving, moreover, a highly comic parody of a tragedy.[80] This treatment of the exile-threat reveals Philemon's greater skill in the creation of dramatic suspense, and takes the stock threat a step further, beyond the traditional pattern. The second change of mood is made possible by the very nature of the characters involved: Eutychus, being a loyal son, does not wish to let Charinus know that Lysimachus, Eutychus' own father, participated in Charinus' father's erotic plans concerning Pasicompsa (915ff.). Thus, the madness-scene is required in order to make Eutychus tell Charinus where his beloved is.

Admittedly, Philemon's version of the exile-motif is unusually elaborate when compared with Menander's treatment of it in *Samia* and in *Synaristosai*, as adapted by Plautus in *Cistellaria*.[81] Nevertheless, I believe that it retains enough of the stock characteristics of the traditional pattern to disclose its link with its Greek ancestors.[82]

The difference between Philemon's and Menander's treatment of the exile-scene may be summarized thus: Philemon tends to elaborate upon the conventional motif in its traditional context of love and despair; his originality extends to plot-movements as well as to the creation of dramatic suspense. The scene is set for the hero's departure into exile long before it reaches its realization on the stage.[83] The variations are restricted to details, including a highly elaborate madness-scene and possibly the absence of a sword, an essential implement for the normal staging of such a scene.[84] *Samia*, however, reveals a completely different approach: while the stock features of the scene remain basically unchanged, the scene itself has been detached from its traditional context of irrational love, and takes the form of a calculated threat. The new ethical dimension, superimposed upon the stock situation, thus receives its strongest possible emphasis. Being an *ad hoc* means of retaliation rather than a plot-motivated development, the exile-motif comes with no preparation at all, and appears, in fact, to be *outside* the formal plot.

We must underline the limited nature of Menander's innovations as evident in *Samia* and, to a greater or lesser extent, in all the examples we have mentioned. Menander does not reject the accepted comic values, but he often reshapes them out of his own insight into the motives of human action. Even though his comedies are built to no small extent on the element of surprise,[85] we find no instance in them of the dramatic reversal of motifs of the kind to be found in abundance in the comedies of Aristophanes and Plautus.[86] While he can choose to reverse the stereotype, as, for example, the character of the soldier in *Misoumenos*, *Perikeiromene* and *Sikyonios* (and also in *Aspis*), this is only done when the circumstances make it credible in terms of the dramatic situation, and when conventional expectations – which are also dealt with in a credible manner, as we have seen – are still preserved in the background.

This last point can be illustrated by a comparison with the character of the soldier Therapontigonus in Plautus' play *Curculio* (unknown Greek source).

From the moment of his appearance in Act IV (533ff.) to the revelation that he is brother to Planesium (641ff.), this character is treated by Plautus in the spirit of pure farce. Therapontigonus is shown as a type of *miles gloriosus*, a bragging soldier, and there is nothing whatever in his character or behaviour to prepare us for the *anagnorisis*, which is generally applied to sympathetic characters.[87] On the contrary, once we have recognized him in the traditional role of the laughing-stock of the play, we expect this line of action to continue and lead up to a farcical climax, towards the end.

The sudden reversal of Therapontigonus' nature is a clumsy and inartistic attempt by Plautus (or the anonymous Greek source) to depart from the conventional character of the soldier, with the obvious intention of cheating the audience of its expectations. We need only to recall the way Stratophanes is presented in *Sikyonios* (he, too, is involved in a situation of *anagnorisis*) in order to evaluate correctly the essential difference between the balanced and restrained manner in which Menander handles the comic repertoire at his disposal, and the totally free approach of Plautus to the matter.[88]

There are only a few cases in the extant fragments of Menander's works of the apparent deliberate overturning of traditional motifs or stock situations. One such instance may be found in the opening scene of *Misoumenos*. Thrasonides stands outside the closed door of his house, declaiming to the Night about his troubled relations with Krateia:[89]

> Oh Night – yours is the largest share of love
> among the gods; in your course of time, most words
> of love and lovers' worries find an outlet.
> Have you ever seen a man more miserable,
> a lover more ill-starred?
> Here I stand, at my own front door,
> in this narrow street, pacing up and down,
> from nightfall[90] – till now when you're almost at your midst,
> while I could sleep and have my love.
> She's inside my house and it's up to me to do it
> and I want it as madly as would the craziest of lovers,
> and yet I don't do it. I choose instead to stand outside,
> in the cold winter, shivering and talking to you.
>
> (A1-A14)

Behind this scene and the ensuing conversation between Thrasonides and his slave Getas, there is a situation typical of love-life in ancient Greece (and perhaps in Rome as well), in which the lover who is barred from entering the home of his beloved registers his complaint by means of a *Paraclausithyron*, a serenade in front of the locked door, in the hope of thus causing the door to be opened.

In Greek and Roman literature, we find innumerable adaptations of this recurrent situation.[91] In comedy, it is frequently used for its own comic purposes.[92]

Menander here stuck to the general traditional outline of the scene – the locked door, the sad lover outside, the nocturnal setting – but the situation of the protagonist himself is in total contradiction to the *topos* and to the realities on which it is based. First of all, the locked door is not that of his beloved, but it is Thrasonides' own house. Secondly: 'This lover has locked himself out, the *exclusus amator* is self-excluded.'[93] And thirdly, the beloved is introduced by her suitor as being most certainly under his power (since the protagonist is a soldier, the spectator is entitled at this stage to assume that he is referring to a bought prisoner of war);[94] and his abstention from having relations with her in *that* situation is a gesture of pure generosity, the result of personal moral choice.

The conclusion to which one is led by all these changes is that Menander deliberately takes liberties with an accepted literary genre,[95] and also with a familiar aspect of the situation of lovers in Greece, in this way indicating to his audience at the very outset of his play how great is the new departure from the accepted romantic story that he is about to show them. The irony of this unusual situation, the result of Menander's unconventional handling of the genre, in itself creates a focus of special interest in the spectator, from the very first lines of the play, in both the protagonist and the girl who is in his power.

As to the actions of the girl herself – to judge by the few relevant fragments in our text – it again appears to have been Menander's intention to upset the stereotype. The complete freedom which the playwright allows her towards her captor – before and after he sets her free – is in total contrast to what we know of the attitude to prisoners-of-war in ancient times, from Homer onwards.[96] It would, however, be somewhat hasty to draw any general conclusions from Menander's comic interpretation of the status of a woman prisoner-of-war in one play.[97]

It is important to note that Menander refrains from spelling out to his audience the novelty of his approach in this play, and prefers to allow the comic situation itself gradually to create the impression that this is an unusual event. In the Latin adaptations of his plays, we find a more direct and somewhat artificial method used by the playwright to emphasize his originality, which does not necessarily stem from the Menandrian original. Thus, in Plautus' *Bacchides*, the slave Chrysalus presents his impressive achievement of 'shaving off' a goodly sum of money from Nicobulus his master in the following terms:

Parmenons and Syruses[98] don't cut much ice with me:
those who rob masters of two or three minas.
There's nothing more useless than a slave
who lacks invention, who doesn't have
mental multipotence ...

(649-52 Barsby)

In Terence's *Eunuchus*, Thais explicitly points out to the audience the difference between her and other *hetairai*. She does it soon after the opening scene of the play in which her relations with Phaedria were represented in a dubious light:

Oh dear, perhaps he doesn't really trust me and
is judging me now from other women's character!
I know what I'm doing, and I certainly know this for a fact,
that I haven't made up any lies, and that no one
is dearer to my heart than this man Phaedria.

(197-201 Brown)[99]

In *Heautontimoroumenos*, the speaker of the prologue notes the uniqueness of plot in Terence's play (which we have to attribute to the Menandrian original!) with regard to his own acting skills:

Pay attention with an open mind; give me the chance to be
allowed to put on, without interruption, a play which
contains more talk than action. That way an old man won't for
ever continually have to play the running slave, the angry
old man, the greedy parasite, the shameless swindler and the
grabbing pimp – at the top of his voice and with lots of
effort. Convince yourselves my cause is just, for my sake,
to lessen some of my exertions ...
In this play we've got talk, talk that is natural and unaffected;
so put my talents to the test – see what they can do
in either line.

(35-47 Brothers)[100]

Apart from *Asp*. 218 and *Epitr*. 1115-17, which could be interpreted as mockery of the hackneyed theme of the girl who is raped
and secretly gives birth without her parents' knowledge – a theme
so popular in New Comedy – we have no direct evidence in Menandrian comedy of any attempt to ridicule the literary tradition in
which he worked and from which he drew his inspiration. There is
some evidence of attempts of this kind in the Latin adaptations, if
we assume that these are elements that originated from his works.
Let us consider, for example, the following speech by Micio con-
demning Aeschinus his adopted son, in Terence's play *Adelphoe*.
There is no reason to suppose that it did not exist in the Greek
original (at least, in its general lines), since it is an integral part of
the father-son relationship, one of the play's main points of interest.
In fact, it is the very climax in the development of that relationship:

> I know your open-hearted spirit, but I'm afraid you don't take
> enough trouble. After all, what city do you think you're living
> in? You raped a girl; it was against the law for you to lay a
> finger on her. That was your first wrong, and a great one, but
> at least it was understandable – you're only human; other
> people have done the same thing often enough, perfectly re-
> spectable people. But after it had happened, tell me, did you
> consider at all? Did you look to your own future at all and ask
> yourself what was to be done, or how it was to be done? If you
> were ashamed to tell me yourself, how was I to find it out?
> While you dithered, nine months went by; you've been treach-
> erous to yourself, to the poor girl, and to your son – as treach-
> erous as you could be. What? Did you think the gods would sort
> this out for you while you were asleep? Did you think she would
> be brought home as a bride to your bedroom without your
> having to lend a hand?
>
> (683-94 Brown)

What we have here is, indeed, a very particular moment in the
long-standing theatrical tradition which is still alive and vibrant,
in which the dramatist invites the spectator to pause for a moment
and consider the moral quality of one of the principal components
of this tradition. Only rarely do we find in New Comedy an ethical
reflection on the banal drama of the rape of a free girl, and her
subsequent pregnancy – and even then, the event is generally

referred to only with brief remarks, mostly of a comic nature.[101] Indeed, *Adelphoe* is the only play known to us in which any serious consideration is given to the problematic nature of the story-pattern under review, a story-pattern which crops up frequently, in different variations and in different plays. From the viewpoint of dramatic technique, we can discern here the same method – the addition of an ethical dimension to a familiar comic situation – which we have earlier defined as particularly characteristic of Menander.

And. 220ff. is certainly a mockery of the New Comedy convention of having the beloved one revealed as a free citizen, a convention applied in the play *Andria* itself. Davus tells the audience, speaking of Pamphilus and Glycerium:

> And now the pair of them are making up some tall story
> that she's a citizen of Athens: 'Once there was an old man in
> the import-export business; he was shipwrecked off the island
> of Andros; he lost his life' – and then she was washed ashore
> and taken in by Chrysis' father as an orphan child! Rubbish!
> *I* certainly don't find it plausible, but they're pleased with their
> story.
>
> (220-5 Brown)

As a matter of fact, this 'invention' of Pamphilus and his beloved is revealed in 923ff. as the truth. Once again, we have a comic combination of events similar to that which Menander used in *Sikyonios*.[102] The analogy between the two plays leaves room for the assumption that the present scorn for comic convention originated with Menander himself and not with Terence.

In this same play, in Act III, two comic *stage* conventions are ridiculed, one after the other. In the first case, the shouts of the mother giving birth are conventionally heard by those standing on stage, coming from within the house.[103] This is Simo's reaction to hearing the shouts of Glycerium:

> What, so quickly? That's absurd! As soon as she heard I was
> standing outside the door, she got on with it. You didn't sort
> out the timing of this properly, Davus!
>
> (474-6 Brown)

The second convention is of someone emerging from the house

addressing those within – speaking through the doorway and creating the illusion that this is the continuation of a conversation which began inside, whose start we can only imagine. Simo, hearing and seeing Lesbia the midwife giving instructions to Archylis the maid on how to nurse the new mother, notes:

> She didn't give her instructions on the spot for what needed doing for the mother; but first she comes out of the house, and then she shouts at the women indoors from the street! Oh Davus, do you have such a low opinion of me? Damn it, do you think I'm the sort of person for you to set about fooling and tricking so obviously?
>
> (490-3 Brown)

In both these cases, the criticism voiced by the character of the stage event is the result of his suspicions that this event is part of an intrigue directed against him. Mocking presentation of this convention, then, is an integral part of the plot, and we are indeed entitled – in both these instances – to regard it as faithfully reflecting the approach of the Greek dramatist to the contemporary stage conventions. The second convention is particularly characteristic of Menandrian technique.[104] We may thus have here amusing evidence of self-mockery on Menander's part.

Our last example is taken from Plautus' *Cistellaria* and contains scorn for the convention of the prologue spoken by a god – a device generally used to give lengthy exposition of the background to the plot. In *Cistellaria*, much of the information is presented by the *lena*, the drunken Madam. Here too, the speech is long and detailed. Nevertheless, the goddess *Auxilium*, Help, who is speaker of the prologue in the play, insists on presenting her version in full, repeating known details, as she shamelessly admits:

> Tattler and tippler both, the old hag! So she has barely left
> a thing for a god to say, in her hurry to tell the tale of
> that supposititious girl! Why, if she had held
> her tongue, I should have told you, just the same,
> and I, being a god, could have made it clearer.
>
> (149-53 Nixon)

The placing of the prologue after the opening scene tallies with Menandrian custom. Furthermore, *Auxilium*'s reference at the beginning of her speech to characters who have just left the stage has a clear parallel in the speech of Tyche, the goddess who presents the prologue in *Aspis*, which also begins in similar fashion (97ff.).

These technical points of similarity between Plautus and Menander, in addition to the evidence in *P. Argent.* 53.1-15 (= Austin, *CGFPR* fr. 252) of mockery, in almost identical terms, in New Comedy itself, of the convention of the god as presenter of the prologue, would point to the present example originating with Menander's *Synaristosai*, the source of Plautus' *Cistellaria*.

The question of the relationship between Menander and the contemporary comic conventions will continue to preoccupy us in various ways and contexts throughout this book. But, already on the basis of the partial evidence reviewed in this chapter, we can conclude that the picture which emerges from Menander's work, as well as the Latin adaptations of it, is of a dramatist who is inclined to confine himself to keeping within the framework of comic tradition, but at the same time makes creative and critical use of its various components. The Menandrian variations tend to rely less on overturning stereotypes than on modifying their extreme comic aspects, often by introducing an ethical dimension into familiar situations and characters and by softening the element of caricature usually associated with them. Herein lies the major difference between the comic art of Menander and that of Aristophanes, his predecessor in this same tradition of comedy.

Artistic Principles

While the main preoccupation of Aristophanic comedy was to present scenes from the life of the Athenian *polis* in terms of fantasy, Menandrian comedy presented scenes from the life of its citizens — mainly from the middle class — in terms taken for the most part from everyday life. The realistic quality of each specific plot varies from one play to the next, sometimes indeed from one scene to the next.[1] However, the artistic principles which guided the playwight in portraying the heroes and their experiences — as can be deduced from his extant writings — appear always to have been identical, and they were three: polyphony, economy and emphasis on human interaction. In this chapter, I propose to demonstrate how these principles are applied, within the narrow framework of the genre.

Polyphony

The most effective way to achieve polyphony is by amalgamating plot-lines of different kinds in a single play.

It has been suggested that Menander apparently avoids developing a double plot even where it might easily have been expected.[2] But a deeper study of the Menandrian corpus would give rise to some objections to this argument. *Dyskolos* is composed of two strands of action essentially distinct in their character and dramatic potential.[3] The first is highly romantic in tenor, and concerns Sostratos' repeated attempts to contact Knemon, either in person or through a third party, in order to obtain his consent to Sostratos' marriage to his daughter.

It is on this strand of action that the main dramatic action of the play is centred. The second strand of action concerns Knemon himself, principally in the manner in which his eccentric character is presented in relation to his human environment. Knemon's misanthropy is portrayed primarily in terms of his reaction to external stimuli, whether or not the other protagonists – the sources of these stimuli – deliberately mean them to have an effect on him. The essentially passive nature of his action in the play thus stands in sharp contrast to the constant over-activity shown by Sostratos, his future son-in-law, at every turn of events. Two minor strands of action are interwoven with these two strands – the sacrificial meal in honour of Pan, and the 'Gorgias plot', by means of which the *peripeteia* in the play is achieved.

What is remarkable about the conjunction of such distinct plot-lines is that the two main components, namely those revolving around Sostratos and Knemon, run separate courses throughout most of the play. In fact, it is not until the incident at the well, in the fourth act, that the misanthrope is made aware of the existence of a suitor for his daughter's hand. Sostratos' attempts to establish contact with him before this turning-point in the play have all proved abortive. Clearly Menander, realizing the potential danger to the integrity of the misanthrope's characterization were he to bring him into contact with the love-plot too early, defers the collision between the two main plot-lines until the need to resolve the dramatic complications renders impossible any further delay in bringing the two strands together.[4]

While admitting Menander's significant achievement in retaining the credibility of the character of his main hero within the restricting framework of a New Comedy-type love-intrigue so vividly represented by the Sostratos strand, it has to be admitted that the way he chose to further his artistic aim nevertheless damaged the structural unity and dramatic development of his play. For it is precisely from Menander's constant effort to preserve the credibility of his main hero's character by shielding him from the romantic action of the play, that the disunity of *Dyskolos* stems. At the same time, it impedes the progress of the plot towards the achievement of Sostratos' marriage with Knemon's daughter – its main aim – which has to be somewhat artificially brought about by Knemon's fall into the well in Act IV towards the end of the play.

It is clear that Menander was aware of the damage to his dramatic action caused by the unusual emphasis he placed on presenting Sostratos as an over-active, impatient lover at critical points in the play – namely, whenever the plot seemed to grind to a halt because of the deliberate separation between its two main strands.[5] The resultant incongruity between the incessant activity of the lover (for which we have no parallel among the comic lovers) and its apparent ineffectiveness, quite apart from providing an infinite source of comedy in the play,[6] thus performs a twofold dramatic function. It enables Menander not only to provide an apparent link between the Sostratos strand and the Knemon strand, but also to maintain an illusion of constant dramatic development, even within the disintegrating framework of the pseudo-dramatic double action of *Dyskolos*.

While in *Dyskolos* the structural disunity of the double plot is the result of character considerations, in *Aspis* it stems directly from the type and the relative importance of the two strands of action involved. The plot-line revolving around Kleostratos' presumed death serves as a background to an intrigue to be directed against Smikrines by the combined efforts of Daos, Chairestratos and Chaireas, who intend to frustrate his plan to exercise his lawful right, as next of kin, to marry his niece, Kleostratos' sister.[7] The intrigue, extending from the second act to the fourth, carries the main burden of the play's action and constitutes its main source of interest. It cannot, however, bring about more than a temporary, illusory solution to the plot complication. The final resolution is provided by Kleostratos' safe return home at the end of Act IV.

What we have here is in fact a double plot in which one line of action (an intrigue) is preceded and concluded by another (an *anagnorisis*). Whereas the *form* of this plot differs widely from that of *Dyskolos*, it nevertheless has the same tendency (although to a lesser extent, since the strands *are* inter-dependent) towards structural disunity, in that the *anagnorisis* strand is presented in two distinct phases.

Much of the dramatic effect of *Perikeiromene* stems from its juxtaposition of a 'serious' love-plot with a farcical one. While Polemon's torments over his separation from Glykera arouse deep sympathy in the audience, the frustration of Moschion (her brother, though he does not know it) because of his failure to attain his ends with her, evokes sheer laughter. Menander, seeking to realize the full comic potential embedded in the contrast between two such widely differing love-plots, develops the two strands in almost the same way, thus underlining the differences between them. Both Moschion and Polemon try to get in touch with Glykera, but to no avail; Moschion's attempt is elaborately depicted at the beginning of the second act, and that of Polemon at the beginning of the third.

Both are instigated to this action by the reports of their respective slaves, Daos and Sosias. Both become the victims of a similar misunderstanding concerning the reasons for Glykera's decision to move out of Polemon's house to that of Myrrhine, believing her action to be due to a supposed love affair between her and Moschion.

Since Glykera is the object of desire of both men, the link (in effect, the overlap) between the two strands of action in which they take part is almost inevitable, the more so when the starting-point of the Polemon plot – his violent act of jealousy against Glykera – is directly connected with Moschion. That this link is maintained principally through the actions of proxies (Daos, Sosias, Pataikos), rather than through a direct confrontation between the protagonists themselves, is revealing. By keeping the main protagonists apart in this way, Menander capitalizes on the comedy of errors which develops as a result of Glykera's decision at the end of Act I to move to Myrrhine's house, without blunting the audience's interest in the Moschion-Glykera-Polemon triangle, which is the focus of the play.

As far as we can tell, *Misoumenos* and *Sikyonios* both fall within the category of dramas with double plots. In the former, Menander seems to combine two love-plots which appear to be essentially different in character (Thrasonides-Krateia; Kleinias-Krateia[?]).[8] The *anagnorisis* between Krateia and her father is apparently achieved through the interaction of these two plots. In the second play, he combines two *anagnorisis* plots (Stratophanes' rediscovery of his parents, followed by Philoumene's rediscovery of her father Kichesias) strongly coloured by love and intrigue.[9] Amatory concerns, conceived in terms of double plot, may also be traced in the scanty remains of *Heros*, *Kolax*, *Dis Exapaton* and *Georgos*.

Of special interest to the present theme are *Epitrepontes* and *Samia*. Although these plays do not fall specifically within the category of double-plot dramas, nevertheless the intricacy and variety of their dramatic action place them on the same level of complexity. In *Epitrepontes*, the process of revelation of the truth about Pamphile's baby extends from the second act to the fourth, and comes about through fragmented and widely differing modes of presentation: a highly elaborate arbitration scene involving Daos, Syros[10] and Smikrines (Act II), followed by an intrigue by Habrotonon against Charisios (Act III), and in conclusion, a series of dramatic confrontations, differing from each other in tenor and style, between Pamphile and her father (overheard by Charisios);

between Pamphile and Habrotonon and between Habrotonon and Charisios (Act IV). The mockery made of Smikrines by Onesimos in the fifth act reveals the truth, at last, to Pamphile's father as well.

In *Samia*, the unfolding of the truth about Moschion's and Plangon's baby is on a more limited scale, only spanning the third and fourth acts. Nevertheless, it involves a series of misunderstandings which significantly complicate the course of revelation. The *dramatis personae* are all involved in one way or another in this process, and fall victim to misunderstandings of one kind or another. In the fifth act, a new strand of action is introduced by Moschion's pretence of going abroad on military service. This pretence comes to clarify yet another, deeper misunderstanding concerning the relations between Moschion and his adoptive father, which had arisen in the course of the dramatic developments of the third and fourth acts.[11]

The picture which emerges, from the extant parts of Menander's plays, of his use of the double plot corresponds very strikingly to the important role played by this twofold pattern in the Latin adaptations of his plays, and this may be taken as evidence of their fidelity to the Greek originals. Indeed, if we exclude *Andria*, the double plot of which must be attributed to Terence (as emerges from Donatus' evidence)[12] and possibly also exclude Terence's *Eunuchus* which, according to Terence's prologue,[13] underwent significant changes during his adaptation, there seems to be no real reason to assume – as some scholars have – that the Latin adapters rather than Menander himself were responsible for any of the double-plot patterns which appear in their adaptations of his plays.[14]

It is difficult not to see the influence of Euripidean drama in this constant emphasis on variety and complexity in the dramatic action, achieved sometimes at the expense of the structural uniformity of the play.[15] This influence, which became an important factor in the general development of Greek dramatic technique shortly after Euripides' death, will have contributed to the introduction of new standards in the approach of New Comedy playwrights to the structure of the comic plot, as reflected so vividly in Menandrian comedy. It seems reasonable to assume that the multiplicity of action achieved by juxtaposing or intertwining disparate plot-lines, as required by these new standards, had rendered the simple, one-dimensional plot of Aristophanic comedy no longer acceptable to a Menandrian audience. Such a plot would be regarded as 'old-fashioned' and 'non-dramatic' compared to the new complex patterns currently provided by Menander and his contemporaries.

Polyphony of the 'literary' kind is achieved by painting the comic event in tragic hues, whether by using the language of tragedy, or by hinting at or imitating situations or motifs taken from tragedy.[16] The inevitable disparity between the comic event and the heavy tragic dimension imposed upon it preserves the essential distinction between the components of the two genres in such a way as to give maximum exposure to the polyphony of the situation. However, in order to savour it fully, the spectator must have some familiarity with the literary traditions behind it.

The recognition scene between Glykera and Pataikos in *Perikeiromene*,[17] with its stichomythical structure, its lofty expressions and its unchanging metrical pattern,[18] well illustrates the advantages inherent in presenting a comic situation (note the farcical element of Moschion's eavesdropping!) in tragic guise (779ff.):

Pa.: Oh Zeus, what is the portion of my fate that now awaits me?[19]

Gl.: Realize your wish – you may learn the truth from me.

Pa.: Tell me, where did you find these articles?
How did they come into your possession?

Gl.: It was in these clothes that I was found as a baby.

Mo.: *(to himself)* Bring yourself forward a little.
[Borne on a tempestuous wave] I have come
at a critical moment for my personal fortunes.

Pa.: Were you left on your own? Indicate that to me.

Gl.: No, not at all. I was exposed together with my brother.

Mo.: That is one of the details I have long[20] been seeking.

Pa.: How then were the two of you sundered from each other?

Gl.: I could tell you all from what I have heard.
But ask me only what concerns *me*, for of that I may speak.
Of all else I swore to her [sc. Myrrhine] that I would remain silent.

Mo.: That which she's told me now, is yet another sure sign.
She gave her word to my mother. Where on earth am I?

Pa.: And who was the one who took you in and brought you up?

Gl.: A woman brought me up, the one who saw me lying there.

Pa.: And what token did she give you of the place?

Gl.: She spoke of a stream and a shady place.

Pa.: The very place described to me by the person who left them.
Gl.: Who is that? Tell me, if you have a right to do so.
Pa.: He who left them was a slave,
      but I was the one who feared to bring them up.
Gl.: You, our father, exposed us? For what reason?
Pa.: Many, my child, works of fate are unbelievable.
      For she who bore you left this life right away,
      and the day before, my child -
Gl.: What happened? I tremble so in my misery.
Pa.: I became a poor man, I who was accustomed to
      having sufficient means.
Gl.: All in one day? How? Oh gods, what a dreadful fate!
Pa.: I learned that the ship which used to bring us our livelihood
      sank beneath the stormy waters of the Aegean Sea.
Gl.: Oh, what a wretched fate is mine! *etc.*

This recognition marks a turning-point and a climax in the plot, as well as in the confrontation between the protagonists. The tragic guise lends due weight to this critical moment in the play, in terms both of its intrinsic dramatic value and of the powerful emotions behind it. Whether he shares those emotions or not, the spectator is called upon to evaluate the importance of this moment and will derive pleasure from the way in which the dramatist blows up the mundane experiences of the protagonists to dimensions generally reserved for the larger-than-life figures of mythology.

A different technique, but with similar effect, is used by Menander in Demeas' second speech in Act III of *Samia* (325ff.). Here the protagonist expresses his tempestuous feelings by a direct quotation from the words of a tragic hero, raising his voice as befits the noble style of delivery in tragedy. But, unlike Glykera and Pataikos in the example quoted above, he immediately becomes aware of the pathetic exaggeration of his heroic stance. Consequently, he lowers his voice to its normal level, and the overdone emotional outburst inevitably gives way to self-irony:

O Citadel of Kekrops' land! O thin-spread aither! O –
Why are you shouting, Demeas? Why are you shouting, you
fool? Restrain yourself. Bear up! …

(325-7 Bain)[21]

While Demeas in *Samia* blatantly suppresses his brief show of tragic emotion, Daos in *Aspis* consciously puts on an outward display of feeling, showing his strict reliance on the tragic mode. He tries to persuade Smikrines that the death of his brother Chairestratos is near, as part of a plan to draw the old miser's attention away from one niece (Kleostratos' sister) to another (Chairestratos' daughter) as a potential bride. To achieve this end, he not merely assumes the pose of the messenger in tragedy, but actually recites a series of quotations from relevant scenes in the tragedies, adding his own critical comments on the texts, and showing off his familiarity with the authors of the respective dramas. The first quotation is missing:

Da.: 'No man is fortunate in everything.' That too is a
    beauty. O reverend gods, what an unexpected grief!
Sm.: Daos, damn you, where are you running to?
Da.: This too is perhaps appropriate: 'The affairs of men not
    prudence but luck controls.' Very good indeed. 'When
    god wishes utterly to destroy a house, he plants the guilt
    in men.' Aeschylus, a noble poet ...
Sm.: Are you citing maxims, you idiot?
Da.: 'Beyond belief, beyond reason, terrible.'
Sm.: Will he not stop?
Da.: 'What of mortal ills surpasses belief?' that's Carcinos.
    'In one day gods make the happy man unhappy.' These
    are all splendid observations, Smicrines.
Sm.: What are you on about?
Da.: Your brother – O Zeus, how shall I say it – is all but dead.
Sm.: The one who was here talking to me a moment ago?
    What happened?
Da.: Bile, grief, an attack of madness, choking!
Sm.: Poseidon and the gods! How terrible!
Da.: 'There is no tale so terrible to tell, no disaster ...'
Sm.: You'll kill me.
Da.: 'For the gods ordained that misfortunes strike without
    warning.' That's Euripides, the other's Chairemon;
    no second-raters.

(407-28 Hunter)

The ostensible purpose of these quotations would appear to be merely to delay the dramatic development by comic means, but the manner in which they are presented by the protagonist, alongside the fact that the entire situation has been staged by him, points in another direction – namely, that we are presented with a parody of the tragic norms of behaviour. This is perhaps the most extreme and artificial of all forms of polyphony.[22]

So far, we have been discussing tragic borrowings relating to the way the characters express themselves in specific situations rather than to the actual substance. In other words, polyphony in these examples is enhanced by changes of tone (whether conscious or unconscious), as the character switches from the mundane language of comedy to the heroic language of tragedy – the result being to produce a theatrical experience full of linguistic variety. This is polyphony in the literal sense of the term. In the following examples, the polyphony depends primarily on analogies of substance (or of structure) which the playwright evokes deliberately, between the current comic situation and earlier traditions of tragedy.

Syros uses an analogy of this kind in his rhetorical argument in the arbitration scene between himself and Daos, in *Epitrepontes*:

> Look at this point, too,
> sir. This child may be a class above us;
> brought up among us labourers, he will one day
> despise all this, and, rushing back to his true
> nature, dare take up a gentleman's preoccupation –
> hunting lions, bearing arms, Olympic running!
> You've watched tragedies, I'm sure, and you are
> familiar with all those stories of how heroes like
> Neleus and Pelias were discovered by an old goatherd,
> dressed in a jerkin just like mine now, and when he realized
> that they were his betters, he told them the whole story
> of how he'd found them, how he'd taken them in.
> He handed them a pouch of recognition-tokens, from which they
> gained a clear and full knowledge of their past history; and so
> these boys, who had been goatherds till then, ended up as
> kings. But if Daos had taken out those recognition-tokens and
> sold them to make a profit of twelve drachmas for himself, they
> would have remained unknown for ever,
> young men of such an age and birth!

It's just not right that I should look after
his bodily welfare, sir, while Daos takes
his hopes of rescue and makes away with them.

(320-40)

The arbitration scene itself, in which the aged Smikrines is asked
to determine the fate of his own grandson, though unaware of the
fact, is clearly a conscious comic reminder of the situation in
Euripides' play *Alope*, in which king Kerkyon plays a role similar to
that of Smikrines, towards his grandson Hippothoon.[23]

In Act V of *Epitrepontes*, a further attempt is made by one of the
protagonists to create an analogy between the plot of this play and
a tragic model. This time it is Onesimos (?),[24] slave of Charisios,
addressing Smikrines who still has not come to terms with the idea
that his daughter Pamphile conceived out of wedlock and has borne
him a grandchild. He remarks:

'Nature willed it, she who heeds no laws.
For *this* was woman born.' Why are you so stupid?
I'll recite you a whole tragic speech from *Auge*,
if you still don't get it, Smikrines!

(1123-6)

When Onesimos specifically mentions the play from which the
tragic quotation is taken – Euripides' *Auge* – the spectator is
inevitably made aware of the comic analogy between the rape of
Pamphile by Charisios and the rape of Auge by Herakles. The brief
mention given by Onesimos of the parallel situation in tragedy
sharply contrasts with Daos' elaborate manner in the above-quoted
example from *Aspis*. For our present purpose, we may overlook the
different dramatic considerations which determine the pace and
nature of the two scenes (in *Aspis* we are dealing with the climax of
the comic situation, whereas in *Epitrepontes* with its resolution).
The assumption behind the behaviour of the protagonist in the
latter play is that the whole dramatic situation is so banal, whether
we were to put it in comic or tragic style, that even its polyphonic
expression becomes just as banal and conventional.

In *Samia* once again we have a situation in which an Athenian
father, Nikeratos, has to deal with the shocking realization that his
daughter has become pregnant out of wedlock (532ff.). Here too, an

example drawn from mythology is used by Demeas, Nikeratos'
interlocutor, in order to soften the initial blow. But Demeas goes too
far in the comparison, developing it *ad absurdum*, to the point where
he identifies the simple and spontaneous act of rape of Plangon by
Moschion with Zeus' sophisticated and carefully planned action in
taking possession of Danaë,[25] actually suggesting that the god
himself is responsible for Plangon's present misfortune. It is Menander's essentially critical approach to the mythological tale that leads
to its revival in this context:

> Tell me, Nikeratos, haven't you heard the tragic actors
> telling how once Zeus turned into gold and, coming down
> in a shower, infiltrated a roof and seduced a girl
> who'd been locked up?
> Ni.: What then?
> De.: Perhaps one should expect anything.
> See if any part of your roof leaks.
> Ni.: Most of it. But what has that got to do with it?
> De.: At one time Zeus turns into gold, at another into rain.
> You see? It's *his* doing. How quickly we've found it!
> Ni.: Are you leading me by the nose as well?
> De.: By Apollo, not I! You're worse by not a little
> than Akrisios, I presume. If he thought proper
> [to seduce] her,[26] then perhaps your own daughter –
> Ni.: Poor me, Moschion has done me in!
> De.: He'll marry her. Have no fear. But what happened
> was divine working, be sure of that.
>
> (589-600)

Samia, like *Epitrepontes*, belongs to a group of comic plays
conceived in relationship to one or more models of tragedy. In the
case of *Samia*, the most likely model would appear to be Euripides'
Hippolytos.[27] Menander's independent approach to the resolution of
the plot-complications[28] takes the spectator back to the ancient
mythological tale, obliging him throughout to judge the drama along
two conflicting planes – the tragic and the comic – which comple-
ment each other to form a rich and multi-faceted picture.

In *Sikyonios*, Blepes' report of the popular assembly that took
place at Eleusis concerning the right of Stratophanes to sole guardianship of his captive Philoumene (Act IV) has a similar effect,

though on a smaller scale (176ff.). The report, which is reminiscent in structure and style of the speech of the messenger in Euripides' play *Orestes* (866ff.),[29] places in a light of comic contradiction the relatively trivial problem facing Philoumene and Stratophanes when compared with the death sentence threatening Orestes in case he failed to convince the people of Argos of the justice of his cause.

Of particular interest in terms of the use of tragic means is the way the stage conditions are shaped for Knemon's apologetic speech in Act IV of *Dyskolos* (711ff.).[30] Knemon's appearance is preceded by Sostratos' report on the circumstances of the rescue of Knemon from the well (666ff.). This report, highly comic in its tenor, contrasts strongly with the traditional messenger speeches of tragedy. Knemon himself is brought on stage by means of *ekkyklema*,[31] a primarily tragic stage device. He is lying in a pose reminiscent of tragic heroes on their deathbed, such as Hippolytos at the end of Euripides' play of that name. Knemon's 'tragic' appearance prepares the spectator for his confession, while still under the impression of the events only just described by Sostratos. But the inevitable contrast between this scene and its tragic antecedents, and between it and Knemon's true situation (unlike Hippolytos he is *not* about to die from his wounds, even though he contemplates the possibility [729ff.]), creates a focus of comedy in a part of the plot-line which is basically serious and humane.[32]

Divine intervention in the human drama of Menander is another kind of polyphony. It is a fertile source in tragedy for the evolution of polyphony. But this subject requires separate study, and it will be discussed in Chapter VI.

These three kinds of polyphony encompass only a small part of a far broader manifestation, which in itself marks one of the more outstanding characteristic traits of Menandrian drama – i.e. that it is basically composed of different types of comedy.[33] In it, we find a broad humour alongside serious expression of moral and human values; emotional and moving scenes alongside a fine irony – all intertwined in such a way as to evoke a complex and varied theatrical experience, as well as to create comic effects.

In addition to the examples cited, it is pertinent to recall Demeas' solemn introspection at the opening of Act III of *Samia* (206ff.), followed by two dialogues of a purely comic nature, the first between Parmenon and the cook (283ff.), and the second between Parmenon and Demeas himself (304ff.); the expulsion of Chrysis later in the act, a highly emotional scene which is toned down by the farcical element of the cook and his irritating comments (357ff.);[34] the opening 'tragic' scene of *Aspis*, followed by the light-hearted comments of the goddess Tyche on the preceding events (97ff.);[35] and the ludicrous siege imposed by Polemon on the house of Myrrhine in Act III of *Perikeiromene*, which prompts Pataikos to launch his serious discussion of the legitimacy of the violent path chosen by Polemon in his attempt to win back Glykera (467ff.).[36]

In Menander's juxtaposition of different kinds of humour, the most impressive element is the balance created between the serious and the humorous in the depiction of the heroes and their experiences – a balance that has no equal in the comedies of Aristophanes, even though there, too, the aim is to present the spectator with a mixture of the serious and the ludicrous, and indeed, in many cases, it was the drama of Aristophanes that provided Menander with his basic tools.[37] Plutarch, comparing Aristophanes with Menander, has the following metaphorical comment on the latter:

> Should the action however demand something fanciful or impressive, he opens all the stops of his instrument, as it were, and then quickly and convincingly closes them again and restores the tone to its usual quality.
>
> *(Mor. 853E)*[38]

The tendency to bring the tone back 'to its usual quality' after a suitable interval appears to be part of the Menandrian technique of juxtaposing different kinds of comedy. This tendency may also be discerned in another characteristic trait of the Menandrian drama that marks an impressive departure from the Aristophanic technique: I refer to the controlled use the playwright makes of the element of *farce* in his plays.

In *Dyskolos*, his early play, three scenes may be interpreted as farcical, and each of them touches upon the personality of Knemon: the entrance of Pyrrhias, deeply shocked at Knemon's violent behaviour towards him in their first encounter (81ff.); Getas' and Sikon's vain attempt to borrow a cooking vessel from Knemon (456ff.); and the mockery of the misanthrope by Getas and Sikon as a punishment for his unpleasant attitude towards them in the above scene (885ff.).

In *Samia*, the element of farce is confined mainly to Acts IV and

V.[39] In Act IV, after a series of particularly amusing misunderstandings between Nikeratos, Demeas and Moschion, the true identity of the mother of Moschion's baby finally dawns on the former two. In Act V, Moschion's plan to punish his father for suspecting him of having relations with his mistress is presented in a ludicrous light.

In *Aspis*, the farcical element is to be found mainly in Act III, where Daos' intrigue against Smikrines is finally accomplished, and perhaps it surfaces once more in Act V, if we accept the proposition that this act includes the mockery of Smikrines, in a similar manner to that of Knemon in Act V of *Dyskolos*.[40]

In *Perikeiromene*, the siege scene (Act III) referred to earlier also has a farcical effect, as does the mockery of Smikrines by Onesimos in Act V in *Epitrepontes* (1078ff.).

This controlled use of the element of farce enables Menander to make sure that the general tone of the play does not rise above the average level of comedy which he maintains in his polyphonic opus. The relatively frequent use of this element at the end of his plays[41] is illuminating: at the point at which the ancient *komos* retains its original force even in the restricting framework of New Comedy, Menander's comic spirit is at its most liberated.[42] This, too, is one of the rare cases in which Menander's artistic purposes appear to coincide with those of Aristophanes.

Economy

This description of Menander's inclination to vary the structure and content of his works might give the impression that we are dealing with a writer inclined to make exaggerated use of the comic and dramatic tools at his disposal, and with a marked preference for expansive dramatic expression over economy. But nothing could be further from the truth, as we discover over and over again while studying the texts of his plays. He was a master of economy, and his ability to present a rich and colourful portrayal of his heroes and convey their experiences, while only rarely digressing from the elements essential for the spectator's full understanding of the dramatic situation, was one of his rare and most valued qualities as a dramatist. We need only recall Plautus' *ubertas sermonis* to appreciate the essential difference between the Latin adapter and his Greek model in terms of artistic intention and technique, even though Plautus, too, occasionally opts for economy and the advan-

tages accruing from it. As to Terence, his economy of writing appears
to follow largely along the road of Menander's.

The Menandrian technique for achieving economy is many-
faceted, varying according to the particular situation. However,
three main methods may be discerned. The first is simply to refrain
from developing motifs and situations where this is feasible, or
alternatively where it is justified psychologically and dramatically.
Consider, for example, the way Menander presents the first encounter between the soldier Stratophanes and Kichesias, whose daughter, Philoumene, he hopes to marry, in *Sikyonios*:

St.:   *(emerging from the house of Smikrines)*
       I'll come back when I've checked these matters, mother.
Dr.:   Stratophanes – this is Philoumene's *father*.
St.:   Who is?
Dr.:   This man here.
St.:   Hello, sir.
Dr.:   This is the man who's kept your daughter safe.
Ki.:   May he be fortunate!
St.:   If you agree, sir,
       I shall become a happy man as well.
Dr.:   Stratophanes, [now let's go] quickly to …

                                                        (377-82)

'The pace of these lines', observe Gomme-Sandbach, 'is extraordinary: no time is wasted over introductions, and Stratophanes is
not allowed to develop his broad hint that he is a suitor for Philoumene's hand. Dromon, whose excitement comes out in the repeated initial vocative *Stratophane*, placed at the line-end to cut in
on the previous speaker, is anxious to reunite father and daughter.
Old Kichesias is too bewildered to say more than three words, and
those he does not directly address to Stratophanes – an excellent
touch.'[43]

We are talking here of a conventional element frequently used at
the end of comedies, a wedding, or more precisely, the preliminary
step towards realizing the wish to marry according to the traditional
norms of behaviour – namely, to seek the consent of the girl's father
in his capacity of her *kyrios*, guardian.[44] If Menander had attempted
to provide a more detailed description of this situation, it would not
only have diverted the spectator's attention from the main subject

of Act V – the expected *anagnorisis* between Kichesias and his daughter (though this is not actually realized on stage, the spectator is continually aware of it) – but would also have been a superfluous elaboration of a theme the normal course and culmination of which were familiar to the audience. This applies both in the specific context of Act V (in which a happy ending is inevitable under the comic convention) and in the light of everyday experience. By refraining from developing this theme further, Menander not only preserves the correct balance in his handling of the components of Act V, but also manages to throw further light on the mental state of his protagonists, even at this late stage of the drama, as Gomme-Sandbach rightly point out.[45]

Another illuminating example of such economy may be found in *Samia*, in the portrayal of Nikeratos' reaction to his discovery that Plangon, his daughter, is the mother of Moschion's baby (532ff.). This contrasts with the detailed portrayal of Demeas' reaction to his discovery of the apparent love affair between Moschion and Chrysis (219ff.). In the former scene, the fact of the discovery is reported to the spectator without any attempt at portraying the precise circumstances:

Ni.: O misery, misery me! What a sight I have seen! I'm rushing
out in a frenzy, pierced to the heart with pain unlooked-for.
De.: What on earth is he going to tell us?
Ni.: My daughter – my own daughter – I found her just now
breast-feeding the baby.
De.: *(To Moschion)* Then your story's true.
Mo.: You listening, Father?
De.: You've done me no wrong, Moschion. But I've wronged you
by suspecting you as I did.
Ni.: You're the man I want, Demeas.
Mo.: I'm off!
De.: Don't be afraid.
Mo.: It's death just to look at him.
(He runs off, left)
De.: What on earth is wrong?
Ni.: Breast-feeding the baby in the house – that's how I've just
found my daughter.
De.: Perhaps she was just pretending.

Ni.:   It was no pretence. When she saw me, she fainted.
De.:   Perhaps she thought –
Ni.:   You'll be the death of me with your perhapses.

(532-44 Miller)

Apart from a wish to vary the dramatic tools used, the difference
of Menander's treatment of the two cases appears to stem mainly
from the different dramatic contexts in which the discoveries are
made, and from the differences in character of the *dramatis personae* involved.

Demeas' discovery is described at the start of Act III, a convenient
timing for a broader exposition, and it serves as a prologue to the
comic events in the scenes that follow, all of which stem from
Demeas' mental, emotional and practical responses to that discovery. In other words, the expansive portrayal here is not only essential for an understanding of the ensuing comic developments, but
also contributes decisively to establishing important aspects of the
protagonist's behaviour, such as his boundless love for his adopted
son, as well as his tendency to analyse events. These two will be the
guiding principles of his future actions.[46]

Nikeratos' discovery, on the other hand, occurs in the middle of
Act IV, as part of a long series of farcical events which follow hard
upon one another at a dizzying pace. In this fast-moving context,
there would have been neither room nor need for a detailed description of the circumstances in which the discovery was made. Everything is subordinate to the theatricality of the individual scene,
including the limited imagination and understanding of Nikeratos
himself, which are so startlingly revealed in the course of this act.

The second important method used by Menander to achieve
economy is the construction of a scene, or part of one, in such a way
as to dispense with the need for a repetition of its factual content,
or further expansion of it.

Thus in *Perikeiromene*, having Moschion eavesdropping on the
conversation of Glykera and Pataikos provides a convenient way of
supplying him with the necessary information on his own family
connection with the protagonists.[47] In this way, the family reunion
promised in the prologue can easily be realized without any further
delays. Indeed, Moschion, unable to control his emotions, steps
forward out of hiding and introduces himself to Pataikos and Glykera, whose relationship to himself he has only just discovered by

pure coincidence. In the lacuna before the choral interlude, the family reunion takes place. This can be kept down to a brief scene, since the important facts are already known to the characters on stage and to the audience.

In similar fashion, in *Misoumenos*, having the monologue of Kleinias follow upon that of Thrasonides at the end of Act III (259-75) responds to the need for *variatio*, and has the further distinct advantage of presenting to the spectator *two* possible lines of action with regard to Krateia, apparently the object of desire of both protagonists:[48]

Th. *(addressing Getas, Krateia's slave)*
It is the father of Krateia, you say, who has arrived? Now it is for you to reveal whether I have become happy, or the most miserable of all men alive. For if he doesn't approve of me and give me her hand in lawful marriage, as it is in his power to do, Thrasonides is done for. God forbid! But let's go indoors: enough with speculations of that sort, we've got to *know*. Hesitant and trembling I enter the house. My soul is foretelling some disaster, Getas. I'm scared. But anything[49] is better than to go on in this uncertainty. Yet, I'd be surprised at all this.

Kl. *(giving instructions to the cook)*
There's one guest, Cook, and me, and third is my girl, if she's indeed come in; for I, too, am torn. Otherwise, it'll be only the guest. For I'll be running all over the town in search of her. But you carry on, Cook, and give ample thought to the matter of speed![50]

Where the Monologue is concerned, there are two further examples worthy of mention, both taken from *Samia*.

The first is Moschion's speech in the prologue, in which a major part of the exposition is devoted to presenting the good character of Demeas (5ff.), enabling the playwright in this way to introduce the audience not only to the general setting of the play, but also to the emotional and ethical aspects of the specific relationship between father and adopted son – the major theme of the play.

The second example is Demeas' speech to Moschion in Act V (695ff.), in which the father displays understanding of the motives behind Moschion's threat to go to Asia as a mercenary, even before his son has had a chance to tell him what prompted him to utter the threat. By attributing to his hero the ability to understand without explanation what goes on in the mind of his son, Menander contributes both to the economy of his play (for Moschion has already explained his motives at some length in his monologue at the opening of Act V), and to a deeper comprehension by the spectator of the profound emotional affinity between father and adopted son.[51]

The third method adopted by Menander to achieve economy in his plays is to exploit motifs and situations for a number of interwoven dramatic purposes, either in the framework of individual scenes or as part of his comprehensive dramatic strategy, in such a way that the spectator becomes aware of them retrospectively at critical points in the play. In *Dyskolos* and *Samia*, extensive use is made of this technique.

In *Dyskolos*,[52] the wild pears which Pyrrhias sees Knemon pick on the hillside (100ff.) – the first external expression of the eccentricities of the misanthrope – soon become a weapon aimed at him by the latter (121); the sun which burns Sostratos as he works in the field (535) – an amusing detail of Sostratos' description of his brief but decidedly unpleasant venture in working on the land – helps Sostratos, the delicate townsman, to be accepted by Knemon as son-in-law (754);[53] the bucket dropped into the well because of Simiche's carelessness (189ff.) – a seemingly accidental cause of the meeting between Sostratos and Knemon's daughter[54] – continues to exert its influence in the course of the vain attempts by Simiche and Knemon to extract it from the well (574ff., 620ff.). In the attempt, Knemon himself falls into the well, and this is the incident which brings about the *peripeteia* of the play; Sostratos' work in the fields, originally a trick devised by the slave Daos in order to set up a meeting between Sostratos and Knemon (366ff.), is derided by Sostratos after it has failed to achieve this aim (522ff.), but nevertheless turns to his advantage when, later in the play, the possibility of his marrying the daughter of Knemon appears for the first time to be a real one (754ff.).[55] Similarly, while Sostratos' description, in Act I (183f.), of the slave Getas as a schemer might appear irrelevant to his character as far as Acts II, III and IV are concerned, Menander takes up the theme in Act V, when he chooses Getas as the initiator and principal performer of the mockery of Knemon (885ff.).

In *Samia*, Demeas' conviction that Moschion is innocent of the charge of betraying him is based on the *kosmiotes* – decency – that had always characterized their relationship in the past (272-4; 344), and harks back to Moschion's self-portrayal in the prologue (18);[56] the expulsion of Chrysis from the household of Demeas in Act III is the realization of a possibility first hinted at towards the end of Act I (79ff.), and which, as Menander would have us believe in Act II, is no longer relevant.[57] Similarly, Chrysis' declaration, at the end of Act I (84-5), that she would never abandon the baby, attains its full significance at the practical level only in Act IV (559f., 568ff.). And finally, there is the antithesis between Athens and Pontos at the start of the dialogue between Nikeratos and Demeas when they reach the scene of the events at the end of Act I:

De.: Can't one notice the change of place already?
     How different are things here from the troubles there!
Ni.: Pontos. Fat old men. Plenty of fish.
     Unpleasant sense of everything. Byzantion. Wormwood.
     Everything bitter, by Apollo! But here are all pure blessings
     for the poor.
De.: Dear Athens,
     may you have all you deserve so that we, who love
     our city, may be most fortunate in everything ...
Ni.: What I found most extraordinary about that place, Demeas,
     was this: at times, it was impossible to see the sun for
     weeks. A kind of thick mist, it seems, was throwing shadow
     over him.
De.: No. He couldn't see anything worth seeing there, so that he
     shone on the people there the minimum amount.
Ni.: By Dionysus, well said!

(96-112)

In the context of their appearance there, this antithesis fulfils four different functions simultaneously:

(1) it symbolically bridges over the geographic distance between the two cities;
(2) it recalls to the audience's mind the old men's stay in Pontos;
(3) it highlights the sense of local patriotism of the protagonists – a gesture of acknowledgement by the dramatist to his audience of fellow Athenians;
(4) it hints at the conflicting characters of the protagonists, each

of whom, while agreeing in principle on the nature of the two locations, expresses his view in his own way, with a style and emphasis of his own.[58]

A fifth function is revealed in Act III, when Nikeratos explains Demeas' sudden decision to expel his mistress Chrysis from his household in the following words:

Demeas is melancholy mad.
Pontos isn't a healthy place.

(416-17)

Thus we find that the contempt shown by both Demeas and Nikeratos for Pontos in Act I is not forgotten, but is taken up by Menander as the logical background (from Nikeratos' point of view) for Demeas' seemingly incomprehensible behaviour.[59]

In each of the cases mentioned, Menander's economy of writing in no way lessens the spectator's ability to understand the characters or the situations in which they are involved. On the contrary, it contributes to a deeper understanding, being a logical result of a specific situation, a natural expression of the character and mental disposition of the *dramatis personae*.

Here we come to the principal difference between the economy employed by Menander and that of Plautus – insofar as it exists – and Terence, where it cannot be attributed to the Greek source.[60]

It should be stressed that Menander, though essentially an economical playwright, was fully aware of the advantages of dramatic expansiveness, and did not hesitate to depart from his more usual practice whenever this appeared to him to be more effective. Outstanding examples of such expansiveness may be found in the arbitration scene in *Epitrepontes* (Act II); Demeas' narrative speech in *Samia* (206ff.); Knemon's apologetic speech in *Dyskolos* (711ff.); and the messenger's speech in *Sikyonios* (176ff.).[61]

Emphasis on human interaction

We have defined the third artistic criterion traced in the works of Menander as emphasis on human interaction. By this definition we do not mean humanism in moulding the characters and their experiences – in itself a significant aspect of Menander's overall artistic approach – but rather his inclination towards developing the personal relationships between his characters and promoting a solution to the plot complications through direct interaction between the *dramatis personae*.[62]

In *Dyskolos*, Sostratos is made to come into contact with a series of people who are not only complete strangers to him, but whose world outlook and way of life stand in complete contrast to his own: Knemon, Gorgias, Daos, and Knemon's daughter. As a result of the close contact established by the playwright between Sostratos and his new environment, positive relationships are developed between him and some of the characters (Daos, Gorgias), which are made to perform an important role in achieving the aim of the plot, namely the marriage of Sostratos to Knemon's daughter.

What is notable about this system of developing relationships is that instead of being a direct continuation of the system of relationships expounded in Pan's prologue as having existed *before* the commencement of the dramatic action,[63] it is based almost exclusively on contacts initiated *in the course of* the dramatic action itself – a rare phenomenon in extant New Comedy.[64] Elsewhere in the plot, a significant change in the relationship between Knemon and Gorgias occurs as a result of the former's fall into the well and his subsequent rescue by Gorgias. Knemon, the misanthrope, who has so far avoided any contact with his stepson and his household, is so deeply impressed by the young man's noble response in this episode, that he adopts him as his son and appoints him guardian over his property and his daughter (722ff.).[65]

In *Perikeiromene*, Pataikos is sent by Polemon to Glykera to try to persuade her to forgive him for his violent behaviour towards her (507ff.). This attempt arouses in Glykera feelings of pride and resentment, and she rushes to Pataikos to present evidence that she is a free-born citizen (708ff.). The following *anagnorisis* (779ff.) is a direct result of the face-to-face confrontation between father and daughter.[66] Towards the end of the play, a second off-stage confrontation between the two persuades Glykera to change her attitude to Polemon, and to resume her relationship with him on socially acceptable terms (1006ff.).

In *Samia*, Moschion and Demeas are shown to reach a deeper understanding of each other after a series of misunderstandings caused by Moschion's decision to pass off the baby borne to him by Plangon as the child of Chrysis, Demeas' mistress. In the fourth act, the misunderstandings between the two over the real parentage of the baby are removed, and in the fifth, those concerning one another. In both cases, resolution of the misunderstandings is achieved through direct confrontation.

In *Epitrepontes*, Menander deliberately avoids bringing together his main protagonists, Charisios and Pamphile, and opts for an indirect manner of revealing their attitudes towards each other. Charisios is made to reassess his relationship with his wife, not through direct confrontation with her, but as a result of overhearing her conversation with her father, when she absolutely refuses to obey her father's demand that she should divorce her husband despite his unacceptable behaviour towards her (714ff., 883ff.). Although the confrontation between father and daughter does not yield the results sought by the former, it nevertheless makes a decisive contribution to the promotion of understanding between the spouses. The fact that this understanding is achieved indirectly, unlike the cases quoted above, emphasizes the independent way in which each of the parties is led towards forming attitudes which will end in the resolution of their dispute.

Similarly, in *Dyskolos*, the representation of the misanthrope as unaffected by his human environment is necessary for the preservation of the credibility of his character. Menander therefore does not let Knemon get involved with his environment until the dramatic moment of the well episode (Act IV). The deep mental shock he experiences here is used by Menander to create a temporary aberration in his character's response to his surroundings. The limited scale of Knemon's relaxation of his misanthropy, as expressed in his monologue and in his subsequent behaviour (733ff., 750ff., 867ff., 911ff.), is an indication of the extent to which Menander is aware of the problematic nature of his hero's essentially unsociable character, though he attempts to dramatize his personal situation in social terms.[67]

In deciding on the extent to which he will develop the personal relationship between characters in the direct manner described above, Menander seems to be guided by two main factors: plot considerations – some of which we have already touched upon in discussing his treatment of the relationship between Pamphile and Charisios and that between Knemon and his environment, in *Epitrepontes* and *Dyskolos* respectively[68] – and the accepted social conventions which Menander, like all playwrights working in the traditions of later Greek comedy, had to take into account if the play was to offer a contemporary image of society, acceptable to his audience.[69]

The effect of these conventions may be seen first and foremost in Menander's tendency to avoid dialogue between a boy and a girl when the latter is known to be a free-born Athenian citizen. Such meetings were strictly prohibited in Menander's Athens, in which seclusion for the female sex was seen as a civic necessity for preserving the purity of the family line.[70] The meeting between Sostratos and Knemon's daughter in *Dyskolos* (189ff.) is an exception, and may be rendered admissible by the fairy-tale atmosphere permeating the play, of which Knemon's 'liberal' education of his daughter is one of the expressions.[71] Nevertheless, this meeting is severely criticized by the slave Daos, who is made to witness it (218ff.).[72]

The absence of public expressions of love between husband and wife in Menander is yet further evidence of the effect of Athenian social conventions on his dramas, since contemporary Greek morality confined such expressions to the privacy of the home. Again, the fact that respectable free-born Athenian women citizens are as a rule restricted to the background of the Menandrian plot, and only rarely come forward to be invested with true dramatic value, may be regarded as a reflection of their actual status in society, which did not allot them any role in public life except on the religious level. It was regarded as natural for them to spend much of their life confined to the women's quarters of the house.[73] One is also reminded of Menander's tendency towards plot solutions shaped by social conventions and according with popular morality, as pointed out by Plutarch:

> Even the erotic element in Menander is appropriate for men who when they have finished drinking will soon be leaving to relax with their wives. For there is no paederasty in all these plays, and the deflowerings of virgins end decently in marriage. As for the prostitutes, if they are audacious and bold, the affairs are cut short by punishments of some kind or by repentance on the part of the young man; but if they are good and return a man's love, either a father is discovered for them who is a citizen or some extra time is allowed for their affair, which brings a humane relationship of respect.
>
> (*Mor.* 712C)[74]

Such solutions, rather than resulting directly from the individual situation of the characters as depicted, more often than not reflect the social and moral framework within which Menander chose to set them as part of his competitive struggle for success. What we are dealing with here is, therefore, a form of drama in which dramatization of human relationships, although playing an important role, is only rarely free from the limiting effects of the underlying social conventions. In this respect, Menandrian drama differs on the one hand from Old Comedy, which shows little interest in developing personal inter-character relationships, and on the other hand from classical tragedy (mainly Sophocles and Euripides) which, although showing great interest in dramatization of human relationships, needs make only very limited concessions, if any, to accepted social norms, since it is drawn from myth rather than from everyday reality.

Neither Plautus nor Terence, in their adaptations of Menander, seem to have fully preserved the dramatic pattern of human relationships as conceived by their prototype. Having their own artistic preferences, they introduced changes in the plot which somewhat detracted from the quality of dramatization of the Menandrian original.[75]

These three principles were applied by Menander in his dramas within a set pattern which appears to have become the norm in his time for the genre of the New Comedy: five acts separated by four choral interludes. We do not know to what extent writers of New Comedy were expected to adjust the pace of the plot development to the division into five acts. Modern attempts to find a common and consistent pattern of such adjustment in Menandrian comedy have not been successful.[76] In fact, apart from a certain tendency on his part to provide a solution to his plot complexities already in Act IV, we have found no set pattern of relationship between plot and acts in the extant comedies. As Holzberg demonstrated, even the exposition in Menandrian comedy is not confined to Act I, but tends to extend to Act II as well, and sometimes even further.[77] Thus, for example, in *Dyskolos*, the character of Knemon is clearly defined only in the encounter between Sostratos and Gorgias, which occurs in Act II.

Nor do the play-endings reveal any permanently set pattern of relationship to the preceding acts – despite their somewhat stereotyped nature.[78] Act V in some cases may include highly significant dramatic developments with regard to the plot as a whole, such as the intrigue of Theron the parasite and the *anagnorisis* that ensues between Kichesias and his slave Dromon (instead of the anticipated *anagnorisis* between Kichesias and his daughter) in *Sikyonios*. However, it can also be confined to events of a purely conventional nature which are characteristic of New Comedy endings, such as an engagement or a wedding feast (as, for example, in *Misoumenos* and *Perikeiromene*) or a mockery of an old character, whether as a separate event (as in *Epitrepontes*) or as part of the traditional marriage situation (*Dyskolos* and *Samia*).[79]

There are also great differences between the plays in terms of preparation for the developments included in Act V.[80] Moschion's attempt in *Samia* to teach his father Demeas a lesson for suspecting him of having an affair with Chrysis comes as a total surprise to the spectator. The same applies to the demand made by Sostratos of his father in *Dyskolos*, that he should consent to accept the impecunious Gorgias as bridegroom for his daughter, as well as consenting to the marriage of Sostratos himself to the daughter of Knemon, Gorgias' step-sister – which is the sole declared purpose of the plot. By contrast, the reconciliation between the lovers and their subsequent weddings in *Misoumenos* and *Perikeiromene* are entirely expected events which stem directly from the preceding dramatic developments.

Menander's flexible approach to plot-construction, as shown by his extant works, contradicts the widely held assumption that there is a typical Menandrian plot-model which can serve as a kind of yardstick by which to measure the Latin adaptations of Plautus and Terence. Acceptance of this basic fact is particularly important for a critical and balanced evaluation of the independence of the Latin playwrights in forming the endings of their adaptations, which are widely regarded as more or less their own inventions to a greater or lesser extent.

III

The Chorus and Related Problems

We know nothing of the nature of the Menandrian chorus (nor, indeed, of the chorus in New Comedy in general), except that it quite frequently took the form of a band of revellers who burst on to the stage at the end of the first act, upon the exit of the actors, and began their song, presumably accompanying this with some kind of dance.[1] In *Dyskolos*, one of Menander's early works, the chorus consists of the followers of the god Pan,[2] and presumably we have here an attempt on the part of Menander to credit his chorus – within the limitations of the diminished role of the chorus in New Comedy – with an individual character which is appropriate to one of the play's motivating agents, the divine prologue-speaker, the god Pan. To what extent such attempts were characteristic of New Comedy poets in general, and Menander in particular, we have no means of knowing until further evidence comes to light.[3] It seems reasonable to guess that in plays incorporating divine prologues, especially those delivered by a divinity which has a specific character familiar to the audience, the band of comic revellers could occasionally appear as representing the outlook of the divinity concerned, although its song need not necessarily be connected with the *plot* within whose frame it appears.

To indicate the moment where the chorus enters the stage, Menander uses a cue consisting of a basic, easily recognized formula, the roots of which are embedded in Euripidean drama (*Phoen.* 196ff.), but which continued to develop into a standard technical device for introduction of the comic chorus during the period of Middle Comedy.[4]

In *Epitr*. 169-71, the formula runs as follows:

Let's go, for there's a bunch of drunk
youngsters coming here.
I don't think this is the time for getting in their way.

Almost identical in expression is *Dysk*. 230-2:

> For I can see these people approaching right
> to this place, some rather drunk Pan-worshippers.
> I don't think this is the time for getting in their way.

Cf. *Asp*. 246ff.; *Perik*. 261ff.; *Fab. Incert*. IV Mette fr. e verso 5ff.; P. Köln 243a 15-17;[5] Plaut. *Bacch*. (= Men. *Dis Ex*.) 106.

The fact that Menander made hardly any attempt, stylistically or thematically, to give variety to the moment when the chorus enters the stage, stresses the purely technical aspect of this moment, as well as its functional value within the framework of the five-act system of New Comedy: this is the point where that part of the play which may be designated as introduction to the plot ends, the stage empties, and the chorus provides a tension-relieving pause in the action until its renewal in the second act. On the other hand, a close examination of the context of the entrance of the chorus in *Dyskolos* and *Aspis* shows to what extent the standard event in itself was exploited by Menander as a source of achieving various dramatic effects while maintaining its interruptive function.[6]

In the former play, the entrance of the intoxicated followers of Pan (230ff. quoted above) takes place at the end of a brief monologue by Daos in which he criticizes Knemon's neglect of his daughter:

> What the devil's going on here? I don't like this at all. A young man doing a girl a service, that's not right. It's your fault, Knemon, damn you! An innocent girl, and you leave her all alone, in a lonely place, with no proper protection. Perhaps this chap knows this, and has slipped in quietly, thinking it's his luck. Well, I'd better tell her brother about this, right away, so that we can look after her. I think I'll go and do that now –
>
> (218-29 Miller)

The sharp contrast between this monologue, which is imbued with deep moral indignation, and the carefree behaviour of the chorus of revellers as it is described by Daos, creates a very striking comic effect which increases the comic potential of the concluding scene of the first act. Daos is unaware of Pan's plan to engineer the marriage of Knemon's daughter to the rich young man – a plan of which the present meeting forms part. His indignation at this meeting, followed by a critical comment on the appearance of Pan's worshippers, thus adds an ironic twist to the entire scene, constituting an additional reminder of the god's involvement in the plot.[7]

In *Aspis*, the appearance of the band of revellers (246ff.) is preceded by two brief episodes in which the cook and the waiter respectively voice their indignation, in the presence of Daos, at their loss of income. They will no longer be required to cater for the party planned for the wedding of Chaireas and Kleostratos' sister, now that Kleostratos is presumed dead:

Cook: *(entering from Chairestratos' house with his assistant. He is unaware of Daos' presence at first.)*
       Every time I get a job, either somebody dies and I have to shuffle off without my wages, or one of the daughters produces a baby that no one knew about, and suddenly the party's over and I have to be off. Fine luck I have!
Da.:   Oh, go away.
Cook: What do you think I'm doing? Here, boy, take the knives, smartly now. After ten days without work, I landed this three-drach job, and this time I thought I'd got the money. Now a corpse arrives from Lycia and steals the lot. *etc.*
Waiter: *(entering from Chairestratos' house as cook and his assistant go off)*
       If I don't get my wages,
       I'll be cut up as much as you are.
Da.:   Go on!
       (Four or five lines are missing or damaged. When the text resumes, the waiter is ridiculing Daos' return from Lycia.)
                                              (216-35 Miller)

These scenes focus our attention on the cancellation of the party, comically dramatizing some of its consequences on a mundane level. The appearance of the band of revellers provides a comic substitute for the cancelled party!

Indeed, the chorus in *Aspis*, truly representing the comic spirit, here retains the optimistic line of the divine prologue-speaker Tyche (97ff.), providing a contrast to the depressed feelings of the characters who have just left the stage. The fact that the revellers' behaviour is approved by Daos here is a fine Menandrian touch, emphasizing the gap between the situation on stage and the hilarious irruption of the chorus:

> There's another rabble
> approaching here, I see, some men, quite drunk.
> You're sensible. What fortune brings is all
> uncertain. Take your pleasure while you can!
>
> (246-9 Arnott)

Nevertheless, the facts that the Menandrian papyrus texts say nothing of the movement of the chorus from the time it makes its first entrance on stage to the end of the play, and that the ancient copyists did not find it necessary to preserve the chorus' songs together with the rest of each play, show how far the chorus was detached from the action of the drama. It seems reasonable to assume that, even if the chorus were to stay in the *orchestra* during the acts (as did the chorus in the classical period) its presence would have had little more than a slender link with the plot. That this is so can be deduced from the absence from the texts of any further entrances after the initial one in Act I or any reference to an exit by the chorus at any stage of the play.

Dyskolos, for example – the only virtually complete Menandrian text extant – could stand perfectly well without any contribution whatsoever from the chorus. This dramatic device had reached that stage in its historical development when it could be regarded as external to the play, and possibly was not incorporated dramatically even into plays in which its presence might have benefited the dramatic situation itself. An example where it might have been used to good effect is found in *Epitr.* 169ff., where Chairestratos refrains from inviting the chorus of revellers to join the party which is being prepared: 'If there were even the slightest necessary link [between the chorus and the play. N.Z.]', observes Sandbach, 'the roistering youngsters of whom it here consists would be most fit company at the party which is being prepared in Chairestratos' house. As it is, they are to be avoided.'[8]

We remember that in our texts, the point of exit of the chorus, in contrast to its point of entrance, is never mentioned by Menander. Neither do we have evidence that it stayed in the *orchestra* to the very end of the play. It is possible that it left the stage during the final act, after its performance in the fourth interlude, bidding the audience farewell, or it could, as in classical drama, have deferred its withdrawal from the stage to the end of the play, when it would have exited without any special ceremony, along with the rest of the cast.

Be that as it may, the Menandrian fragments provide clear evidence of the growing decline in the importance of the chorus as a dramatic factor within the general design of the play on the one hand, and of the restriction of its function to that of providing an inter-act division on the other. The absence of any specific reference to its participation in the wedding celebrations, which are characteristic of the end of many Menandrian comedies,[9] demonstrates most emphatically that in Menander, and presumably in other contemporary poets as well, there was a diminution even in its traditional dramatic function of heightening the level of the comic spirit at critical moments. This fact is all the more evident when we bear in mind that the Menandrian chorus was composed of a band of revellers who could easily have been fitted into festivities of any kind.

The almost total detachment of the chorus from the action of the play, and its conventional appearance as a band of revellers regardless of the dramatic situation, caused a break between the various parts of the play to a degree which we do not find in classical drama, where the songs of the chorus, even if they do not always stem directly from the plot (e.g. in some plays of Euripides) invariably retain a certain link with it. Menander, aware that this element might damage the integrity of his plot, tries to bridge over the break between the individual acts by various link devices.[10]

The most important of these devices involves two characters making an entrance at the beginning of a new act while immersed in a conversation which, the playwright would have us believe, they began during the break between the acts. The entrance of Gorgias and Daos at the beginning of Act II and that of Kallippides and Sostratos at the beginning of Act V of *Dyskolos* are two examples of this device. When the subject of the conversation, moreover, was already broached in the previous act – as, for instance, in the meeting between Sostratos and Knemon's daughter, or in the conversation between Smikrines and Chairestratos in *Asp.* 250ff. (Smikrines' intention to marry his niece) – the effect of this device is not only to achieve continuity of action, but also to clarify the story-line, by filling in details of events which are presumed to have taken place during the interval. Menander extends his use of this link device to create a bridge not only between acts, but also between the scenes of which the acts are composed. Thus, for instance, the entrance of Sostratos and Chaireas engaged in conversation at the beginning of the first act of *Dyskolos* (50ff.) bridges the artificial break between Pan's prologue and the commencement of the actual dramatic action.[11]

The appearance of fresh characters at the end of an act, introducing new strands into the action, is also employed by Menander as an important device for achieving continuity in his plays.[12]

In *Dyskolos*, for example, the appearance of Kallippides at the end of Act IV focuses the audience's attention on a question the answer to which will be provided at the beginning of Act V – namely, will Kallippides agree to his son marrying Knemon's daughter? The audience at this point knows nothing about Kallippides apart from his excellent financial situation and his competence in managing his lands (774f.). This first appearance of Kallippides in the play, with the questions it raises about his possible reactions to the situation, creates a point of suspense and interest entirely new in the play,[13] and strong enough to keep alive the audience's expectations throughout the fourth interlude, which is intended principally to cover the length of time needed for Sostratos to obtain his father's assent to the marriage.[14]

An identical technique is employed in Daos' first appearance at the end of Act I in the same play. In his speech (see above), which concludes the act, he announces his intention to inform Gorgias of the meeting between Knemon's daughter and a young stranger. This is a new line of action which serves to introduce a new character, Gorgias. The subsequent interlude provides the necessary period of time required for the realization of this intention, as the audience is made aware at the very beginning of the second act. Similarly in *Samia*, the appearance of Demeas and Nikeratos at the end of the first act (96ff.) serves to inform the audience of their agreement to marry off their children, Moschion and Plangon, to each other. The practical consequences of this decision, made during the choral interlude, will become apparent to the audience at the start of the second act, through the monologue of Moschion and a dialogue between him and Demeas.

In all these cases,[15] the strong thematic link between the end of one act and the beginning of the next, consists of characters and events which give new impetus to the plot at the very point at which there is a break in the action on stage. This creates an illusion of continuity of action by means of which the choral interlude finds its proper and natural place – filling in the real time needed for performing extra-dramatic actions connected with the situations which are represented. In other words, the above examples focus our attention on the linking function of the concluding scene of one act and the opening scene of the next which we often find in Menander's plays. They show us how Menander resolves the problem of overcoming the break in action on stage caused by the traditional choral interlude.

Not only the subject matter, but also the stylistic formation of these scenes or parts of them, are important Menandrian devices for retaining the continuity of action. This may be demonstrated by two examples. The first is taken from the third act of *Samia*,[16] where Demeas has learnt that Moschion is the real father of the child whom Chrysis had previously made him believe was their child. This has led him to the erroneous conclusion that Chrysis had betrayed him with his adopted son, a conclusion which prompted him to expel her from his house together with the baby. Nikeratos, his neighbour, taking pity on Chrysis, has offered her shelter in his house. The act ends with Nikeratos' words of comfort to Chrysis:

> Demeas is melancholy mad.
> Pontos isn't a healthy place.
> Follow me inside to see my wife.
> Cheer up! What's the matter? He'll come to his senses
> when he thinks over what he is doing.

> (416-20)

These words[17] prepare the audience for the solution of the plot-complication in the next act, which opens with a brief speech by Nikeratos addressed to the members of his household (421ff.). This speech takes the audience back to the events which took place at the end of Act III, while emphasizing the unpleasant consequences of the entire affair for Nikeratos, which apparently began during the preceding interval. Like Nikeratos' previous comments at the end of the third act, his present ones also end with a reference to Demeas' moody state of mind:

Demeas
will stick at nothing.[18] By Poseidon and all the gods, he'll bewail
his stupidity.

(426-8)[19]

The second example is taken from *Perikeiromene*. At the end of
Act I, Glykera is seeking shelter with Myrrhine, Moschion's mother.
A lacuna of 70 lines prevents us from knowing whether she moved
to Myrrhine's house during this first act, or whether this move was
supposed to have taken place during the interval between Acts I and
II.[20] In any case Daos, Moschion's slave, who is aware of his master's
passion for Glykera, refers to Myrrhine's acceptance of the arrangement as a *fait accompli*, and therefore decides upon the following
course of action:

I must look for my young master.
It seems to me to be the right moment for him
to come here straight away, so I think.

(264-6)

These lines conclude the first act. At the beginning of Act II, Daos
and Moschion stand in front of Myrrhine's house planning the best
strategy for approaching Glykera without Myrrhine's knowledge.
Part of the irony of this situation lies in the way Daos' assumption
that Moschion's arrival at this moment is opportune (266) is gradually revealed to be totally mistaken, as Daos himself is forced to
admit when reviewing the chain of events that has just transpired:

Things are not as clear-cut as I thought then.

(353)

These words, which conclude the opening scene of Act II, constitute
a kind of epilogue for the line of action which began with Daos'
personal decision, at the end of the first act, to urge Moschion to
return home in order to be able to meet his beloved Glykera. This
decision, and Daos' acknowledgement of his mistake, round off this
part of the plot, forming a structural unit (ring-composition) into
which the choral interlude is conveniently integrated.

Whatever the nature of the choral interludes in New Comedy, and
whatever the degree of their impact on the form and content of the

plot, it is clear that in Menander their main function was to afford the passage of dramatic time necessary for performing an off-stage action, which is either unusually important or such as requires a longer period of time than that afforded through the short passage from scene to scene during the act itself.[21] Let us provide a few examples.

In *Aspis*, the break between the second and third acts covers the period of time necessary for the preparation of the intrigue against Smikrines, including arrangements involved in inviting Chaireas' friend to present himself disguised as a doctor who has to come to examine Chairestratos and pronounce him moribund.

In *Dyskolos*, Sostratos goes off to his father's nearby country estate to fetch his slave Getas towards the end of Act I, and he returns to Phyle empty-handed shortly after the start of Act II – a longer trip than the one he makes within the region of Phyle itself (from Pan's shrine to Gorgias' land) during Act III (573, 611).[22] Also covered during this interval is the time needed for Daos to find Gorgias and inform him of the meeting between the young stranger – Sostratos – and Knemon's daughter. The break between the second and third acts is meant to cover the lengthy preparations for the sacrificial feast in honour of Pan (435-7), the implication of which for Knemon forms the focus of interest in Act III. It is between the third and the fourth acts that Knemon falls into the well. It appears that Menander chose to present this turning-point in the plot as an off-stage action, in order to make the most of the element of surprise in Simiche's announcement of this event *after* the interlude (620ff.). The break between the fourth and fifth acts provides the length of time required for Kallippides to enjoy his sacrificial meal, and for Sostratos to obtain his consent for his marriage to Knemon's daughter.

In *Sikyonios*, Stratophanes and Theron travel to Eleusis at the end of the third act. In the second scene of Act IV, a messenger returns from Eleusis with information about the deliberations taking place there, with Stratophanes' participation, about who should be entrusted with the care of his beloved, Philoumene (176ff.).

In *Samia*, Demeas goes off at the end of Act II to prepare whatever is necessary for the wedding celebration. At the beginning of Act III, preparations for the feast are at their height. It is reasonable to assume that during the interval between the first and the second acts in *Perikeiromene*, the moving of Glykera from Polemon's house to Myrrhine's has taken place;[23] in any case, it adequately represents the length of time required for Daos to seek and bring back Moschion.

Of special interest is the break between the second and third acts in *Epitrepontes*, which represents the passing of dramatic time during which there is no progress in the dramatic action as such, nor is any offstage action reported that would require a significant passage of time. At the end of Act II, Onesimos announces his intention to present his master Charisios on the following day with a ring which is to prove, so he believes, that his master is the father of a baby left exposed together with the ring and other identifying articles (412ff.). At the beginning of Act III, he explains why, in spite of the long period of time which is supposed to have passed, he has not yet been able to carry out his plan:

> Half a dozen times I've embarked on the business of going to my master and showing him the ring: and half a dozen times I've got very close to it, been right on the brink of it – and then I funk it. I'm sorry now I ever told him anything. He keeps on saying, 'God damn that blasted tell-tale.' I'm afraid he'll make it up with his wife, and then get rid of the tell-tale, who knows too much for comfort. Best not stir in another ingredient to the mixture we've already got: the present stew's quite bad enough.
>   (419-29 Miller)[24]

What we have here is a unique example in New Comedy of a break between acts serving exclusively as an aid to characterization. Assuming that the morrow has come with Act III,[25] the way Menander avoids exploiting the interlude for dramatic purposes other than to emphasize the hesitant behaviour of his character is quite striking.

It is interesting to note how rarely Menander and his contemporaries exploited the possibility of using the choral interlude to represent an indefinite period of time, in order to expand the time circle of the plot beyond a single day.[26] Like their predecessors in tragedy and comedy, New Comedy playwrights preferred to express themselves within the limitations of the 'Unity of Time' – 24 hours.[27] Apparently, the introduction of irrelevant choral interludes into later Greek comedy did not significantly alter this traditional mode of presentation.

The Latin adaptations were written for continuous performance. They dispensed with the chorus, and this inevitably affected the pace of the action.[28] The difference is readily apparent in Plautus' adaptation of Menander's *Dis Exapaton* in his play *Bacchides*.[29]

Technical Variety in the Use of Motifs

One of Menander's techniques, we find, is to return to certain situations, motifs and behaviour patterns in different ways in the course of the same play. I would like to quote only the most outstanding examples of this technique, which is deeply rooted in Greek drama pre-dating Menander, both tragedy and comedy, in order to demonstrate the functions of this frequently employed device in his plays.[1]

At the start of *Aspis*, Smikrines meets Daos and learns from him of the death of his nephew Kleostratos. In Act III, the two meet again and once again Daos imparts to Smikrines news of the death of a relative – this time it is Chairestratos his brother (399ff.). Whereas the first encounter conveys the atmosphere of a genuine tragedy (the protagonists do not know that Kleostratos was in fact saved from death and is being held prisoner), the second concerns a tragic event but one invented by Daos as a means of diverting the greedy old man's attention from his desire to marry his niece, sister to Kleostratos.

The internal contrast between these two encounters, offset by their apparent external similarity (the two characters behave in an almost identical fashion in the two scenes), highlights the reversal which has taken place in the situation of the protagonists from the start of the play to the stage before its climax. This is the same Smikrines, revealed as a money-grubbing miser in a situation involving the death of a relative and, ostensibly, this is the same Daos – deeply moved by the death of his master's uncle. Yet how great is the difference between the present situation and their former encounter. Smikrines, formerly the arch-plotter, has now unwittingly become victim of the schemes of other characters. Daos, the humble and obedient slave of Act I, here emerges as the manipulator of intrigues against the old man.[2]

In the arbitration scene and in the scene which follows it, in Act

II of *Epitrepontes*, the effect of role-changing, based on reverting to the same situation from a different viewpoint, is more limited in scope, and its ironic significance is restricted to the scenes in question.

In the former scene, Syros the charcoal-burner claims ownership of the belongings of the baby which was handed over to his care by the slave Daos. But no sooner has his claim been granted than he is forced to give up a ring found among these belongings. It is Onesimos, slave to Charisios, who in the subsequent scene puts him in this inferior position by claiming that the ring is his master's property (391ff.). Finding himself in the same situation as Daos was in the previous scene, Syros does not lose hope and declares:

> I'll wait.
> Tomorrow I'm quite ready to entrust the matter to any
> arbitrator you choose – just like that! I've not done so badly
> so far, either. Still, it looks as though I must give up all my
> occupations and practise the pleading of cases.
> This is how everything is preserved nowadays.
>
> (414-18)

In Act II of *Perikeiromene*, Daos' repeated failures in his attempts to set up a meeting between Moschion and Glykera show, by means of the careful use of gradation of dramatic irony, how ludicrous is the situation of Moschion: he is unaware of the fact that he is actually related to the woman he so desires. In his ignorance, he thinks that Glykera's moving from the house of Polemon to his mother's house, is a proof of her secret desire for him, and is eager for an opportunity to realize his erotic fantasies about her (301ff.).

Similarly, in Act V of *Samia*, Parmenon repeatedly defers carrying out Moschion's demand to bring him a cloak and sword from inside the house (660ff.). The effect of this repetition is to hold up to ridicule Moschion's threat to set out for Asia to do military service there.

Both *Samia* and *Dyskolos* are noteworthy for their repetitive character. In the former, apart from the example already quoted, we find Moschion appearing as protector of Chrysis and the baby against Demeas in Act II and in Act IV, but for different reasons and in different circumstances.[3] Chrysis herself is thrown out of Demeas' house in Act III, and out of Nikeratos' in Act IV. At the end of Act III, Nikeratos gives her shelter, and close to the end of Act IV Demeas does the same. The chiastic pattern, based on repeating scenes but with different male protagonists, creates the impression of a rhythmic, multi-faceted comedy with infinite changes of mood, but balanced in its structure and in its approach to situations and the *dramatis personae*.

Nikeratos and Demeas both fall victim to the mistaken belief that Moschion has had an affair with Chrysis, but, as Hunter points out: 'It is a mark of the difference between them that Demeas' anger soon gives way to calmer reflection, whereas Nikeratos' anger and frustration merely vents itself in farcical action.'[4]

We find this same tendency of Menander — to highlight the differences of character between the two by means of their different reactions to one and the same situation — on two other occasions in the play: the first, Demeas' restrained reaction upon seeing Chrysis nursing the baby (265ff.) as opposed to the emotional outburst of Nikeratos upon discovering his daughter at his house nursing the same baby (532ff.).[5] The second case concerns Moschion's show of apparently setting out for military service in Asia, in Act V. While Demeas immediately realizes that this is a deliberate move by his son, and displays understanding and sensitivity to the motives behind it (695ff.), Nikeratos, blind to Moschion's mental anguish, perceives only the unpleasant consequences for his daughter of apparently being abandoned by his intended son-in-law (716ff.).[6]

In *Dyskolos*, the scenes of borrowing from Knemon which recur in Act III, together with their farcical re-enactment in Act V, clearly have a comic purpose. However the repetition here is also a successful attempt to attain symmetry of form. A similar attempt of this kind may also be discerned in the repeated presentation of the events which lead to the incident of the well by means of emotional outbursts on the part of the characters involved, accompanied by an exchange of words between them and another character on stage (189ff.; 574ff.; 620ff.). The changing of interlocutors (Knemon's daughter with Sostratos; Simiche with Getas; Simiche with Sikon), the difference in their reactions to the event portrayed, and the gradual way in which the dramatic development reaches its climax (Simiche's dropping the bucket into the well; her vain attempt to recover it, resulting in the mattock falling into the well; and finally

Knemon himself falling into the well in a vain attempt to recover both bucket and mattock) are variations within a set framework and provide a convenient way to highlight the differences in character between the protagonists. We have already cited the confrontation between Sostratos and Knemon's daughter,[7] the first link of this tripartite chain of events. Let us now have the remaining two confrontations:

Simiche-Getas:

Sim.: *(emerging from Knemon's house, not noticing Getas' presence)*
Oh calamity, calamity, calamity!
Get.: Oh, Hell! Here's the old man's woman.
Sim.: What's to become of me? I wanted to get the bucket out of the well, if I could, by myself, without telling master; so I tied the mattock to a poor rotten old piece of rope, and it promptly broke on me.
Get.: *(aside)* Oh, great!
Sim.: Oh, dear! Now I've dropped the mattock into the well too, as well as the bucket.
Get.: *(aside)* Then all that's left is to throw yourself in after them.
Sim.: Unfortunately, he wanted to shift some dung that was lying in the yard, and he's been running round for ages looking for the mattock, and yelling – oh, there's the door: here he comes.
Get.: Run, run, poor woman, he'll kill you. Better no, defend yourself!

(574-88 Miller with alterations)

Simiche-Sikon:

Sim.: *(coming out from Knemon's house.)*
Who'll come and bring assistance? Oh dear me!
Who'll come and bring assistance?
Sik.: *(emerging from shrine)*
O Lord Heracles!
By all the gods and spirits, do let us get on

with our libations! You insult and clout us, you –
may go to hell! What an incredible
house!
Sim.: Master's in the well!
Sik.: How did that happen?
Sim.: How? He was going down to fish the mattock
out and the bucket, then he slipped while at
the top, and so he's fallen in.
Sik.: Not that crabby old terror?
Sim.: Yes.[8]
Sik.: By Heaven, he's done himself justice! And now it's up to
you, my dear old girl!
Sim.: How?
Sik.: Take a mortar or a rock,
or something of the sort, and drop it on
him from above!
Sim.: Dear fellow, do go down!
Sik.: Poseidon! Like the victim in the fable, fight
the dog inside the well?[9] Never!

(620-34 Arnott)

This emphasis on the stylized formation of the various stages of the *peripeteia*, in an attempt to show up the characters of the protagonists, is perhaps one of the most impressive aspects of this play.[10]

In sharp contrast to the technique of repetition described above, we have the exploitation of unfulfilled motifs, a technique by which motifs are introduced for the sake of superficial immediate effects and do not have the consequences which we are led to expect. This takes the spectator by surprise; his expectations are first built up and then he is let down,[11] as illustrated in the following scenes.

Towards the end of Act II of *Epitrepontes* (412ff.)[12] Onesimos the slave announces his intention the next day to present his master Charisios with the ring which had been found among the recognition-tokens of the anonymous baby, in an attempt to check whether there is anything to the notion that Charisios might be its father. The spectator is made to anticipate that Onesimos will carry out this plan in the time-gap between Acts II and III, but at the start of Act III, he is let down in this anticipation when Onesimos reveals that he has failed (or rather refused) to put his plan into action because of the destructive effects he feared it would have for him (419ff.).[13]

Similarly, this same Onesimos prepares the spectator for his master entering in an emotional outburst on the verge of madness (878ff.), following his discovery that his wife Pamphile has unexpectedly refused to obey her father's wishes and divorce him, a discovery which makes him feel the deepest remorse for his own unfair treatment of her:

> He's mad, I swear it, quite loopy, really raving, absolutely
> crazy! My master, I mean, Charisios. He's fallen into black
> depression, or something very like it. There's no other expla-
> nation ...
> He reproaches himself savagely, eyes blood-shot, all worked
> up. I'm terrified, my mouth dry with fear. In this state, if he
> sets eyes on me, who told him about his wife, he might kill me.
> That's why I've stepped quietly out here. But where to turn?
> What to do? I'm finished, done for. Oh, there's the door, he's
> coming out. O God, save me if you can!
>
>   (878-907 Miller)

But when Charisios appears on stage, he is pefectly calm. Indeed, his attitude is carefully controlled and spiced with self-mockery, and his general approach reflects a totally objective evaluation of his relations with his wife, a pattern of behaviour diametrically opposed to what the spectator was led to expect after the preliminary remarks of Onesimos (908ff.).[14]

Again, in Act I of *Samia*, Moschion's apprehension of the approaching encounter with his father (61ff.) arouses expectations in the spectator that he will not easily obtain Demeas' consent to his marriage with Plangon, daughter of their neighbour Nikeratos. It soon becomes evident in the following scene that this was a false impression, for it emerges that Demeas is not only very keen on this match, but he has already come to an agreement with the father of the bride on the formal aspects, without even taking the trouble to consult his son first (113ff.).[15]

Equally misleading is the refusal of the slave Daos in *Asp.* 189ff. to accede to the request of Smikrines to let himself get involved in his dispute with his brother Chairestratos. Daos' pretext is that such an intervention would not merely be going beyond his sphere, but would also touch on matters totally alien to his Phrygian background, namely the law concerning *epikleroi*, 'heiresses'.[16] Consequently, whatever understanding he might display for these matters, or whatever help he could offer, would be practically useless:

Da.: Smikrines, I think the old saying 'know yourself' enshrines a profound truth. Let me stand by it. Anything that concerns an honest servant, you can refer to me and question me about.
(One or two lines are missing, and the following four lines are seriously damaged.)
... any seals, contracts he made when abroad – all that I can tell you. If so instructed, I can explain them one by one, giving place, occasion, witness. But property, and marriage to an heiress, and family, and differences of relationship – heavens, Smikrines, don't ever involve Daos in that! You're free men, you deal with that yourselves.
Sm.: For heaven's sake! Do you think I'm doing anything wrong?
Da.: I come from Phrygia. Many things that you Athenians approve of seem shocking to me – and vice versa. Why ask for *my* opinion? Yours is naturally better than mine.

(189-209 Miller)

However, later on in the play, we find this same Daos acting as a very keen partner in the family intrigue directed against Smikrines – in fact, as its initiator and chief implementer (320ff.).

Finally, several examples from *Dyskolos*, the play in which, more than in any other of his extant dramas, Menander uses the technique of letting down the expectations built up in the spectator, in order to achieve complex dramatic effects.[17]

Towards the end of Act I, Sostratos leaves for his father's house in the village with the clear intention of returning in the company of Getas, his father's scheming slave, hoping he will initiate an intrigue against Knemon (181ff.); yet when the spectator is informed, in Act II, that Sostratos could not find Getas at his home (259ff.), his anticipation of the intrigue for which the dramatist has whetted his appetite has not been fulfilled. A similar effect is created later in the play: Sostratos refrains from seeking the good offices of Getas when the delayed meeting of the two does take place (551ff.).[18]

Furthermore, Getas' behaviour throughout the play, apart from the final phase (885ff.), does little to justify his characterization by Sostratos in Act I (183f.) as an astute schemer with a special talent for invention and intrigue.[19]

We find this same tendency to disappoint the audience in their anticipation of intrigue once again in the play, in the ironic presentation of the scheme of Sostratos and Gorgias – in Act II – to engineer a meeting between Sostratos and Knemon. The planned meeting never takes place, because Knemon unexpectedly decides to stay at home and not go out to work in his fields, as he usually does every day (454f.).[20]

The possibility of Kallippides opposing his son's marriage to the daughter of Knemon is first hinted to the spectator at the end of Act IV, when Sostratos advises Gorgias to put off his meeting with his father until after his father has finished his meal (778ff.). Sostratos' complaint, at the beginning of Act V (783-4), creates the initial impression that this is indeed the case, but the minute Kallippides starts to respond to his son, it is immediately evident that not only is this an entirely mistaken impression, but also that the subject of Sostratos' complaint is not at all what the spectator had been led to expect. For the problem now is Kallippides' objection to the marriage of his daughter to Gorgias, an entirely new element in the plot, which Menander chose to introduce at this specific point in the play, without preparing the audience for it in any way whatsoever in advance.[21]

In his extensive use of this technique,[22] Menander appears to be following the example of Euripides, who also tended to play on the audience's expectations in order to achieve a heightened dramatic effect in his plays.[23] It would be unsafe to regard this use of unfulfilled motifs as showing that Menander was careless or sloppy in his development of these motifs. This is not a matter of carelessness but a deliberate means used by the playwright to create continual dialogue between his work and the audience, a dialogue based on working *against* the expectations of the audience rather than working *with* them. The clear advantage of this technique is that it adds an extra element of flexibility, naturalness and, of course, surprise to the Menandrian plot. Together with his other techniques, it offsets the conventional and formal elements of the play, such as the expository prologue; the systematic division into five acts; the set-piece choral interludes and the traditional concluding festivities, showing Menander's ability always to give a new twist and an extra dimension to his characters and to the events portrayed.

In determining the movements of the actors on stage, Menander sometimes shows the same preoccupation with dashing the expectations of the audience as we have found in his exploitation of unfulfilled motifs and situations. An outstanding example of such a deliberate 'choreography' may be found in the way Menander deals with the movements of the protagonists in the scene of Chrysis' expulsion in Act IV of *Samia*, and in the scene of Moschion's apparent departure for overseas in Act V of the same play.

In Act IV, Nikeratos, encouraged by Demeas, enters his house with the obvious aim of expelling Chrysis from it (517ff.). The spectator expects the immediate implementation of this intention, but what actually happens is something quite different. In line 532, Nikeratos emerges from his house, overcome with emotion and shock at the sight of his daughter nursing the baby of Moschion and Chrysis (as he had believed). In the ensuing conversation with Demeas, the question of expelling Chrysis nowhere arises. Nevertheless, when Nikeratos goes back into his house (547), the spectator anticipates that he will complete the process begun when he first entered the house (520) and nipped in the bud by the sight of Plangon with the baby. Nikeratos' reappearance without Chrysis (556ff.) thwarts that anticipation. For a moment it appears as though the plot is about to take an entirely new turn, following Nikeratos' revelation that Chrysis refuses to give him the baby, and that she has persuaded his wife and the entire household to deny his suspicions concerning the baby's parentage (558ff.).

This antagonistic female behaviour comes as a complete surprise to Nikeratos, who had clearly expected the women in his house to admit the truth, even if it meant incurring his rage (549). His threat to kill his wife (560f.)[24] complicates the situation even further, and temporarily diverts attention from Chrysis, who is still under threat of expulsion from the household. In line 562, Nikeratos enters his house for the third time. Judging by his behaviour so far, the spectator would have been justified in expecting him to emerge from his house once more, so as to report on the state of affairs inside, where crisis point has been reached. But Menander chose not to follow this pattern, and here again did not fulfil the expectations he had raised in the spectator. This time, it is Chrysis herself who appears, carrying the baby in her arms (568f.). Only then does Nikeratos make his third entrance, as expected (570).

Thus, some 50 verses after it is first introduced into the plot, the expulsion of Chrysis from Nikeratos' house at last becomes stage reality. It is the delay in implementing this dramatic act, engineered by the special arrangement of the entrances and exits of the *dramatis personae* and the motives attributed to them, that helps create the effect of playing upon the audience's expectations which Menander strives for here.

An identical technique, with similar effect, is applied by Menander in Act V of *Samia*, with the presentation of Moschion's plan to teach his father Demeas a lesson for suspecting him of having intimate relations with Chrysis. In 658ff., Moschion takes the first step towards implementing this plan: he sends his slave, Parmenon, to Demeas' house to fetch a cloak and sword, in the deliberate aim of arousing Demeas' suspicions as to his son's intentions. He expects Demeas to appear in person and try to persuade him to give up the idea of going to Asia (664ff.), and the spectator is led to share that expectation. Instead, Parmenon reappears empty-handed, and reports on the preparations being made in the house for celebrating Moschion's wedding to Plangon, clearly believing that his master is unaware of these preparations (670ff.). But Moschion, angry with Parmenon's failure to carry out his orders, sends him back again in the hope that this time his plan will work. Again, the audience expects the appearance of Demeas and again it is disappointed, because once more Parmenon appears instead – now carrying cloak and sword as instructed (687).[25]

Parmenon's negative reply to Moschion's question as to whether he has seen any of the family when he took these objects (688ff.), ostensibly leads the situation to the point of stalemate. 'It looks as if the stratagem had entirely miscarried (690). But no sooner has the spectator been thus led not to expect to see Demeas than out he comes.'[26] Demeas' gentle condemnation of Moschion's behaviour (695ff.) comes as a further surprise to the spectator and to the young protagonist himself, who was prepared for two possible reactions on the part of his adoptive father – either entreaties not to leave him or sending him off on his way in anger (664ff., 682ff.).

Parmenon's failure to reappear on stage after he re-enters Demeas' house (693-4) is also significant in terms of the aspect of Menander's technique under discussion. His absence contradicts his declared intention to join Moschion without delay in his travels to Asia (*ibid*.). The reason for this lack of consistency appears to be the dramatist's need to abide by the rule of three actors[27] – and, indeed, the actor who plays Parmenon is allowed to reappear immediately after Demeas' speech, in the person of Nikeratos (713). Thus, with Demeas and Moschion, he forms a group not exceeding three actors with speaking parts. Parmenon's failure to reappear goes unnoticed in the emotional context of the final scene of *Samia*.[28]

Between Comedy and Life

Between the final years of Aristophanes and the beginning of Menander's career, Attic comedy had undergone a great many changes, the most important of which seems to have been the separation of the chorus from the dramatic action. This change, combined with the decreasing interest in mythological parody on the one hand, and in social and political criticism on the other, paved the way for the introduction by the comic poets, towards the end of the fourth century, of a new form of comedy which we may here designate realistic. Thus we find that the comic plot is no longer conceived in terms of extraordinary events illustrating by way of paradox some negative aspect of the communal life; rather, it is the ordinary and the domestic that the playwrights of the new era seek to portray in their works. And while comedy as a whole has now become conventional in the extreme, a growing tendency towards individualization of characters and their experiences can nevertheless be observed.

Menander played an important role in this development. His successful attempt to make Greek comic conventions more lifelike is frequently referred to by the ancients, who recognized it as one of his greatest achievements as a playwright. It also won him much of his reputation in antiquity and the admiration of two of the most severe critics of the classical world: Aristophanes of Byzantium and Quintilian. The former went as far as to suggest that Menander's realism was indistinguishable from the actual life it portrayed: 'O Menander and Life, which of you imitated which?' was his famous saying (K.-T., *Testimonia* 32). Similarly the latter, in praising Menander's versatile rhetorical qualities, credited him with perfect representation of every reflection of human existence (*Inst. or.* X.i.69).

However, modern scholars do not all share the ancients' favourable view of Menander's realism. Some complain that Menander misrepresented Hellenistic society in laying too much emphasis upon the seemingly immoral activities of that society. Others regret the absence of any treatment in his plays of Athens' contemporary political experience and of many important aspects of its social life. 'It is usual to praise him without stint', writes Tarn, '... but to the writer he and his imitators seem about the dreariest desert in literature. Life is not entirely composed of seductions and unwanted children, coincidences and recognitions of long-lost daughters, irate fathers and impertinent slaves. Doubtless he had met these things; but, though his characters were types, the life was not typical. The world, however, has decided that it *was* typical, and on material drawn from the New Comedy is chiefly based the traditional belief in Athens' decadence.'[1]

Such criticisms evidently ignore the limitations of the literary framework within which Menander's realism was expected to be expressed, limitations which Menander's audience had been brought up to accept as natural. Nor do they seem to have sufficiently taken into account the differences between the ancients' concept of realistic drama and our own.[2] In the following pages, an attempt will be made to discuss the question of Menander's realism in terms more appropriate to the context in which this question first presented itself to his readers, namely, to treat it as an essentially artistic problem rather than as a historical one. For that purpose, the two best-preserved plays by Menander, *Dyskolos* and *Samia*, have been chosen. The analysis of these plays will show that Menander's realism is precisely what we would have expected it to be, given the particular context in which it is applied – a vivid dramatic tool, constantly subjected to character and plot considerations as well as to the moral attitudes of the contemporary spectator, and invariably reflecting the numerous artistic possibilities immanent in that very special zone where comedy and life meet.

Dyskolos

In *Dyskolos*, through the interference of the prologue-speaker Pan, a rich young city-dweller named Sostratos falls in love with the daughter of the peasant Knemon while he is hunting in Phyle, and wishes to marry her. Knemon is a misanthrope, and therefore all Sostratos' efforts to establish contact with him, whether directly or through an intermediary, come to nothing. It is only after Knemon's fall into the well in his courtyard, an incident which may be interpreted as the last link in the chain of events set in motion by Pan's manipulation of the play's action,[3] that the hoped-for turning-point is reached. Sostratos and Gorgias, the girl's half-brother, a poor but proud peasant, cooperate in rescuing Knemon from the well. The misanthrope, grateful to his stepson for his help, adopts him as his son and appoints him guardian of his property and daughter. Obtaining Knemon's grudging consent, Gorgias betrothes his sister to Sostratos. The latter manages to persuade Kallippides, his father, a landowner known for his wealth, to agree not only to his own marriage to the misanthrope's daughter but also to his sister's marriage to his future brother-in-law Gorgias. The play ends with a celebration of the double marriage, an unusual combination of two families so widely divergent in status and financial position, and with the misanthrope being forced to participate in the happy event.

Much of the play's charm lies in the manner in which the accepted social norms and the provisions of the law are applied to the fairy-tale plot,[4] whose romantic focus and whose main hero fail so conspicuously to conform to the expectations current in the every-day life of that period.[5]

The opening events plunge us straight into a socially unexpected situation, which is capitalized throughout the first act, creating an atmosphere of general laxity with regard to social conventions. First we have Sostratos' hasty use of the mediation of his slave, Pyrrhias, to obtain Knemon's consent to his marriage with his daughter. As Chaireas the parasite explains before he discovers that Sostratos has already sent his slave out on the mission (57ff.), hastiness is a mode of action suitable to an ephemeral love affair with a *hetaira*, but marriage requires a serious examination of the girl's family background (*genos*), her character (*tropoi*) and her financial situation (*bios*).[6] Sostratos, in his eager impatience,[7] not only omits to carry out this investigation, an incontrovertible social obligation in contemporary Athens, but even chooses to entrust his affairs to a slave, an entirely inappropriate action in view of the importance of the issue at stake, as he himself cannot help admitting (75ff.).

The second irregularity concerns the violent reception of Pyrrhias by Knemon. According to Pyrrhias' report of the incident (97ff.), Knemon has immediately expelled him from his premises without any apparent reason, before he had even had a chance to start conveying his message. Needless to say, Knemon's behaviour here was entirely unacceptable, even for a peasant, according to the social norms of his day, and calls forth an apology for the decivilizing effects of the life of hardship led by Attic peasants (129ff.).

In the following scene, Sostratos would have been expected to take advantage of Knemon's pursuit of Pyrrhias on to the stage, in order to try and mention his proposal of marriage to the person whom he is traditionally expected to address: Knemon, after all, is legally the *kyrios*, guardian, of his daughter. Yet he is discouraged from approaching Knemon by the latter's misanthropic outburst, during which he completely ignores the presence of others on the stage (145ff.). Left with no alternative, Sostratos considers resorting to intrigue in collaboration with his father's slave Getas (181ff.). This fresh approach, like the previous one involving a slave, contrasts sharply with the behaviour expected of a prospective son-in-law. This is the third (potential) irregularity in this act.

The fourth is found in the encounter between Sostratos and Knemon's daughter towards the end of the act (189ff.). In Athens of the classical and the Hellenistic periods, in which the purity of the family line (*genos*) was a civic necessity, complete segregation between the sexes was observed until, and even after, marriage.[8] Respectable free-born female citizens, like Knemon's daughter, would appear in public only to participate in religious festivals or funeral rites. Only at such formal occasions could a young Athenian set eyes on a free-born girl, and New Comedy often capitalizes on these situations as starting-points for its plots.[9] Knemon's daughter, by going out unaccompanied to draw water from the nearby Nymphs' spring, by falling into conversation with a young man who is a complete stranger to her, and by accepting his offer of help, exhibits a pattern of behaviour completely unexpected of the average Athenian girl.[10] The slave of the girl's half-brother Gorgias, Daos, an accidental witness to her meeting with Sostratos, blames Knemon for allowing his daughter to roam around unsupervised in this secluded spot (218ff.).[11] His strong criticism of Knemon's attitude as a father, and his decision to report what has transpired to Gorgias, put this stage-event into perspective from the point of view of everyday social expectations.

The first act thus ends with neither Sostratos nor Knemon, nor his daughter – the main protagonists in the romantic story unfolding before us – conforming to the social conventions of the day. In

the second act the norms of social (and legal) behaviour begin to
assert themselves and gradually increase their hold on the characters throughout the rest of the play.

The primary representative of these norms is Gorgias. In the
prologue to the play, he is characterized by the god Pan as a young
man who has matured early because of the hardships he has
endured in life. (Gorgias scrapes a livelihood from cultivating a tiny
plot of land inherited from his father, and supports his mother,
Knemon's estranged wife and mother of his daughter, who had
separated from him after a life of incessant quarrelling. Gorgias'
only help in his labour is Daos – 22ff.) His first reaction on hearing
Daos' report of his half-sister's encounter with the stranger confirms
this characterization. Gorgias criticizes Daos severely for not having intervened in the affair (233ff.): he should have immediately
approached the stranger and warned him not to show his face in the
area again; but instead, Daos has refrained from any action, as
though the girl involved had been a stranger rather than one of the
family: 'One cannot escape blood ties, Daos', exclaims Gorgias. 'My
sister is still my concern. Her father wishes to ignore the family
connection between us; let's not copy his ill-nature. For if her
chastity were to be blemished, her dishonour would also be mine.
The outsider judges only of events, not of who was responsible for
them' (239-46). Gorgias therefore concludes that he has no choice
but to confront the misanthrope directly, even at the risk of ill-treat-
ment at Knemon's hands, in order to acquaint him with the danger
threatening his daughter's chastity (249-54). Gorgias braces himself for the meeting, stationing himself near the misanthrope's
house with Daos.

In his attitudes and in his decision to confront Knemon, Gorgias
conforms fully to the expectations of the average Athenian, for
whom the duty of maintaining the family honour is paramount.[12]
Gorgias continues to reflect these expectations in the morally severe
attitudes he expresses towards Sostratos during their first meeting,
before he becomes aware of the serious nature of the lover's intentions. Sostratos returns to the scene after his failure to find Getas,
his father's ingenious slave, whose skills he had hoped to employ in
devising an intrigue against Knemon (259ff.). His destination, like
that of Daos and Gorgias, is Knemon's house. He plans to confront
Knemon directly this time (266-7) and to broach the marriage
proposal to him (a suitable approach by any standard, were it not a

misanthrope with whom he has to deal). He is about to knock on Knemon's door when Gorgias accosts him, outlining his view of the unsuitability of Sostratos' behaviour from the moral, social and legal standpoints (269ff.).

He makes the following points: first, Gorgias claims a close connection between the material prosperity of a man and the correctness of his moral attitude to life: Sostratos, he claims, is endangering the very financial basis of his existence by his immoral behaviour (270-87). Secondly, one should not imagine that the weakness of the poor in relation to the rich may be exploited by the latter without penalty. A poor man who has been wronged has an acute sense of outrage, so one must be doubly wary of arousing his anger (293-8). Thirdly, Sostratos, who is seeking to shame a freeborn girl, is planning a crime that deserves death many times over (289-93).

On the first two levels, Gorgias' claim reflects the typical ancient Greek outlook.[13] On the third, although the ultimate legal sanction was not regularly resorted to in everyday life (marriage with an abused girl or an appropriate financial compensation to her family were the normally accepted solutions to the problem), it nevertheless posed a threat to the very life of the seducer.[14] The fact that these claims are irrelevant, considering Sostratos' honourable attitude to the girl and to her social environment, creates a comic effect, and underlines the gap between the reactions of Gorgias (which were only to have been expected) and the romantic character of the plot.

Sostratos' reaction to Gorgias' charges puts his love for Knemon's daughter and his plans for their union into a proper perspective:

> I saw a girl here, I love her.
> If that's the crime you're talking about,
> then perhaps I *am* guilty.
> What else can one say? Except that I've come here
> not for her, it's her father I'd like
> to see. I'm free-born, of adequate
> means, willing to take her
> without a dowry, and give assurances always
> to cherish her.
>
> (302-9)

Two aspects of this reaction deserve our attention: the first is

Sostratos' emphatic declaration of his real intention to marry the girl, made at his first meeting with Gorgias, even before his discovery that Gorgias is a blood relation of his beloved (306-9). The second is his renunciation of any expectation of a dowry. In the first, we find a foreshadowing of the act of *engyesis*, 'betrothal', which is to take place at the end of the fourth act between these same two protagonists (761ff.).[15] Sostratos' statements at this point will be used later by Menander when he comes to give shape to this dramatic moment in the play. Thus, for instance, the would-be bridegroom will not need to express formally his acceptance of the terms of the *engyesis* or his commitment to his duty to take care of his wife, as is usual in real life, and as Menander himself made other comic lovers do.[16] Above all, this first expression of Sostratos' intentions also provides a firm basis for the development of the relationship between Gorgias and Sostratos as the play proceeds. Gorgias, who has never experienced love in his life and, as a hard-working farmer, considers it a luxury (341ff.), is less impressed by Sostratos' romantic feelings than by his readiness to marry his half-sister. As far as *he* is concerned, *this* is the major factor, the first brick on which the friendship will be built.

Sostratos' generous gesture in renouncing a dowry contains an element of surprise, not in itself (such gestures may be found elsewhere in New Comedy)[17] but in that, although in the fourth act the misanthrope will nevertheless dower his daughter with half his property (738), Sostratos (and his father) will continue to refuse it (844ff.).[18] Since the dowry was a desirable but not an essential constituent of a valid Athenian marriage,[19] the lover's renunciation does not detract from the legitimacy of the proposal of marriage. At the same time, Menander, through his unusual treatment of the dowry theme and the relatively important emphasis placed on this motif in the play, succeeds in reflecting its significance for a Hellenistic audience. Thus the romantic convention of the play will be sustained within the framework of normal Athenian marriage customs.

The pragmatic side – the actual marriage proposal – of Sostratos' reaction stands in sharp contrast to the apparently inappropriate context within which it is expressed. Gorgias may be impressed by the seriousness of Sostratos' intentions, but at this stage he does not see any possibility of their coming to fruition, owing to the misanthropic nature of Knemon. Unwilling to arouse vain hopes in Sostratos' breast, and out of consideration for his feelings, he describes to him the misanthrope's character, way of life, financial situation and relationship with his daughter (323ff.). Thus Sostratos becomes acquainted with the *genos*, *bios*, and to a certain extent the *tropoi* of the girl he intends to marry, but as *negative factors working against his hopes*. Menander here capitalizes on the tension between everyday norms which seek to assert themselves and the idea that they cannot be fulfilled in the present situation because of Knemon's eccentric character.

Gorgias' account is finally confirmed by Knemon's own statement, reported by Gorgias himself, that he will marry off his daughter only when he finds a bridegroom of his own nature (336f.). This statement by Knemon shows him in an ambiguous light: on the one hand the misanthrope is well aware that he ought to marry off his daughter; on the other hand, he imposes unrealizable conditions which reduce the prospects of finding a match for her almost to nil (see also 337f.). In the specific social context of contemporary Athens, the absurd element in his behaviour may be thus defined: Knemon speaks as the *kyrios* of his daughter (cf. the use of the term *ekdosein*, 'give in marriage' in 336),[20] but does not fulfil the obligations implied by this legal position.[21] He thus risks the extinction of the *oikos*, family, of which he is in charge. The intrinsic contradiction in Knemon's behaviour creates a deliberate tension in the plot.

The special relationship which Menander invents between Knemon and his daughter, as described by Gorgias in lines 333-5, is utilized to provide Menander with an opening between Knemon and the outside world. It shows Knemon's potential ability, limited though it is, to establish contacts with his human environment, the significance of which will gradually emerge in the course of the fourth act. On the other hand, it is important to observe that the close relationship between father and daughter has been determined by their regular cooperation in agricultural work – an upbringing uncharacteristic of contemporary girls of citizen status (who, as we have already noted, were normally confined to the women's quarters in the house).[22] This unusual habit of theirs – working side by side – inspires Sostratos later in the second act, for obvious reasons, to join forces with Gorgias and Daos in their work in Gorgias' field, which borders on that of Knemon (358ff.). Thus it is against this background of divergence from normal social conventions that the intrigue of Sostratos, Daos and Gorgias against

Knemon evolves, an intrigue designed for bringing about a meeting between Knemon and a supposed agricultural labourer, Sostratos.

On the other hand, another illumination of Knemon's internal world, and the relation between it and everyday reality, is the assumption shared by Gorgias and Daos that Sostratos' urban background (which can so easily be deduced from his smart appearance and mode of behaviour), constitutes a seemingly insuperable obstacle to obtaining Knemon's consent to his marriage to his daughter (356-70). Athenian social norms favoured union between social peers, whereas the play confronts us with the assumption that it is possible to bridge substantial social and economic gaps.[23] When Knemon later agrees to his daughter's marriage to Sostratos (753ff.), he will do so while under the impression that his would-be son-in-law is an industrious agricultural worker like himself, unaware that he is dealing with a rich, pampered city-dweller. His initial point of view is identical with that of Gorgias, who supports marriage between peers as a matter of principle and later attempts to apply this principle to himself, although he is overborne by argument (823ff.). Menander in this case assigns to Knemon an entirely realistic outlook.

This outlook contrasts with the romantic conception of the play, according to which rich and poor may successfully intermarry. What we have here is an interplay between fiction and reality in which the conventional presuppositions of the characters are turned upside-down by the unconventional reality of the play itself. The dramatic importance of the second act of the play depends largely on its contribution to this interplay.

It must be pointed out at this juncture that the misanthrope owns property estimated by Gorgias to be worth two talents (327f.), a considerable sum of money in contemporary terms,[24] yet he is regarded as poor throughout the play (130, 604ff., 795 [with reference to his daughter]). His 'poverty', in other words, is an artistic fiction, a necessary convention in a play whose plot is based on a sharp distinction between rich and poor. It is this fiction which permits the ambivalent approach to the theme of Knemon's daughter's dowry, which we have discussed earlier. But above all, it provides the audience with an objective standard by which to measure Knemon's misanthropic character: his style of life – one of poverty and hard work – is not a matter of necessity but of free choice.[25]

Sostratos' final speech in this act (381ff.) focuses on the character of Knemon's daughter, a result of the independent manner – by contemporary standards – in which her father has brought her up, keeping her far from the damaging influence of women (as Sostratos conceives it). It is the special circumstances of the girl's life which attract Sostratos to her.[26] Knowledge of her unusual character, already partly revealed to him in his first meeting with her in Act I, is the last constituent needed for Sostratos as suitor to be able to form the complete background picture of his potential bride, in the manner depicted by Chaireas the parasite in the first act (64ff.). Equipped with this information on the *genos*, the *bios* and the *tropoi* of the girl, and with his acquaintance with one of her close blood-relations as a temporary substitute for acquaintance with her father, Sostratos fulfils the social requirements for initiating a marriage connection with a free-born girl. All that is left for him to do is to obtain her father's consent to the marriage. The manner in which this consent is to be obtained is one of the main sources of interest of this play.

The third act presents Knemon in the midst of his negative reactions to everyday situations – a sacrificial meal in honour of Pan offered by Sostratos' mother in the god's shrine which is situated next to Knemon's house (431ff.), and an attempt by those in charge of the preparation for this meal (Getas the slave and Sikon the cook) to borrow a cauldron from him (456ff.). By presenting Knemon the misanthrope against the background of such situations, Menander contrasts the eccentric with the conventional. The resultant effect is mainly comic, but at the same time this confrontation reflects a subtle interplay between fiction and reality. For instance, at one of the climactic comic points of this interplay, Sikon the cook identifies Knemon's unusual behaviour as characteristic of the inhabitants of the whole region of Phyle! (520f.; cf. 129-31 and 604-6). Knemon himself criticizes what he perceives as the religious hypocrisy of those participating in the sacrificial meal, in terms vividly reflecting Theophrastus' argument in his treatise *On Piety* (447ff.).[27] Of similar effect is the use made by Knemon and his interlocutor Getas of the technical terms *symbolaion* (a contract, bond – in acknowledgement of a loan), *chreos* (a debt), *kleteres* (summoners, witnesses that gave evidence that the legal summons had been served) in lines 469ff., which demonstrates Knemon's awareness of current legal terminology, showing that he is not completely cut off from everyday life.

The confrontation between Knemon and his human environment as it is expressed in these scenes prepares the way for Knemon's 'punishment' at the end of the play and creates an effective contrast with the moment in which Knemon himself is in need of external help, when he falls into the well in the interval between the third and the fourth acts. But even within the confines of the third act itself, this confrontation has a thematic significance which extends beyond the scenes just described, namely the creative tension between the two polarities of action on the stage, Knemon's evasion of his environment on the one hand, and Sostratos' development of his social connections on the other. While Knemon recoils from the social occasion of the sacrificial meal held in honour of Pan and reacts by shutting himself in at home, Sostratos welcomes it wholeheartedly, seeing it as a heaven-sent opportunity to promote his affairs (557ff.). He is quick to turn this opportunity to his own advantage by inviting Gorgias and Daos to participate in the meal to be held after the sacrifice, completely ignoring the social gap between them and himself and his short acquaintance with them (note Getas' reaction, 608ff.). Menander stresses the contrast between Sostratos' social behaviour and the anti-social approach of Knemon as regards the sacrificial meal by putting in Sostratos' mouth the expression *philanthropeusomai*, 'I'll be generous' (573) as characterizing his completely different social attitude.

The end of the third act deals mainly with Knemon's attempts to retrieve the mattock and the bucket which his maid-servant Simiche has carelessly dropped into the well (574ff.). This scene serves as a preparation for the fall of Knemon himself into the well, of which we learn at the beginning of the fourth act. Here again we find Menander contrasting unconventional behaviour with the norm by making the slave Getas, a bystander during these proceedings, see in Knemon's unnecessarily violent behaviour towards Simiche and in his senseless refusal to avail himself of the aid of others a typical pattern of behaviour for an Attic farmer (604-6). Knemon, who refuses to turn to Daos for help (595f.), is an exception in a society which tended to rely on the help of friends and neigbours in everyday life.[28] On the other hand, Simiche, who offers to call Daos to help (594), represents the norm. The same applies to Sostratos, whose appearance in the company of Gorgias concludes the third act: Sostratos recruits friends to help him, in contrast to Knemon, who rejects any help. Now Sostratos has even managed to persuade Gorgias, in spite of his initial reluctance, to participate in the sacrificial meal as his guest (611ff.).

Even before Knemon's fall into the well is related to Sostratos and Gorgias, at the beginning of the fourth act, the friendship between these two has been placed on a firm moral and social basis, as a preparation for Sostratos' participation in the family rescue-operation and for his immediate betrothal to Knemon's daughter. Sostratos, aware of the significance of the link which is being forged between him and Gorgias, does not broach the idea of intrigue in his meeting with Getas (551ff.), as he had previously intended to do (181ff.); instead, he concentrates on fostering his new friendship with his would-be brother-in-law. This he does in a socially acceptable manner by inviting Gorgias to take part in the family sacrificial meal arranged by his mother. This invitation formalizes his newly created relations with Gorgias by offering him an introduction to his family, and constitutes a formal expression of the seriousness of Sostratos' intentions towards Gorgias' sister. Gorgias himself feels secure enough in his relationship with Sostratos to accept as natural the latter's readiness to take an active part in the rescue of Knemon (637-8).

Menander's choice of *Gorgias* as Knemon's rescuer in the fourth act raises the question of his thematic preferences in the play. It has long been recognized that Menander's main concern in *Dyskolos* is *not* the love element but a character-study of the misanthrope.[29] In the second act, the question of Knemon's responsibility for his family emerges in full force, and in the third act – as a continuation of the first – the question of his social attitudes as a whole. Had Sostratos been Knemon's rescuer, he would not have been able to effect the normalization of the relationship between the misanthrope and his world, except, perhaps, in the limited realm of obtaining his consent to his marriage with his daughter. Even then, there would have been a danger of damaging the integrity of the misanthrope's character and, needless to say, of reducing the intrinsic value of the mental change which is to take place in him, by presenting him as being affected unconsciously by the act of a lover motivated by self-interested considerations.[30]

In order to avoid this danger, and to bring about as comprehensive and as credible a solution as possible to the problem of Knemon's relationship with his close environment (of which Sostratos' marriage constitutes only a part), Menander, in complete contrast with the audience's expectations from the romantic conventions of the play, assigns the central role in rescuing Knemon to *Gorgias*, while presenting Sostratos' function in the proceedings in quite a ridiculous light. In so doing, he significantly extends the scope for integrating everyday norms into the play far beyond the limited confines of Sostratos' love-story: Gorgias, who has been maltreated by the misanthrope but bears him no grudge (722ff.), succeeds in making the misanthrope face the implications of his duties to his family and in rectifying his distorted world outlook. Thus the way is paved for the formal restitution of Knemon's *oikos* (731ff.) as a *preparation* for Sostratos' marriage with Knemon's daughter – a development which would hardly have been expected had the role of the rescuer been assigned to Sostratos himself. In this manner, an important realistic dimension is added to the play, to counter-balance the romantic convention.

An amusing, and for the present study significant, detail of Sostratos' behaviour in the course of the rescue operation, is the way he has to restrain himself from taking advantage of his proximity to Knemon's daughter:

> When he was safely out, I came out, and here I am. I couldn't control myself any longer – I very nearly went up to the girl and kissed her. That's how madly in love I am.
>
> (685-9 Miller)[31, 32]

Sostratos is well aware of the girl's citizen status. His adherence to the rules of morality here fits in with the serious nature of his social relationship with her.[33]

The dramatic shape which Menander gives to the apology scene (690ff.), the climax of the play, indicates the nature and scale of the legal implications this scene will encompass even before the misanthrope begins his speech. The wounded Knemon is brought on to the scene supported by his daughter and Gorgias. Sostratos takes care to stay in the background; he is not yet one of the family (753). To complete the family tableau, only Myrrhine, mother of Gorgias, wife of Knemon and mother to his daughter, is missing. She, as has already been mentioned, has long been separated from Knemon and lives with her son. Knemon orders her to be summoned immediately and she arrives without delay (698f., 709). The whole family is now gathered together ready for the full restitution of the *oikos*. All that is lacking is the setting out of the legal terms under which this restitution will be fulfilled and an explanation from Knemon of how he now feels able to offer these terms.

Surrounded by his family, Knemon begins his speech of apology, written by Menander in the trochaic tetrameter in order to emphasize the special significance of the moment. Knemon admits that he was wrong in thinking it possible to live in complete isolation from human society, and in believing that this society is composed exclusively of egoistic individuals motivated merely by materialistic considerations (713ff.). His deliberation reflects contemporary arguments about the relation between the individual and society.[34] He attributes this change in his world outlook directly to his experience of his stepson's noble behaviour (722ff.).

Gorgias is, in fact, the thread linking Knemon with the external world, and will continue to function as such following a series of legally valid decisions which Knemon now enumerates (729ff.). These decisions encompass all those present, with the exception of Sostratos, of whose existence Knemon is not yet aware. They satisfy the demands of comedy for 'poetic justice' for the *dramatis personae* in the way most intelligible to an Athenian audience, by bringing the situation into line with the provisions of the *law*. Indeed, Menander is not interested in any personal change in Knemon's character which remains detached from everyday reality, but in a change that would have practical implications for the *oikos* – the main focus of interest in New Comedy. This accords with Menander's general approach in the play, which is that of showing Knemon's personal fortunes as inseparable from the fate of his family.

The moment when Knemon adopts Gorgias as his son, appoints him as his heir and *kyrios* of his daughter, transfers to him the right of *engyesis*, of 'promising her in marriage', sets aside half of his property for Gorgias to use as dowry for her, and entrusts him with the welfare of his mother and himself – this is the point where Menander employs the forces of everyday reality to encroach on fiction in the story of the misanthrope (729-39).

Knemon behaves as would an average Athenian head of *oikos* who has recognized his inability to continue functioning as such through his mental and physical limitations (his fall into the well has persuaded him he may be about to die).[35] Not having a son of his own to inherit his property, he adopts one of his relations. As an adult free-born Athenian citizen with no legitimate male heir, he fulfils all the criteria required for an adoption. His choice of Gorgias, a relation of his wife, corresponds to everyday practices.

One might have thought that there would be a certain difficulty in the fact that Gorgias is the only son of his deceased father. By allowing himself to be adopted by Knemon, he deprives his real father of the only male offspring who could preserve his cult, since he is legally obliged by adoption to sever all previous family ties and to transfer completely to the new *oikos*. Athenian law did not explicitly *prohibit* an adoption in such circumstances, but it was morally frowned upon. Menander has pointedly kept Gorgias' deceased father in the background; after the prologue, he is not mentioned in the play. On the other hand, the act of adoption of his stepson by Knemon seems a *natural, logical* result of the type of relationship which has developed between the two following the well incident. One assumes that the Athenian audience, like the *dramatis personae* themselves, would therefore have given little thought to the way Gorgias' real father is deprived of his natural rights at this climactic moment in the play. The reality of the scenic moment has wiped from the audience's mind what would have been a vital contemporary legal consideration at this point.[36]

Knemon's instructions to Gorgias appear to have the character of terms in a will (729-31), a detail which conforms with the Athenian practice of combining adoption with a testamentary disposition. The size of the dowry – half the property – which Knemon allots to his daughter is, as far as we know, higher than the norm,[37] but it is this generosity which most tangibly expresses the special relationship between the misanthrope and his daughter, emphasized so strongly in the play by Menander in preparation for this moment. Similarly, Knemon's inclusion of Gorgias' mother with himself as objects of Gorgias' care conforms with the audience's expectations of a reunion between Knemon and his wife (which does indeed materialize, although within the limitations of the personality of the misanthrope – 735), expectations which arose for the first time when Knemon summoned her to the scene before beginning his speech.

Menander paves the way for the fulfilment of these expectations by leaving open the question of whether Knemon is divorced from his wife. A modern audience might assume that Gorgias' mother, by leaving her husband's house for that of her son (22), had taken the first step towards divorce – desertion – or, to use the Greek term, *apoleipein*.[38] But an Athenian audience, familiar with the contemporary divorce procedures, would have known that the termination of a marriage, if initiated by the wife, could only be legalized if she took the further step of handing a written statement to the magistrate.[39] Mention of such a step is deliberately omitted in *Dyskolos* in order to leave open to the couple the path of reconciliation.[40]

It is against this background of the reunion of Knemon's family that the solution to the problem of Sostratos' marriage to his daughter is set, through the transfer of the guardianship of Knemon's daughter to her half-brother Gorgias. As a result of this act, a new legal situation is created which renders unnecessary any personal involvement of Knemon in the marriage procedure, thus enabling Menander to retain the integrity of his character as a misanthrope.

Indeed, Knemon, who now sees himself free of any formal obligation towards his daughter, strongly rejects Gorgias' attempt to make him participate in choosing a bridegroom for her (751ff.). Even his consent to Sostratos' marrying his daughter – a necessary condition for the validity of the marriage while he was her legal guardian, but now merely a gesture of concession to his position as father and devoid of any legal force – is given simply because of Gorgias' pressure on him, with a complete lack of interest in the identity of his would-be son-in-law (Gorgias appeals to Knemon's sense of duty and gratitude by presenting Sostratos as one who was involved in rescuing him from the well [753]. Sostratos' brief 'agricultural' experience also helps to remove any possible objection on Knemon's part on grounds of difference in status and way of life [754f.]). This change in the misanthrope's legal status in relation to his daughter, moreover, permits him to be absent from the ceremony of the *engyesis* which takes place in the subsequent scene between Sostratos and Gorgias (761ff.). Thus yet another important dramatic means is found to preserve the credibility of the misanthrope's character.

In order to retain the unity of the scenic moment, Menander allows Gorgias and Sostratos to perform the ceremony of the *engyesis* even before consent to the marriage is obtained from the groom's father Kallippides. His consent, unlike that of Knemon, *is* necessary for the proposed marriage,[41] and it is indeed given retrospectively, so we must assume, in the interval between the fourth and the fifth acts (785ff.). Menander himself draws the attention of the audience to this irregularity of procedure by making Sostratos twice reject Gorgias' offer to communicate his plans to his father, the first time *before* the *engyesis*, under the pretext that his father's consent is assured in advance (761) and the second *after* the ceremony, claiming that it will be easier to persuade Kallippides, now arrived to participate in the sacrificial meal, after he has satisfied his hunger (778f.). The strong emphasis laid here on the need to obtain the consent of the groom's father to his marriage to Knemon's daughter – an unusual match in contemporary terms – creates a new point of suspense in the plot near the end of the fourth act. At the same time, it puts the dramatic situation into perspective *vis-à-vis* everyday reality.

The ceremony of the *engyesis* itself (761ff.), a conventional realistic element in Menander's comedy,[42] is here formulated by the playwright in a quite exceptional manner, with the clear purpose of making it conform as much as possible to the romantic conventions of the love-story of which it forms the climax. The normal considerations behind the *engyesis* were practical ones, intended to ensure the future of both parties, not only from the economic point of view but also from that of the continuity of the family line.[43] Quite surprisingly, the approach adopted by Gorgias, the pragmatic peasant, differs from the one normally expected, being based on moral considerations and putting much weight on personal virtues. For instance, while announcing his half-sister's betrothal to Sostratos, Gorgias claims that Sostratos deserves to marry her because of his exemplary behaviour and noble character as revealed in the course of events before the *engyesis* (764ff.). This evaluative reference replaces the usual formulae concerning the dowry and the continuation of the family line which would be expected in a betrothal ceremony.

The ceremony has yet another distinctive feature in this play: it takes place exclusively between Sostratos and Gorgias, the two protagonists whose contribution to the fulfilment of this dramatic moment in the play is the greatest. The absence of witnesses to the ceremony does not detract from its legitimacy, for their presence was a matter of convention, not a legal requirement.[44] As a substitute for flesh-and-blood witnesses, Sostratos and Gorgias content themselves with the gods (762), an expression of the great faith they have in one another after what they have been through together.

At the beginning of Act V, the audience is presented with a surprise: Sostratos, not content with obtaining his father's consent to his marriage to Knemon's daughter, successfully persuades him to arrange a match between his sister and Gorgias (791ff.). The introduction of this motif by Menander in the final stages of the play has been interpreted as an attempt to do 'poetic justice' to this positive character, in accordance with the conventions of New Comedy.[45] But in the context of Sostratos' marriage – the *leitmotif* in the plot of *Dyskolos* – the motif of this extra marriage seems to have a significance far beyond the realization of this conventional purpose.

Gorgias' marriage, like that of Sostratos, forms part of the comic convention of the play, which bridges the gap between rich and poor. But there is an essential difference between the two: while Sostratos' marriage is a love-match, Gorgias' marriage is arranged, devoid of any sentimental basis at least in its primary stages. This difference epitomizes the gap between fiction and reality which Sostratos' love for Knemon's daughter in *Dyskolos* so vividly represents. For it is not Sostratos' marriage, but that of Gorgias, which better reflects the specific character of the Athenian institution.[46] Menander here makes a striking contrast between the values of everyday life and those of comedy, giving the world of reality a blatant entrance into the fictional framework of his play. The process of rendering the plot of *Dyskolos* 'realistic', begun in Sostratos' first meeting with Gorgias in the second act, culminates here in the introduction of a distinctive realistic element which forms an antithesis to the romantic thesis of the play (although still within the limitations of the comic convention mentioned). The fact that it is the unconventional Sostratos who proposes the arranged marriage of Gorgias ironically emphasizes the powerful influence of social convention, inescapable even in the theatre.

Since Gorgias' marriage to Sostratos' sister is conceived by Menander as an antithesis to Sostratos' marriage to Knemon's daughter, it is necessarily accompanied by all those down-to-earth considerations, and that firm insistence upon fulfilling the finer points of the law, which were absent from the development of Sostratos' match.

The financial consideration is raised by Sostratos' father (795f.)

and rebutted by Sostratos, who affirms the fragility of materialistic success and the value of true friendship in the hour of need (797ff.). Kallippides is convinced by these two weighty arguments, and gives his consent to the arranging of a marriage between his daughter and Gorgias, in stark contrast to his statement earlier in the act that *love* is the cement of marriage (788-90). The difference in economic status is raised by Gorgias himself (823ff.) and is considered by Sostratos and Kallippides as irrelevant to the present case. Moreover, the formula of the *engyesis*, 'for the sowing of legitimate offspring', which was not mentioned by Gorgias in the betrothal ceremony between his half-sister and Sostratos, is here pronounced by Kallippides, and the exact amount of the dowry is specified (842ff.). Gorgias uses his own receipt of a dowry on his betrothal to initiate a belated attempt (doomed to failure) to give a dowry to his half-sister (844ff.), an element which had been omitted in the actual betrothal ceremony in the fourth act. The dowry proposed by Gorgias (upon Knemon's instructions, 737-8) – one talent – is significantly less than that proposed by Kallippides for his own daughter – three talents – but both were apparently very generous in contemporary terms.[47] Thus, even with concessions to the comic spirit of exaggeration, the stress on the economic gap between the two families is retained.[48]

When the argument over Gorgias' proposed betrothal to Sostratos' sister has been settled, the time has come to celebrate the double marriage. Here the question of Knemon's participation in the family occasion is raised. In order to retain the credibility of Knemon's misanthropic character, Menander presents him as refusing to attend the wedding feast (867ff., 874ff.). But the social norm naturally required him to attend the marriage celebrations of both his daughter and his adopted son. The solution to this problem is found in the actions of Getas and Sikon, who, because of their grudge against Knemon, force him to join the circle of dancers against his will (931ff.). Getas' and Sikon's revenge upon Knemon for the way he treated them in Act III is carried out in the spirit of the ancient *komos*[49] and has, on the whole, an unrealistic character. This is shown, on the one hand, by the hyperbolic employment of elements drawn from the borrowing scene in Act III,[50] and on the other hand by the musical accompaniment to the scene (879f.) and its catalectic iambic tetrameter. But the *function* which it is intended to fulfil is entirely realistic. It is in this spirit of creative tension between comedy and reality that *Dyskolos* ends.

Samia

Samia is a family comedy composed almost entirely of realistic elements which, in their dramatic-comic presentation, reflect the bourgeois aspirations of contemporary Athens.[51] The balance between realism and comedy is maintained throughout the play. This sets *Samia* apart from *Dyskolos*, the fairy-tale play whose plot is set firmly in the mould of romantic convention and in this respect has little to do with real, everyday life. It is important to establish from the outset that social and legal norms are applied in *Samia* under dramatic conditions fundamentally different from those in *Dyskolos*. This may be attributed to the desire of the playwright to present various relationships between stage reality and everyday life, not only in terms of the contents of his plays but also of their quality and essence. So that while in *Dyskolos*, the lives of the protagonists fluctuate between extremes – between town and country, between rich and poor, between family and strangers – in *Samia* we find ourselves in an intimate encounter between two urban families – the families of Nikeratos and Demeas – who are next-door neighbours and have evolved a network of close relationships.

The economic gaps between the two families, insofar as there are any,[52] are not emphasized, nor do they constitute an obstacle to a possible union between the two houses through marriage of their children, as we discover in the early stages of the play. These differences serve mainly to point out the contrasts between the characters of the two heads of *oikos* – Nikeratos and Demeas. Their existence allows Menander to pick and choose from among dramatic options, and this in turn adds spice and interest to the plot.[53] Certainly, in *Samia*, no artificial or deliberate attempt is made to bridge the gap between rich and poor by means of comic conventions – as is the case in *Dyskolos*.

Another important element in *Dyskolos* is absent from *Samia*: the creative tension between the eccentric and the ordinary. There are no Knemons in *Samia*. All the characters are ordinary; their aspirations are conventional, and the entire plot takes place in the context of the familiar and the ordinary. Even the romantic convention, which is so important in *Dyskolos*, is subjugated in *Samia* to considerations of real life. This is in accordance with the general thrust of the plot, whose purpose – in sharp contrast to *Dyskolos* – is to show how the integrity of the *oikos* may be preserved against the irrational forces which threaten to break it up.

The play opens with the appearance of a young man named Moschion who, in a long and detailed monologue addressed to the audience, confesses to disgraceful conduct while his adoptive father, Demeas, was away in Pontos. It is in the course of this confession that the background to the plot and the characters of its protagonists are presented.

Moschion, a shy and modest young man, was adopted as a child by Demeas, a wealthy Athenian bachelor. Over the years a close and deep friendship developed between the two and Moschion, out of gratitude to Demeas, always endeavoured to live up to his father's expectations (7ff.).

When Moschion reached adolescence, Demeas fell in love with a *hetaira*, a courtesan of Samian extraction, named Chrysis. At first he was ashamed of his sentiments and tried to conceal them from his son. But Moschion was not to be fooled, and thought it advisable to set his father's mind at rest, particularly against approaches by young rivals to his mistress, by prevailing upon him to bring Chrysis into his own house (21ff.). The extant parts of the monologue do not allow us to reach a positive conclusion about Chrysis' precise status; though in line 577 she is referred to as free, she may very well have been bought by Demeas as a slave, and subsequently liberated by him.

Chrysis became friendly with the womenfolk of the poorer household next door, that of Nikeratos. During the absence of Demeas and Nikeratos, who had left home for Pontos on business about a year earlier, Chrysis invited Nikeratos' wife and daughter Plangon, and some other women, to join her in celebrating the festival of Adonis (35ff.).[54] It was on this occasion that Moschion, under the influence of the relaxed atmosphere of the party, lapsed from his normally virtuous behaviour and succumbed to the temptation to make love to Plangon (41ff.). The girl became pregnant, and the baby that was born in due course was handed over to the care of Chrysis, who had in turn become pregnant by Demeas but had lost her child.[55] Moschion never tried to deny his guilt; in fact, he assumed full responsibility. He promised Plangon's mother, under oath, to marry the girl as soon as his father returned from his voyage, but in the meantime Chrysis was to pretend that the baby was born to Demeas and herself (49ff.).

There is nothing in this that departs from everyday experience, as we know it from the sources of the period.[56] For example, rape committed during religious festivals was not an infrequent occurrence and New Comedy often used it for its own purposes.[57] In *Samia*, the absence from Athens of the two fathers at the time the rape was committed adds a realistic dimension to the dramatic situation, and it makes their ignorance of this event appear entirely natural. This is a marked departure from other comedies, in which the rape and the subsequent pregnancy occur under the very noses of the parents, though they have not the slightest inkling of what is going on.[58]

Moschion's behaviour following the rape and the birth of his son is also determined by everyday norms. Legal sanctions in cases of rape of a citizen girl ranged from a heavy fine (500 drachmas) to the death penalty, depending on the circumstances and the type of charge made (civil or private).[59] Marriage to the victim was considered a proper solution – unless there was some definite obstacle preventing it. However, for such a marriage to be valid, the consent of the rapist's father was an essential condition, so long as the young man came under his legal authority as *kyrios*. But the father's consent was not to be taken for granted, particularly in a case of rape which could result in the loss of the dowry.[60] So Moschion, in postponing his marriage to Plangon until his father's return from Pontos, was acting entirely in accordance with *the existing legal and social options*. Demeas and Nikeratos, Plangon's father and her *kyrios*, held the fate of the couple in their hands.

The Athenian father was not deemed to have a specific duty to bring up his own offspring.[61] Consequently, if Moschion had abandoned his baby – the evidence of Plangon's lost virtue, in a society which regarded preservation of the family honour as a vital civic need[62] – Menander's audience would have accepted this with understanding, and perhaps with a certain degree of indifference, in the light of the circumstances. For while modern Western society would condemn such behaviour, it was a familiar element in everyday life and in the plots of New Comedy.[63] But Chrysis' aborted pregnancy made such a solution unnecessary, while in itself opening the way to social and legal complications of an entirely different kind, due to the new situation it created. A substantial part of the human drama about to unfold before us stems from the remarkably humane approach (in terms of the accepted attitudes of the period) of Moschion and Plangon to their offspring.

What is so distinctive about Moschion's narrative are the powerful bourgeois emotions he displays, as an individual and as a citizen; he is ashamed of himself and ashamed before the audience of his deed (47f.); he suffers deep remorse for his act which contrasts sharply with his past moral conduct (3, 17f.); he feels the pain of failure in his relations with his adoptive father (6ff.) – emotions that run through the entire confession of the young protagonist. While we may assume that Moschion's somewhat pathetic exaggeration in describing the weight of this single moral lapse in the generally positive pattern of his life would have brought a smile to the lips of his audience, there is no doubt that his conservative attitudes, as revealed in his opening speech, corresponded to their general aspirations, and thus helped them identify with the situation presented on stage. Menander, in setting the views of Moschion in the context of contemporary social and moral thinking,[64] thus preserves the realism of his drama, as well as maintaining the appropriate 'comic level' in his description of everyday considerations.

In the exposition in Act I, of which Moschion's speech is a major part, Demeas' desire for Chrysis is defined as the romantic element in the play about to unfold before the audience (21ff.). Moschion's relations with Plangon, as described at this stage (at any rate in what survives of his monologue), lack all emotional basis. Only in Act II will these relations begin to assume a romantic hue which will grow increasingly strong as the play progresses, until it reaches its climax in Act V.[65] On the other hand, the relations between Demeas and Chrysis gradually emerge as secondary in importance to Moschion's relations with his adoptive father Demeas – an aspect of the drama whose tremendous impact on the story is prepared for in the opening scene.[66]

This shift of emphasis at the romantic level of the drama plays an important role in establishing Menander's realistic approach. In a lively and surprising manner, it reflects the true state of relations between the different components of the *oikos* – the legitimate (Moschion and Plangon) and the illegitimate (Chrysis), emphasizing the obvious social superiority of the former to the latter. While, in his exposition, Menander creates the impression that Chrysis' status in the home of Demeas is unshakeable and is hardly of less

importance than that of Moschion himself, we must bear in mind
the fact that in legal terms there is a great disparity between the
position of Chrysis in the *oikos* and that of Moschion, and it is
entirely to her disadvantage. Moschion formally belongs to the *oikos*
by virtue of his adoption by Demeas;[67] but this is not the case with
Chrysis who, because of her alien origin, cannot marry Demeas. She
must content herself with the status of *pallake* (of an inferior kind
in her case); in other words, with the status of more or less perma-
nent mistress, but without any of the rights enjoyed by legitimate
members of the *oikos* in which she lives.[68]

Much of the realism of the play may be attributed to the treatment
of the implications of this difference of status between Moschion and
Chrysis – both of whom are 'alien elements' brought in 'from the
outside' by Demeas, the head of the *oikos* – even though the opening
monologue seemed to point to a more romantic approach on the part
of the playwright. The full significance of this difference comes to
light in Act III, when Demeas has to confront the need to choose
between his son and his mistress. The ordeal he has to face is not
only as father and lover but also, and perhaps more significantly,
as head of an *oikos* which, because of its problematic structure,
inclusive of 'external' elements, is in a highly sensitive situation to
begin with.[69]

The end of Moschion's speech has not been preserved; nor has the
greater part of a speech delivered by Chrysis during a brief interval,
when Moschion appears to have left the stage in order to return
together with his slave Parmenon. The latter breaks the news that
he has seen Demeas and Nikeratos in the port, back from their
journey, and urges the hesitant and embarrassed Moschion immediately to settle the business of his marriage (61ff.). Chrysis joins
the conversation, declaring that she is ready to go on pretending
that the baby is her own, in spite of the apprehension voiced by
Moschion and Parmenon over the possible consequences of such an
act. She is confident of Demeas' love and of her ability to appease
him (69ff.). Parmenon and Chrysis take their leave. Moschion
retires in order to rehearse a speech he intends to make to Demeas
when they meet (88ff.).

This latter scene arouses in the spectator expectations of possible
objections on the part of Demeas to the proposed marriage between
Moschion and Plangon, and makes him wonder whether Demeas
will accept Chrysis' baby in his household. These are both realistic

expectations in terms of the attitudes of the period: marriage between a wealthy bridegroom and a poor bride was certainly a rarity in Hellenistic Athens (just as in Athens of the classical period) and the possibility that the bridegroom's father might object to such a marriage had to be taken into consideration even where there had been a rape (in fact, Demeas will not discover the fact of the rape until Act IV).[70] Furthermore, a *pallake* who bore a child to the head of the *oikos* without first getting his permission would have anticipated her expulsion from the *oikos*, unless its head decided to give his consent *post factum* and accept the *nothos*, bastard son, into his household.[71]

The opening scene of Act II illustrates precisely this second point, whereas the concluding scene of Act I totally dispels the fears provoked in the audience of possible objections to the marriage. Demeas and Nikeratos make their appearance. Their dialogue makes it plain that, *quite independently of what has been happening in Athens*, they have agreed that Plangon should marry Moschion. All that remains to be done is to decide on a date for the wedding (113ff.).

The wedding plan of the two fathers brings to an end the romantic story-line that had begun to evolve in the previous scene – the traditional struggle to obtain the father's consent to the wedding of his son – which was so common in New Comedy. What distinguishes the situation in this play is the fact that the economic gap between the two families is no obstacle, right from the start, to an official marriage link between them.[72] This is a marriage contract between two neighbouring families who know each other well and thus fulfil the normative requirements for successful wedlock between their offspring: familiarity with the *genos* (family line), the *tropoi* (character) and the *bios* (financial situation) of the prospective marriage partner. This situation is markedly different from that in *Dyskolos*.[73] It was for the heads of the two *oikoi* to decide on the marriage contract without necessarily first consulting their children. For though love was considered a desirable element, it was not essential for the nuptial link, which was specifically intended 'for the procreation of legitimate offspring', an everyday reality in its most prosaic form.[74]

The marriage plan contracted by the two fathers, quite independently of developments at home, reveals the dual nature of the marriage process in the play: what appeared to Demeas and Nik-

eratos a matter of free choice for them as heads of *oikoi* was actually
a vital imperative for them if they were to preserve the honour of
their families and avoid the social and financial damage which
would result from litigation – or, in the case of Moschion, avert a
possible sentence of death for raping a free citizen girl.

Demeas and Nikeratos are ignorant of the truth behind the
marriage and only discover it towards the end of the play, in Act IV,
when appearance and reality meet and the truth about the baby's
origin is revealed to them. Both aspects of this two-dimensional
marriage process – it needs to be stressed once more – are totally
realistic, and the dramatic irony thus created is the result of their
reciprocal influence in the play.

With our attention focused on Demeas, it is important to stress
that it is Demeas the *father*, *head of the oikos*, whom we encounter
on this first appearance, and not Demeas the *lover*, of whose devo-
tion Chrysis is so confident. It is in this role of head of the *oikos* that
he appears once again at the opening of Act II, when the question of
the future of Chrysis and 'her baby' rises to the surface. Menander,
frustrating the expectations aroused in the audience by Moschion's
speech and Chrysis' own description of the strength of Demeas'
romantic feelings for her (80ff.), deliberately refrains from according his hero any sentimental qualities. This technique ultimately
has the effect of highlighting the centrality of the *oikos* and his
future heir in Demeas' evaluations. At the moment of truth, when
he has to choose between his son and his beloved mistress, the choice
he makes accords with the prevalent values of his time.

The second act has survived only in a very partial and fragmentary state. Moschion comes back to say that, rather than rehearse
his speech, he was carried away by daydreams about the wedding
(120ff.). He runs into Demeas emerging from his house – now furious
with Chrysis, his 'lawfully wedded courtesan' (130) because he has
been led to believe that she has borne him a child without his
knowledge. Moschion protests against Demeas' initial intention to
drive her away together with the baby (134ff.). In spite of the gap
of about 28 verses missing from the text at this point, there is little
doubt that Demeas allows himself to be persuaded. They then
proceed to discuss the marriage of Moschion and Plangon (145ff.).

Menander raises the issue of the baby's future even before the
subject of Moschion marrying Plangon has been discussed, thus
highlighting the real option faced by Moschion – should he reveal

to his father the baby's true origin and restore his legal rights to him in an honourable manner without doing harm to his social position? Moschion, however, does not take advantage of this option. Given his natural shyness and fears of his father's reaction, he opts instead to philosophize on the rights and wrongs of differentiating between a bastard and a legitimate son (137ff.), preferring the original plot of intrigue to an open showdown with his father:

> In my view, it's not birth which makes one man better than another, but if you look at it justly, it is the good who is legitimate and the bad who is a bastard and a slave ...
>
> (140-3 Hunter)

Menander here plays upon the expectations of his audience, suggesting the possibility of an immediate and reasonable solution to the complexities of the plot only to reject it as inappropriate because of the inhibitions of the protagonist. This technique has significant implications for the realization of everyday norms in the play; if we remember that the subject of marriage is raised by Demeas *after* an ostensible solution has been reached to the question of the baby's future, we may understand that Menander here contrasts a normative solution to the problem of Moschion and Plangon, i.e. marriage, with a partial and fundamentally false solution for their son, namely, his acceptance as a *nothos*, a bastard son, in the household of Demeas. It is through this contrast that the options open to the protagonists for applying the legal and social norms to their mutual relations can be appreciated by the spectator already at this early stage of the play.

The shortcomings of the arrangement arrived at between Moschion and Demeas are particularly evident in the light of the baby's presence in Demeas' home. While the latter accepts the baby into his household, the terms are such as to rule out any possibility of his ever being considered a fully-fledged member of his *oikos*.[75] So, while the accepted norms of life are applied in one section of the stage situation, distortions which call out for reform are highlighted in another.[76] This technique, as we shall demonstrate, is characteristic of the plot of *Samia*.

Moschion's appeal to Demeas to drop the legal barrier between the *nothos* and the *gnesios* — between the bastard and the legitimate son – is absurd in the context of the period.[77] However, it fits in with a convention encountered from time to time in Greek literature, when a conception of ideal values is presented, even though it is never applied to reality.[78] Just as in *Dyskolos*, Kallippides accedes to the exaggerated demands of his son Sostratos,[79] so in *Samia*, Demeas accedes to Moschion's appeal and allows Chrysis to bring up 'their' child in his household, despite his inner objections to this arrangement.

But Demeas' decision does not depart from what is known to us of the accepted attitude to illegitimate children in Athens. In terms of the concepts prevailing at the time, Chrysis' son could not be treated as anything other than a *nothos*, whether he was conceived in her relations with Demeas or was the offspring of Moschion, as Demeas begins to suspect in Act III.[80] In this scene, there is special significance to the emphasis placed on the illegitimacy of Chrysis' son, since Demeas believes that the baby is his own flesh and blood. In this way, Menander highlights the vast gap between Demeas' loving attitude to his adoptive son Moschion and his marked indifference to his natural 'son', the fruit of his relations with his mistress Chrysis. This difference in attitude displayed by Demeas towards his two 'sons' corresponds to the prevailing standards of the period, which accorded the *gnesios* superiority over the *nothos* in all aspects of social life, from the narrow confines of the *oikos* to the broadest framework of the *polis*.[81] Thus, throughout the idealistic arguments put forward by Moschion, and Demeas' reluctant acceptance of his son's request, the realistic hard nucleus of the situation is preserved almost in its entirety.

Moschion's ardent desire to marry Nikeratos' daughter is taken by Demeas to be an expression of his love for her (153ff., 165f.). But the spectator, aware of the legal implications for Moschion's status as a rapist,[82] may also be conscious of another aspect of the protagonist's ardour – one that has nothing whatever to do with any emotion of love – the fear of legal sanctions being applied to him in case of failure to arrive at some arrangement which will satisfy the victim and her family.[83] That is the 'dark' pragmatic side of Moschion's behaviour, which totally escapes the notice of his father.

Just as his son had seen to it that circumstances would be favourable for his continued affair with Chrysis (23ff.), Demeas also seeks to help Moschion attain his heart's desire; and he does so in a most fitting manner – within the framework of the law – by bringing forward the date of the wedding (154ff.). The fact that his son actually loves his intended bride is purely coincidental to the marriage plan itself. Menander places special emphasis on this idea by having Demeas make the following statement:

> It seems that the accidental is indeed
> a divinity and looks after many of the things we cannot
> see. Not knowing Moschion was in love, I ...
>
> (163-6 Bain)

However, when Demeas discovers that Moschion is in love with Plangon, he is overjoyed to learn it, and this is immediately trans-lated into concrete action: he asks Nikeratos to stage the wedding without delay (170ff.). Demeas' reaction to the marriage of Moschion and Plangon reflects, more than anything else, the very limited emotional expectations the Hellenistic spectator would have had of the Athenian institution of marriage.

Nikeratos, however, is reluctant to accept Demeas' suggestion that the wedding should take place that very day. Only after Demeas repeatedly implores him does he accede to this request (176ff.).

Given the fragmentary condition of the extant text, it is not possible to determine the precise reason for Nikeratos' objections. They might be due to his poverty, which makes him unable to purchase, at such short notice, all the fine foods required for the wedding feast. Demeas anticipates opposition from Nikeratos' wife as well (200f.). Her view is not as important as that of the head of the *oikos*, Nikeratos, and lacks all legal significance in itself. Yet her opinion is given due consideration here,[84] and this highlights the irony behind the situation of the heads of the two *oikoi*. In their ignorance of the real state of affairs, they could hardly realize that Nikeratos' wife would not merely refrain from voicing opposition to so early a marriage, but would even support the idea with enthusi-asm. The playwright does not show as much interest in Chrysis and *her* attitudes, thereby revealing an important realistic aspect of the situation: as a *pallake* in Demeas' household, no one would consult her for her views on any issues affecting the future of the *oikos*. There was no need to ask her opinion, and in any case it would not have been taken into consideration by Demeas when setting the date of the wedding.

In terms of contemporary attitudes, the idea of holding the wedding on the very same day is not unreasonable, even though two or three days were required to complete preparations for the formalities of the wedding ceremony itself.[85] Weddings in Athens were a *family affair*, and the *polis* did not interfere.[86] The law and social norms determined only the limitations of choice of a marriage partner – for example, incest and marriage to a foreigner were banned. No formal legal procedures, such as registration with the *archon*, were required as a basis for the matrimonial link between the parties, from the moment they expressed their wish to live together to form a family, whether they did so directly or through the *kyrios*. The intimate, informal nature of the Athenian institution of marriage, combined with the ancient theatrical convention of Unity of Time (the action covers the span of a single day), enabled Menander's audience to accept as perfectly natural the haste with which the marriage of Moschion and Plangon was arranged (as was the case with *all* the weddings in New Comedy).[87]

At the end of Act II, the wedding preparations begin (Parmenon is sent by Demeas to buy the foods needed for the wedding feast and to hire a cook, 189ff.), and these continue through the rest of the play until the final scene, in which the engagement ceremony, the *engyesis* of Moschion and Plangon, takes place. The frequent mention of the wedding preparations (which appear to reflect everyday life),[88] and the effect this has on the characters, build up a steadily realistic plot-line that is a constant link between stage events and real life, whatever the dramatic twists of the plot may be.

By the end of Act II, it appears certain that the wedding will take place. All that remains to be done is to translate the plan into fact by means of the *engyesis* ceremony and the wedding itself. But before this can be achieved, the real human drama of the play unfolds. Demeas' suspicion of his adopted son Moschion develops into a conflict, which will lead to realization of the *engyesis* at the price of the other, more romantic, option – Demeas' love for Chrysis.

We shall soon see that all the developments and ramifications of this drama serve a single aim – the preservation of the *oikos* against the irrational forces which might threaten to destroy it. This defence of the *oikos* occupies a central position in the social values of the Greek *polis*. From the beginning of the play, the behaviour of the protagonists is circumscribed by the limitations of the law, and this is certain to lead to *engyesis* at the end. This is only to be expected in a comedy whose point of departure is the rape of a free citizen girl. What in *Dyskolos* was the romantic aspiration of the lover is here presented as an element naturally stemming from the pragmatic considerations of all the characters.[89]

The legal framework is used by the spectator as a yardstick by which to measure the behaviour of the characters, particularly that of the two major protagonists, Demeas and Moschion, in the specific area of their commitment to the continued existence of the *oikos*. It is in this context that the fundamental differences between father and son are revealed, reflecting the gap between youth and old age. Moschion, who is aware of the facts, forgoes the chance to restore his baby son to his rightful parents at the end of Act II. In Act III, Demeas, unaware of the true story, suspects that Moschion and Chrysis have conducted an affair behind his back and that the baby is the issue of that affair. He chooses to sacrifice his love for the sake of the happiness of his adopted son and to go ahead with the wedding procedures. He does this out of his deep commitment to Moschion, and, so we must assume, to the *oikos* of which he is head.

There is no doubt that Demeas emerges victorious from this ordeal. Unlike Knemon, who becomes aware of his commitments as head of *oikos* only after the traumatic experience of his fall into the well,[90] Demeas is fully aware of these duties from the start, and acts accordingly even at times when he has to take the most painful personal decisions. His firm position as head of *oikos* adds an important realistic dimension to the plot.

While in *Dyskolos*, Menander chose to shift the plot from the conventional romantic context to the realistic plane only towards the end of the play, in Act IV,[91] in *Samia*, a clear preference for pragmatic, realistic considerations over the romantic options latent in the specific dramatic situation emerges already in Act III. This difference in technique is no coincidence. It illustrates the differences in the quality and range of the realistic *mimesis* that Menander seeks to achieve in the two plays. A brief review of the events which occur in Act III will help us discern the extent to which the stage situation is adapted to the realistic expectations of his audience at this central point in the play.

Preparations for the wedding feast are at their height when Demeas appears at the beginning of Act III. In a long monologue he informs the audience that he has heard Moschion's old nurse talking to the baby in a way which shows clearly that Moschion is his father

(236ff.). Demeas is still engrossed in his reflections about what to do next when Parmenon returns from the market together with the cook (280ff.). Demeas attempts to extract the truth from Parmenon but the latter, having confirmed that Moschion is the baby's father, makes off in order to spare himself further interrogation (295ff.).

Left to his own thoughts, Demeas now reaches the conclusion that Moschion, far from trying to wrong him, has done his best to escape Chrysis' evil influence by means of a hasty marriage to Plangon (328ff.). Chrysis alone is to blame for what has happened. It was she who tempted Moschion when he was drunk, and since he was naive and inexperienced he fell victim to her charms (338ff.). The only way to set the situation right is to expel Chrysis without delay, in spite of his love for her (349ff.).

Having resolved to be as good as his word, Demeas orders Chrysis to leave his house immediately, together with the baby and her old maidservant. Chrysis, shocked and amazed at the sudden change in his attitude towards her, demands an explanation. Demeas mentions the baby to which she has given birth without his knowledge, and repeats his command (369ff.). He takes his leave from his mistress by painting a sombre picture of her future social and economic predicament (390ff.). Nikeratos returns from the market to find Chrysis standing in tears at the door of his house, together with the maid-servant and with the baby in her arms (399ff.). After a short inquiry, he takes her into his house, suggesting that the whole business is nothing but a passing whim of Demeas, a result of their long stay in Pontos (416ff.).

In *Samia*, as in *Dyskolos*, Menander's main interest lies outside the sphere of love – in exploring the specific human relations within the *oikos*. Evidence of this may be found in Demeas' reaction. Demeas the father, the head of *oikos*, has the upper hand over Demeas the lover in a situation whose objective circumstances could, with the same degree of probability, have led to the very opposite line of plot-development. Such a different plot-development we find, for example, in Theseus' preference for his wife Phaidra over his son Hippolytos in Euripides' play *Hippolytos* – a tragic association which might readily have sprung to the mind of some members of the audience.[92]

Demeas' insistence on Moschion's innocence (328ff., 343ff.) can hardly be reconciled with the incriminating circumstances described by him. Menander himself draws the spectator's attention to this by means of the protagonist's confession: 'This may seem a hazardous statement, gentlemen, but it's true' (328-9). However, it is precisely this obstinacy which reflects, more than anything else, the special relationship between father and adopted son, heir to his rites of worship[93] – a relationship which, unlike Demeas' superficial ties with Chrysis, obliges him to give due consideration to the problematic aspects of the incriminating evidence he has stumbled upon.

This special relationship which Menander has invented for the protagonists as the opening condition of the play enables him to lead his hero Demeas along a road which would make it possible for him to preserve the honour of the family and its integrity at a critical phase of the plot. Thus there will be no need even for a temporary *apokeryxis* – disowning[94] – of Moschion by his father (contrast Nikeratos' approach, 509f.), while on the other hand only those elements which are not regarded as legitimate members of the *oikos* (Chrysis and the baby) will be harmed. This is a twist of the plot which, though due to an error, undoubtedly responded to the attitudes of the audience, composed for the most part of respectable citizens, many of whom were themselves heads of *oikoi*.

To oust Chrysis, the *hetaira*, is ultimately an act signifying that preference is given to the interests of the *oikos* over those of the private individual. Chrysis, the stranger, is at this point perceived by Demeas as the source of danger to the *oikos* because of her destructive influence on Moschion. Demeas believes that the marriage of his son to Plangon is intended by Moschion solely to provide him with means of escaping from the clutches of Chrysis (335ff.). It is therefore vital to pursue the road to the wedding and ensure its successful conclusion. But whatever happens, Chrysis will have to leave (348ff.). There is much irony in this situation: Demeas' attempt to set his house in order has an even more drastic effect on the position of Moschion's son, his own grandson, who is to be excluded from the house as an undesirable element together with his 'mother'.

Here we have a further example of the ambivalent manner in which everyday norms are applied – a manner so characteristic of Menander's technique in *Samia*.

The legal argument on which Demeas bases the need to expel his mistress from his household – the apparent fact that she conceived the baby against his will (354f., 374, 387) – accords with the accepted norms of the period.[95] Demeas, in using this argument, applies a sanction against his mistress which he had been persuaded by Moschion not to apply only a little earlier (see the opening events in Act II), thereby creating an apparent external contradiction in his behaviour. Menander uses this contradiction to obtain a more complex realistic effect. On the one hand, we have the *logical* reaction of Demeas, as head of the *oikos*, to the changing state of affairs in his home as he perceives it: what was earlier an optional path for him, becomes now, after discovering Chrysis' apparent infidelity, an essential measure for preserving the integrity of the *oikos*. Demeas' plan to expel Chrysis, already familiar to the spectator from Act II, surfaces once again, this time with added force, as a *fait accompli* in the chain of events. On the other hand, the belated implementation of this plan, as well as Demeas' powerful emotional outbursts, are bound to be interpreted by the other characters (unaware of the reasons for his behaviour) as an indication that he has become unbalanced, possibly as a result of his long and wretched stay in Pontos (416ff.; cf. 437ff.).[96] Their confusion reflects the gap between what society would have expected from a head of *oikos* who is responsible for the rational organization of his household, and what appears to be the failure of a specific individual – Demeas – to live up to these expectations.[97]

There are other ways in which this situation is presented realistically. In Act III, for example, placing the blame on Chrysis may be traced to the deep-seated tradition of hostility towards women in Greece – intensified even further in the attitude of the protagonist because of Chrysis' former calling as a *hetaira*.[98] Demeas' understanding of the circumstances in which she tempted Moschion is also a reflection of widely held social attitudes:

> Obviously she got hold of him when he was getting drunk,
> when he wasn't in control of himself. Unmixed wine
> and youth work many silly deeds, when a man finds
> by him someone who has contrived a plot with these as aids.
> $$(339\text{-}42)[99]$$

The prevailing realistic tone of this act, however, is ultimately determined by two principal factors. First, the fundamental difference, which Menander takes care to stress, between Demeas' attitude to Chrysis, his mistress, and to his beloved adopted son – a difference which reflects the contrast between Demeas' familiarity with the characters of the two and the relative depth of his feelings for them. It also reflects Demeas' priorities as head of his *oikos*. Moschion is his *poietos*, adopted son, but Demeas attaches no importance to the fact of adoption, as he himself points out:

> It just doesn't seem credible to me
> that he who has been so well-mannered and moderate in his
> dealings with everyone else, should behave like this towards *me*,
> not even if he's ten times adopted, not my son
> by birth. For it's not his origins I look to, it's his character.
>
> (343-7)[100]

On the other hand, Chrysis' new role as *gamete hetaira*, 'a lawfully wedded courtesan', to use Demeas' own paradoxical phrase (130),[101] is totally unacceptable to him. However passionate Demeas' desire for her may be, he never loses sight of the fact that Chrysis the Samian is an alien element in the household of an Athenian citizen.[102]

The second factor concerns the specific nature of the relations between Chrysis and Demeas. A hint as to the limited character of this relationship may be found already in Act II, in Demeas' sarcastic reference to Chrysis as *gamete hetaira* which we have just mentioned, as well as in the fact that he is ready to throw her out of his house when he learns of her one-sided decision to raise the child whom she presents to him as the fruit of their union.

In Act III, the implications of the restricted nature of the relationship between Demeas and Chrysis come to the fore. Demeas – in marked contrast to Polemon in *Perikeiromene*, who is also under the mistaken impression that his mistress has betrayed him – shows no inclination whatever to think of himself in terms of a betrayed *husband*.[103] Aware of Chrysis' past as a *hetaira*, he continues to regard his relations with her as with a concubine – a relationship that here lacks any connotation of marriage, even when the emotional tension between the two reaches its climax (376ff.).

If anyone expects Menander in Act III to make Demeas change his emotional attitude towards his mistress and behave like a betrayed husband, he is going to be let down by the events on stage, since it is precisely the opposite scenario which evolves. The unfaithful Chrysis is regarded by Demeas as no better than a street whore who, in tempting his son, has reverted to her true nature. 'The creature's a common whore, a pestilence!' (348 Bain), to use his words. Throughout the scene of her expulsion, his attitude to her as a *hetaira* is emphasized. Even though her motives were material, he claims, she has not yet learned to appreciate the economic benefits of living under the roof of so well-established a householder as himself (376-86); her own belongings, her *parapherna*, are returned to her, as is the custom when relations are severed with a *pallake* and a *hetaira* (as well as a wife);[104] she is doomed not to continue to live in the relative comfort and respectability of a contractual concubine of Demeas, but to return to a life of prostitution far harsher than any she has known before:

A fine figure![105] Once you are in town,
you'll see yourself precisely for what you are.
The others of your sort,[106] Chrysis, who charge just ten
drachmai, run to dinner parties and drink themselves to death
on unmixed wine, or else they starve if they're not willing and
quick enough to do this. You'll get to know this, I'm sure,
as well as anybody, and you'll realize what a woman you are
and what a mistake you've made.

(390-7)

Menander, in refraining from attributing a matrimonial character to the relations between Chrysis and Demeas, on the one hand, and in stressing her professional past on the other, preserves a consistently realistic situation.

Revelation of the facts behind the events – an essential condition for a solution to the complexities of the plot in the spirit of comedy – takes place in Act IV. It is important to note that in this act, unlike the previous acts, Menander shows a marked inclination towards farce, based almost entirely on repetition or reversal of situations and motifs which we have encountered in the earlier stages of the play. To understand the realistic aspect of the farcical situation presented here, let us examine the close thematic link between Act IV and the preceding scenes.

At the beginning of the act, Nikeratos emerges from his house in order to talk to Demeas about Chrysis. He meets Moschion, who is waiting for his wedding which is to begin after nightfall, and tells the impatient bridegroom of the latest developments (428ff.). His report is interrupted by the appearance of Demeas, who vents his fury at members of his household for the commotion caused by Chrysis' expulsion from his house, and assures the audience of his determination to go ahead with Moschion's wedding, regardless of the mental agony it will cause him (440ff.). Unaware of Demeas' suspicions that he is having relations with Chrysis, Moschion appeals to him to take her back into the family home (452ff.). Demeas is shocked at what he considers to be his son's impudence, and his indignant refusal is followed by a dialogue full of comical misunderstandings, which soon develops into a bitter confrontation between the two.

This confrontation between father and son, if we compare it to the previous clash between the two in Act II (a comparison that is inevitable in the light of the clear analogy between the two situations), reveals an interesting fact: while in Act II the reasons given by Moschion for *not* expelling Chrysis are couched in terms of pure logic which are divorced totally from the realities of the period, his claims in Act IV as to why she should be taken *back* into the household of Demeas are based primarily on *the need to abide by social conventions*. 'What do you think our friends will say when they find out?' (458-9 Bain), Moschion asks Demeas, encouraged to do so by Nikeratos. He points out to him how embarrassing it would be if Chrysis, the *pallake* in the home of the bridegroom's father, did not attend the wedding feast, particularly since her relations with the family of the bride are so close. Referring to himself Moschion adds:

I'd be behaving badly if I let you do this.

(460)

Menander here exploits the difference which emerges (after the events of Act III) between Demeas' approach to the wedding procedures and that of Moschion and Nikeratos – a difference which, while stemming from a basically comic misunderstanding, reflects the totally realistic attitudes of the protagonists. On the one hand, there is the approach of Demeas, who views the anticipated *engyesis* as a means of protection for his son (and his *oikos*) against his treacherous mistress; on the other, Moschion and Nikeratos think of the ceremony as a purely formal proceeding (and as far as Moschion is concerned, a vital one) intended to unite Moschion with Plangon, in accordance with social conventions. This explains their repeated demand for Chrysis' participation in the wedding celebration.

The spectator is well aware of these differences of motivation and approach, and appreciates the ironic tension which exists between the formal wedding situation and the considerations of the main protagonist, Demeas, towards the ceremony.[107] These considerations, though basically logical, have no basis in the facts behind the events. The spectator would thus derive added pleasure from the complexity of such a normal wedding ceremony in the ordinary domestic drama played out before him.

A further realistic element in the present confrontation is Demeas' growing sensitivity to his status as head of his *oikos*, a not unexpected development in the light of his suspicions concerning the relations between his adopted son and his mistress. This growing sensitivity finds its first expression in his reaction to Moschion's remark quoted above: 'Will you try to stop me?' (461).[108] When Moschion confirms that he will oppose his father's attempt to exclude Chrysis from the wedding ceremony, Demeas loses his imposed self-control and apparently addresses the audience[109] as follows:

> You see? This is the limit!
> This is more terrible than the terrible things that took place
> earlier.
>
> (461-2)

Demeas' feeling that his position as head of *oikos* is being challenged grows when Moschion, totally ignoring his adoptive father's objection, not only dares to appeal to Nikeratos to summon Chrysis (464),[110] but goes even further when he tells Demeas that he is duty-bound to take Chrysis back into his household (467): 'But you must, father.'[111] Demeas' replies (467-8): 'Must I?[112] Am I not to be master (*kyrios*) of my own household?' Moschion, who realizes that he has gone too far in making such a blunt and outright demand upon his father, softens the tone of his address to Demeas, but nevertheless repeats his request – this time in a manner more befitting an obedient and respectful son: 'Grant me this favour' (468). But Demeas, locked in his suspicions of his son, interprets this humble request as a hidden threat to his standing as head of *oikos*. Ironically, he suggests that perhaps *he* should move out and leave the house to his son and mistress:

> What favour?
> It sounds as if you're asking me to quit my own house
> and leave the two of you alone together. You let me go on with the
> wedding, let me go on with the wedding, if you have any sense!
>   (468-71)

On the face of it, there is an element of unreason in the way Demeas, at this critical stage of the confrontation, still stands by the original marriage plans. This, however, could be explained by his deep commitment to his son and the *oikos* of which he is the head. This commitment is stressed by Menander once more in this confrontation when Demeas, forced finally to share with Moschion all that he knows of the affair, tries desperately to keep the family disgrace hidden from Nikeratos, but to no avail. Moschion's open support for Chrysis and his apparent indifference to the revelations of Demeas (481ff.) provoke the latter to reveal the shameful family secret to Nikeratos, who is a stranger to their *oikos*.[113] As Demeas himself puts it to Moschion:

> It's your fault he's got to know of everything.
>
>   (500)

We may note, incidentally, that Moschion's indifference to Demeas' discovery, while due to a failure to understand what Demeas thinks he has discovered, represents an extreme change of attitude on his part to the rape he committed against his future wife Plangon, as compared with the attitude he displayed at the beginning of the play. His profound inner shame at his deed, accompanied by his sense of shame in the face of his human environment, and his exaggerated perception of his single lapse in his otherwise unblemished record as a son and a citizen, have given way to a commonplace truism:

> But, father, what I did isn't such a terrible crime.
> I'm sure thousands of men have done it before.
>   (485-7 Miller)

Here Menander clearly chose to detract from the integrity of his hero's character in order to reinforce the farcical element of the scene. However, we cannot ignore the impressive realistic dimension which is added at this decisive point in the play to the rape situation, this time putting it in its proper perspective in terms of its relation to reality.

It is worth drawing attention to two other declarations by Demeas in the course of this confrontation: the first is a part of his reaction to Moschion's remark (473) that his efforts on behalf of Chrysis were actually meant to be for the benefit of *Demeas himself*:[114]

> I call you as witness,
> Apollo. Someone is conspiring with my enemies.
>
> (474-5 Bain)

We may trace here a concept characteristic of Greeks in antiquity: to divide their human environment into friends and enemies.[115] Here the essence of Demeas' attitude to Moschion's behaviour is presented unequivocally, and in a realistic light: Moschion, in his support for Chrysis, has *betrayed* his father by allying himself with a person whom the latter has ousted from the circle of the *oikos*, thereby virtually dubbing her officially as an 'enemy'.

Demeas' second remark refers to a later phase of the confrontation, in which he is forced to come to the unpleasant conclusion that Moschion, contrary to his expectations, is ready to accept responsibility for his alleged relations with Chrysis (482ff.). This is the real moment of crisis for Demeas, and he addresses the following sharp question to Moschion:

> Do you so completely reject and renounce me?
>
> (484 Gomme-Sandbach)

Menander, in a desire to emphasize the irony of the situation of Demeas, who has become increasingly entwined in the network of his suspicions of his son, allows him to get into a situation in which the normal set of relations between son and heir and father and head of *oikos* is reversed. According to the accepted norms, it would be the father who would have the authority and the power to renounce his son if he found it necessary,[116] but that precisely is the one sanction which Demeas did not apply to Moschion in Act III, when the truth about the baby's paternity dawned on him.[117]

Let us now turn to Nikeratos. His response to the notion that Moschion has had relations with the mistress of his adoptive father, and that she has borne him a son is clearly portrayed in such a way as to present a complete contrast to Demeas' response in Act III (492ff.). This appears to be a grossly exaggerated reaction. It lacks all logical and human considerations, and is expressed largely through comparisons from mythology which are far more extreme than the situation in the play (495ff.).[118] The solution proposed by Nikeratos – that Chrysis be sold and Moschion renounced by *apo-keryxis*[119] – is quite unrealistic as far as Chrysis is concerned.[120] To implement this idea would also mean destroying the *oikos* and publicly exposing the family disgrace – two consequences which Demeas wishes to avoid. Furthermore Nikeratos, in contrast to Demeas, appears temporarily to confuse the latter's relations with his mistress with a marriage-like relationship. Putting himself in Demeas' place he comments:

Ni: You're no better than a slave, Demeas.
     If he *had sullied my couch*, he would have *wronged* no other
     man nor would his *bedmate*. I'd be the first into the market
     tomorrow, selling my concubine and disowning my son.
     Everyone would know. No barber's shop, no colonnade
     would be empty. Everyone would sit from morning on
     talking about me and saying that Nikeratos was a real man,
     because he was doing the right thing and prosecuting his
     son for murder.
Mo.: What *murder*?
Ni.: I consider it murder when someone rises up
     against me and does such things.

                                        (506-14 Bain)

The words he uses in describing the betrayal would be more appropriate to a betrayed *husband* than to a *lover* who has fallen victim to the intrigue of his professional mistress[121] (although he does also talk of selling his concubine). Should we not then say that the pattern of behaviour presented by Nikeratos in Act IV is less realistic than that presented by Demeas in Act III? Not necessarily. For the unconscious distortion of the situation and uncompromisingly moral and over-emotional approach reflect the viewpoint of the *ordinary man* in a lively and credible manner:[122] *he* would have undoubtedly perceived the crime attributed to Moschion and his partner as a clear case of *asebeia*, impiety,[123] calling for an immediate and firm reaction in order to save the honour of the family.

Nikeratos, in other words, represents the ordinary man, with his over-simplified black-and-white approach, and is here portrayed by Menander as a conventional alternative to the more rational, sophisticated and unconventional Demeas. Nikeratos who, like Demeas, is also the head of an *oikos*, believes in the justness of his ways and is also conscious of the duties stemming from his status. There is, however, an unbridgeable intellectual gap between the two, which inevitably finds expression in their contrasting approaches to the issues which arise in the play.

Nikeratos rushes into the house to evict Chrysis and 'her' baby, and Moschion seizes the opportunity of finding himself alone with Demeas to inform him that the baby's real mother is Plangon (520ff.). Demeas has hardly digested this startling news, when Nikeratos darts out again with cries of woe: he has just seen his daughter bare her breast to give suck to the baby (532ff.). Moschion runs away in fright. Nikeratos returns to his house to convince himself that he has not been imagining things; but when he reappears on the scene, he looks as though he has completely taken leave of his senses. This time he vents his rage on Chrysis, whom he accuses of stirring up his wife and daughter against him and of refusing to hand over the baby to him (556ff.). He then rushes back into the house, threatening to kill his wife.[124] He emerges again in hot pursuit of Chrysis, who flees, carrying the baby in her arms, totally at a loss. Demeas rescues her and offers her shelter in his house (568ff.). He insinuates the truth about the baby to the furious Nikeratos, using the myth of Zeus and Danaë as a parable (589ff.). Nikeratos, who has by now been assuaged, and Demeas, return to their respective homes to get on with preparations for the wedding.

This farcical chain of events is an even more extreme and comic variant of the theme developed in Act III with the expulsion of Chrysis. However, while in the earlier act the outcome was the elimination from the *oikos* of elements which are not fully-fledged members (Chrysis and the baby), in the current act the thrust of the plot is to restore them to it. The baby's true identity is acknowledged, and thereby, one may assume, the path is set for the change in his status – from *nothos* to *gnesios* in the new *oikos* to be founded by its parents. Chrysis is also taken back into the household of Demeas, where she resumes her former place as his mistress.

This 'conservative' solution to the complexities of the plot parallels in scope the outcome of *Dyskolos*, with one significant difference. Whereas in *Dyskolos*, a *new* legal framework is required to attain the solution in its full extent,[125] in *Samia*, the existing framework – the wedding plan and, in particular, Demeas' determination to go ahead with it – is enough for attaining the same purpose.

The realistic dimension of the course of events portrayed in Act IV finds expression in the reactions of the protagonists themselves – reactions which, despite their farcical guise, represent patterns of thought characteristic of contemporary society. Thus, for example, Nikeratos' anger and frustration upon discovering the disgrace of his daughter (532ff.) are precisely the reactions which would have been expected of the average Athenian father concerned for the honour of his family. Such a father would have had the utmost difficulty in accepting any kind of challenge offered to his authority by his wife and daughter, particularly when inspired to it by his neighbour's *pallake* (558ff.). Many of the heads of *oikoi* and *kyrioi* in the audience would undoubtedly have shared these emotions and reactions.

The same applies to Demeas: his scale of priorities as father and head of *oikos* continues to be completely consistent with the concepts of the period. Thus, when he learns the truth about the baby's origin, his first concern is for the effects this discovery is liable to have on his relations with his *son*. 'You've done me no wrong, Moschion,' he declares. 'But I've wronged you by suspecting what I did' (537-8 Miller)[126] – but not a word about the possible effects it might have on his relations with *Chrysis*. The *pallake* continues to be of secondary importance to him – as indeed she should be – and she will remain so until the end of the play.[127]

When Demeas discovers the truth about the baby, this also arouses in him the first stirrings of pride as a *grandfather*, so that when Nikeratos in his fury threatens to burn the baby, Demeas, all of a sudden – for the first time since learning of its existence – becomes anxious for its fate (553ff.).

Both he and Nikeratos display a familiarity with the law in the brutal argument which breaks out between them over Demeas' open and unexplained support for Chrysis:

Ni.: You began this. I call witnesses to this effect.
De.: *You* are taking a stick to a free woman and
       pursuing her.
Ni.: Blackmailer!
De.: The same goes for you!
Ni: Bring out the baby to me!
De.: Don't be absurd! The baby's mine.
Ni.: It isn't.
De.: It's mine.
Ni.: Ho! People!

(576-80 Bain with alterations)[128]

This argument finally ends on a realistic note. Once again we find Demeas urging Nikeratos to make all the necessary preparations for the wedding feast (612ff.), but this time the marriage (which earlier was regarded as a purely formal arrangement) has come to represent the vital interest of *both* parties. Nikeratos' attempt to portray Moschion's legal situation in terms of a seducer caught in the act (612) – i.e. in circumstances that could lead to his being killed without trial – is cut short by Demeas. What might be uttered at a moment of high tension, during a first encounter between strangers, as when Sostratos meets Gorgias in *Dyskolos*,[129] is best left unsaid between the heads of two closely allied families who have already decided that their children are to wed. Nor is there any place here for that sense of discrimination between the poor and the rich that so typifies Gorgias' attitude to Sostratos in their first meeting. This element is entirely absent from the closing scene of Act IV, as indeed from the previous scenes of the play.

Also conspicuous for their absence from Act IV are any expressions of remorse on the part of Demeas and Nikeratos for their earlier unfair treatment of Chrysis, or of praise for her noble behaviour towards their grandson, the illegitimate son of Moschion and Plangon. They are far too concerned for the future of their children to give any thought to the *pallake*.

The same applies to Act V. Repairing the damage done to the relations between Moschion and Demeas by the misunderstandings which arose between them in Act IV is so central to Act V, that there is hardly room for any thought to be given to the issue of the moral responsibility to Chrysis of Moschion, Demeas and Nikeratos. She has meanwhile returned to Demeas' household and resumed her role of concubine. Menander places her in the background, and she virtually disappears from the scene as a *dramatis persona* in her own right, except for one brief moment when Demeas addresses her with instructions for the preparations for the wedding feast (730).

What might appear superficially to be Menander's negligence in applying 'poetic justice' to his sympathetic heroine[130] is in fact a deliberate means to highlight the *real* drama in the play, the ebb and flow in the relations between Demeas and his adopted son.

The Menandrian spectator was conditioned in advance to accept the centrality of the male in the Athenian *oikos* and the basic inferiority of the alien *pallake* who, though she lives in the household, has a status which lacks all connotations of marriage. He would hardly be likely to have been troubled by the lack of concern displayed by the *dramatis personae* for Chrysis or by her sudden disappearance from centre stage once the complexities of the plot have been solved. If he harboured any expectations whatsoever of 'poetic justice' with regard to Chrysis, these would in all likelihood have been fully satisfied once Chrysis was taken back into the home of Demeas. Menander, aware of these limited expectations, refrains from expanding further the role of Chrysis. In this way he not only attains the specific dramatic effect which he sought, but also contributes to consolidating the realistic approach which runs through his play.

The solution to the complexities of the plot in Act IV makes the spectator anticipate a smooth, swift and conventional ending to the play in Act V – something along the lines of the ending of *Perikeiromene*, centred on the engagement ceremony of the young couple, and followed by the traditional wedding feast. But Menander, contrary to these expectations, chooses to devote the last act to a re-examination of the relations between Moschion and Demeas, deferring the conventional developments to the very end of the play. In this way, these relations are given maximum exposure, and their central place in the poetic world of *Samia* is accorded its final and most impressive exposition.

The act opens with a monologue delivered by Moschion, who finds it hard to forgive his father's suspicions and proclaims his intention to teach the old man a lesson. He decides to feign a departure for Asia to serve as a mercenary (616ff.). He orders Parmenon, who reappears after a long absence from the stage, to fetch a cloak and sword and awaits Demeas' arrival (657ff.). Parmenon returns with the news that preparations for the wedding are at their height (670ff.). Moschion sends him away again, hoping that this time Demeas will notice him and come out. Yet it is Parmenon who comes back, bringing the cloak and sword (678ff.). Moschion hardly manages to conceal his disappointment. At this point Demeas appears, already informed by Parmenon (as it turns out) of Moschion's intention to join the army (690ff.). He immediately sees through the motives for Moschion's conduct and asks for his forgiveness (695ff.).[131]

In presenting even the deepening of the relations between father and son in farcical guise, the play ends still in character with the accepted form of play-endings of New Comedy.[132] But even here, there is nothing unrealistic.

To deal with this situation, Menander chooses to capitalize on a practice quite common in his time; young Greeks from Athens and other cities would set out to seek their fortune in foreign countries as mercenaries. The close link between comedy and reality here places Moschion's pretence from the start on a familiar and credible basis both from the viewpoint of the other characters, who are unaware of his hidden motives (except for Demeas), and from that of the spectator, who is of course fully aware of these motives.

By removing this motif from the erotic context which is traditional in comedy (623ff.) to the conflict between father and son,[133] Menander paves the way to a more significant treatment of this conflict. When Moschion decides to punish Demeas, the special relationship between father and son is revived, this time for *both* of them. The great gap between youth and age and between their powers of discernment and perception emerges: the responsible and reasoned behaviour of Demeas points to the immaturity of Moschion's reactions with particular emphasis.[134] While Demeas earlier stood by the painful decision he had made despite the personal sacrifice which it involved, his son, in a similar context of serious emotional affront, is capable only of an act of role-playing. Furthermore, while Demeas kept Moschion's disgrace a closely guarded secret, abiding by the rules for the preservation of family honour, Moschion breaks those rules in exposing his father's error publicly, as Demeas himself tells Moschion:

I accused you unjustly,
in ignorance, in error, in madness. But be sure[135] of that:
I may have acted wrongly towards all others, yet I took a good
care of *your* interests, *and* I kept to myself whatever I was
mistaken about. I did not let it out for the entertainment of our
enemies. But you now are making public my mistake and calling
witnesses to testify to my folly. I don't approve,
Moschion. Don't remind me of the one day in my life
when I slipped badly, and forget the days that went before!
(702-10)

The role played by Nikeratos in this scene deserves special
attention. When he emerges from the house, burning with eagerness
to go ahead with the wedding ceremony, he catches sight of
Moschion, dressed to set out on a journey (715ff.). He immediately
suspects that Moschion is about to abandon his daughter to her
shame and break his promise to marry her. As before,[136] he feels
duty-bound to draw attention to the legal implications of this
situation, thus steering the play at its conclusion from farce combined with sentimentality to a more down-to-earth realism:

Ni.: Hey, what's this?
De.: I've no idea, by Zeus.
Ni.: You have no idea?
      He's got a military cloak! It looks as if he's planning to go
      abroad.
De.: That's what he says.
Ni.: He says so? Who will allow him, a seducer, caught in the act
      and self-confessed? I'll tie you up without delay, young man.
(715-18)

Nikeratos' intervention accelerates the pace of developments and,
after a brief and comic exchange between the bridegroom, his father
and his prospective father-in-law, the way is open to the ceremony
of *engyesis* (726ff.). The ceremony itself, unlike the engagement of
Sostratos and Knemon's daughter,[137] is a precise copy of reality. It
is held in the presence of witnesses; the engagement formula '... I
give you this girl to keep for the production of a crop of legitimate
children' (726-7 Bain) is carefully adhered to by the bride's father;[138]
a dowry is promised – here in the context of a 'will': '... and I offer

as dowry all my property, whenever I die – which god forbid (– may I live forever)' (727-8 Bain).[139] In fact Moschion, as a *moichos*, a seducer who marries the girl he seduced (717), could not have expected a dowry.[140] The mention here of a dowry by Nikeratos helps to mitigate the bridegroom's past moral lapse. The bridegroom gives his consent to the terms of the engagement (728-9).

The *engyesis* in *Samia*, contrary to the engagement of Sostratos to Knemon's daughter, is an unexciting and routine event and is deliberately presented in this manner as the climax of a typical marriage procedure in a play whose protagonists are average Athenians with bourgeois aspirations and whose every action tallies with these aspirations.

Divine Interventions and Human Agents

In silence the god accomplishes everything

(Men. fr. 462K.-T.)

The presentation of the dramatic situation as the product of the initiative of a divine prologue-speaker, and its outcome as the inevitable fulfilment of a plan conceived by him, is a stock feature of Menandrian comedy.[1] This feature, utilized in varying degrees in the Plautine *Rudens* and *Aulularia* (adapted from Diphilos and conceivably from Menander respectively) may have emanated from the world of tragedy, Euripides' *Hippolytos*, *Bacchai* and *Ion* being cases in point.[2] Working within the traditions of New Comedy, Menander applies the mythological motif to social and domestic concerns, for it is within the framework of the family and of contemporary social conventions that the divine speaker is seeking to achieve his aims. This process, later to be paralleled in the above-mentioned Plautine adaptations, particularly *Aulularia*, could have been a contemporary modification, possibly Menandrian, of an earlier pattern, portraying god-man relationships in the spirit of New Comedy. Thus it is possible that the motif in question was much less common in Old and Middle Comedy, and did not come into prominence until the poetic conventions of the later period, particularly those of Menandrian comedy, led to its stock appearance in New Comedy.

The influence of the divine speaker on the characters and their actions was, most probably, Menander's attempt to turn his plots into something more complex, deep and subtle than a mere dramatization of everyday reality, thus revealing a higher artistic control over traditional expectations. When Menander portrays his characters as working under divine guidance, fulfilling a scheme originally conceived by the divine prologue, attributing to themselves a measure of success or failure in the accomplishment of that scheme, he is in effect juxtaposing *two* perspectives: that of natural realism in which the dramatic characters act and behave in accordance with contemporary social conventions, and that of quasi-mythological dimensions, in which divine intimations are superimposed on to the generally realistic course of events. Such a juxtaposition could not fail to appeal to his highly sophisticated audience, brought up in an atmosphere of growing scepticism towards traditional religious values and beliefs, yet nevertheless constantly searching for substitute concepts and ideas.[3] Moreover, Menander must have drawn a further advantage from the interweaving of elements drawn from the divine sphere into the intimate domestic atmosphere of his plays, for the resultant disparity created comic and ironic effects, such as the occasional magnification of his characters and their experiences. The introduction of the divine scheme also provided Menander with a logical link between the divine speaker and the plot. In other words, in turning the divine speaker into a factor in the play's action, Menander was not only achieving the particular dramatic and comic effects he was seeking, but also rendering the plot as a whole more coherent from the point of view of both form and matter.

Let us now turn our attention to those of Menander's plays whose divine prologue has survived the centuries, whether wholly or in part – *Aspis*, *Perikeiromene* and *Dyskolos* – in order to examine the employment of the mythological pattern. As we shall see, each play exemplifies a different aspect of divine influence on the human plot, thus further underlining Menander's versatility as a playwright.

We begin with *Aspis*. The background to the plot is basically outlined by the goddess Tyche, Fortune, in a delayed prologue which has survived almost in its entirety (97ff.).[4] Smikrines' and Chairestratos' elder brother has died, leaving a son named Kleostratos and a daughter. Kleostratos has set out to seek his fortune in Asia as a mercenary, having entrusted his sister to the guardianship of his uncle Chairestratos, who, unlike his elder brother Smikrines, is distinguished for his rectitude and good nature. When Chairestratos realizes that Kleostratos' stay in Asia is dragging on, he decides to marry the latter's sister to his step-son, Chaireas, himself providing the dowry. The date of the wedding is fixed for the day on which the plot begins to unfold, and, as the play starts, preparations for the occasion are at their height.

The appearance of the slave Daos, Kleostratos' pedagogue and personal attendant (Act I, sc. 1), upsets the marriage plans. He enters bearing his master's shield, followed by a large retinue of slaves, maidservants and pack-animals, loaded with booty. He reports to Smikrines his young master's death in battle, exhibiting the shield as evidence. Old Smikrines, who is greedy and ill-natured (114ff.), realizes immediately that Kleostratos' death has put his sister in the position of *epikleros*,[5] heiress to his considerable property. He is thus likely to make use of his legal right to marry her as next of kin, a point which is developed at some length by the divine speaker (138ff.), thus focusing the audience's attention on the play's main centre of interest.

However, the goddess Tyche makes it plain that Smikrines will be inexorably frustrated in his attempt to marry his niece: she reveals to the audience that Kleostratos is still alive and that the body of another soldier, with whom he had exchanged shields, had been mistakenly identified as his own. In fact, although he is at present in captivity, he will soon return safely (99ff.). And Tyche goes on to specify the irony of the situation into which Smikrines has manoeuvred himself unawares:

> Our villain, who heard just now about the six hundred gold pieces, and got a look at the foreign slaves, pack-mules and girls, will want to have the heiress himself: and his age gives him a prior claim.[6] But he won't succeed! He'll cause a great deal of trouble, and show the whole world what he's really like – and then he'll be back where he started.
>
> (138-46 Miller)

Now, had *Aspis* been a simple variation of New Comedy's stock portrayal of domestic reality, Smikrines' frustration would have remained an exclusively intimate, exclusively humanly motivated experience, but Menander chooses to elaborate the theme by making Tyche refer to herself in terms explicitly indicating her deep involvement in, and absolute control over, the dramatic situation:

> What's left
> is yet to tell you my name. Who am I, the controller
> and manager of all this? Fortune.
>
> (146-8)

While such a representation of the divine prologue's relationship
to the plot would have no parallel in the remains of Greek New
Comedy or in its Latin adaptations, it nevertheless conforms most
readily with the Hellenistic conception of Tyche as a divine force
dominating human affairs.[7] To quote but one typical example,
Demetrios of Phaleron's saying in his treatise *On Fortune*, written
c. 317 BC:

> If you were to take not an indefinite time, nor many genera-
> tions, but just the fifty years before this, you could see in them
> [sc. in the Macedonians and the Persians] the violence of
> Fortune. Fifty years ago do you suppose that either the Mace-
> donians or the King of Macedon, or the Persians or the King of
> Persia, if some God had foretold them what was to come, would
> ever have believed that by the present time the Persians, who
> were then masters of almost all the inhabited world, would
> have ceased to be even a geographical name, while the Mace-
> donians, who were then not even a name, would be rulers of
> all? Yet this Fortune, who bears no relation to our method of
> life, but transforms everything in the way we do not expect and
> displays her power by surprises, is at the present moment
> showing all the world that, when she puts the Macedonians
> into the rich inheritance of the Persians, she has only lent them
> these good things until she changes her mind about them.
> (*Fr.Gr.H.* IIb 228.39 = Wehrli 81)[8]

Indeed, Menander's audience, who were accustomed to conceive
of Tyche's control over human affairs in absolute terms, undoubtedly thought her representation here of the relationship between
herself and the plot of *Aspis* to be a natural reflection of their own
outlook, putting the comic characters and their experiences into a
comprehensible perspective for them. In other words, in thus outlining the extent to which the plot of *Aspis* as a whole is dominated
by its divine prologue-speaker, namely Tyche, Menander was not
only increasing the comic potential of his play, but also rendering
the comic situation more credible to his audience, urging them to
regard Smikrines' frustration – the plot's main objective and centre
of interest – in relation to their own daily experiences.

By sharing her plans with the audience, Tyche puts them in the
position of judging the stage characters' reaction to events in an

objective manner. The gap between the limited knowledge of the *dramatis personae* and the broader awareness of the audience engenders a high degree of dramatic irony which is maintained throughout the play. The audience's superior knowledge enables them to see the meeting between Smikrines and Daos at the beginning of the play in a new thematic light: that of the divine and the human planes and the gap between them. One has only to remember Smikrines' initial reaction to Daos' report about Kleostratos' death: 'Oh Daos, what an unexpected *tyche*!' (18) in order to appreciate fully the absurd position into which the old scoundrel has manoeuvred himself.

This, indeed, is how Tyche's plan functions from the moment she discloses it at 143ff. Immediately after the prologue, Smikrines reappears on the stage. His monologue makes it clear to the audience that Tyche's influence is inexorably at work, and that its destined victim, Smikrines, is proceeding according to expectation on the way to his destruction:

> This wedding they're preparing –
> I intend to give them notice to call it off.
> Perhaps it's odd even to mention it. It's no time
> for wedding, now that news like this has come.
>
> (158-61)

This impression is strengthened when Smikrines proclaims to Daos his intention to marry his niece, but Daos refuses to support him in this initiative. Hurt and offended by Daos' evasive attitude, he asks the latter: 'For heaven's sake! Do you think I'm doing anything wrong?' (205 Miller). Daos' reply, 'I come from Phrygia. Many things that you Athenians approve of seem shocking to me – and vice versa' (206-8 Miller), may be taken to express criticism of the Athenian law on *epikleroi*;[9] but, given the present context, there is a specific aspect to Smikrines' behaviour which lends an ironic colour to the discussion as a whole: in his attempt to exercise his *legal right* to marry the girl, Smikrines is in effect *wrong* from the point of view of the gods, represented here by Tyche.

Daos' emotional address to Tyche when Smikrines has left the stage emphasizes the irony in the situation of the characters in the play, who are involuntarily carrying out the plan of the divine prologue:

> Oh Fortune,
> what a master you're entrusting me to, after the one I had!
> What comparable wrong have I done you?
>
> (213-15)

Even more significant is his assertion at the end of the first act that 'the affairs of *tyche* are inscrutable' (248-9). This statement reaffirms the gap between the limited knowledge of the stage characters and the broader awareness of the audience, a gap which is to become a major source of comedy.

At the beginning of the second act, Smikrines reiterates – this time to his brother Chairestratos – his intention to marry his niece. Chairestratos attempts to dissuade him, to no avail (253ff.). The argument between the two sheds light on the power of the *nomos* within the framework of which Smikrines acts, and puts into its proper perspective Chairestratos' limited ability to influence Smikrines. But at the same time, there is in this argument a preview of the way in which Tyche will continue to influence the course of action in the play, by temporarily subverting the social order through manipulation of the *dramatis personae* themselves. Indeed, here we clearly observe that Tyche who – to repeat Demetrios of Phaleron's words – 'bears no relation to our method of life, but transforms everything in the way we do not expect and displays her power by surprises'. It is her power that Menander wishes to emphasize. This emphasis, attained by the exploitation of a concept completely opposed to Tyche in its nature – namely *nomos*, law – must have appealed to the Athenian audience, lending an intellectual dimension to the plot as a whole. The power of *nomos* is reiterated emphatically at the end of Chaireas', the erstwhile prospective bridegroom's, speech:

> In future, I don't even expect to see her.
> She is assigned to another by that law
> which judges my claim null and void hereafter.
>
> (296-8)[10]

Chaireas and Chairestratos are already in profound despair when the idea occurs to Daos to exploit Chairestratos' melancholy for an intrigue against Smikrines. Chairestratos should pretend to be dead, and his own daughter would thus also pass for an heiress, yet with a property four times larger than that of Kleostratos' sister. This would undoubtedly prove too great a temptation for the avaricious Smikrines, who would certainly prefer the new heiress to the previous one. Thus the way to Chaireas' union with his beloved would be cleared (329ff.).

Daos' intrigue is, in fact, a variation of that chain of events, the product of Tyche's planning, the initial imposition of which on Smikrines we have already seen at the play's inception. In both cases, we are dealing with a supposedly deceased relative (Kleostratos/Chairestratos), a presumed heiress (Kleostratos' sister / Chairestratos' daughter), and with the greed deeply embedded in Smikrines' character exploited (by Tyche/the *dramatis personae* seemingly without Tyche) to achieve the desired ends. While in the first case there is no question of private initiative by the characters involved, this is far from being so in the second case. Here, the wishes of the protagonists coincide with those of Tyche, when they proceed to carry out unawares the final and most decisive stage in the perpetration of Tyche's overall plan. The analogy between the situation arising from Kleostratos' presumed death and that arising from Chairestratos' feigned decease and its implications for Smikrines highlights the close connection between the divine and human plans. So does Daos' amused answer to Chairestratos' question 'What am *I* to do?' (380): 'What we planned./ Die and good luck (*tyche*) to you!' (380-1).[11]

Daos' plan is approved and immediately put into effect. Smikrines is informed by Daos that Chairestratos has suddenly been taken ill and is in a critical condition (419ff.). With Daos' repeated reference to the element of chance which rules human affairs,[12] a new dimension is added to the situation: the human protagonist here presents the feigned events as being caused by chance, while participating unwittingly in the plans of a divine entity of which chance, from the human point of view, is the main characteristic. This is dramatic irony at its height.

A friend of Chaireas appears disguised as a doctor, and confirms to Smikrines that Chairestratos is about to die (431ff.). At this point 205 verses are missing, and for the rest of the play we have barely fragmentary evidence (almost nothing remains of Acts IV and V), so that we cannot examine the human-divine relationship in the play beyond this point.

It is reasonable to assume that Smikrines was tempted to believe in Chairestratos' death and acted as expected. At any rate, near the end of the play (Act IV?) Kleostratos returns home and is warmly welcomed by his slave Daos (491ff.). In the fifth act, a double marriage apparently took place – that of Chaireas with Kleostratos' sister, and that of Kleostratos with Chairestratos' daughter (521ff.). It is tempting to believe that the end of the play contained a 'punishment' scene in which Smikrines was pestered by Daos and the cook after the manner of Knemon's treatment by Getas and Sikon at the end of *Dyskolos*.[13]

While in *Aspis* the goddess Tyche exploits the protagonist's – Smikrines' – natural tendencies – greed, wickedness and selfishness – in order to fulfil her plan, in *Perikeiromene* the divine prologue speaker, Agnoia, Ignorance, achieves her aim by introducing into the protagonist's – Polemon's – behaviour an element which is in sharp contrast to his normal disposition. The fact that we are dealing here with a *negative* pattern of behaviour explicitly exploited by the goddess, in order to achieve an aim which is *positive* in essence, lends the play a special character and sets it in a different category from both *Aspis* and *Dyskolos* from the point of view of human-divine relationships. But before proceeding to dwell on the dramatic and thematic significance of this intervention of Agnoia which preceded the opening of *Perikeiromene*, let us outline the background to the play, as presented to us in the almost entirely extant divine prologue and deduced by us from later scenes.

Some eighteen years before the dramatic opening of the play, a Corinthian (?) merchant, Pataikos, shocked by his wife's death and by the sinking of his ship in the Aegean sea, had exposed his new-born children, his son Moschion and his daughter Glykera. The children were saved by an old woman, who kept Glykera for herself and handed Moschion for adoption (?)[14] to a wealthy woman named Myrrhine. Subsequently, when Corinth was afflicted by war and troubled times, the old woman gave Glykera to a mercenary of Corinthian descent named Polemon, and, before her death, revealed to Glykera the truth about her origin and her brother's identity, depositing with her the swaddling clothes of both foundlings. Glykera, unwilling to damage Moschion's social status and future career, refrained from publicizing their kinship, and even when she and Polemon moved next door to Myrrhine, she maintained her silence. Moschion, a loose and unruly young man, soon took a fancy to his pretty neighbour. One evening, as she was standing in her doorway giving orders to her maidservant, he fell upon her, smothering her with hugs and kisses. Knowing that this was her brother, Glykera showed no resistance, and when he took leave of her and promised to see her again, she burst out crying for not being permitted to see him as much as she pleased. Her conduct aroused Polemon's jealousy. Whether he himself had witnessed what had happened, as is implied by lines 157-8, or whether he was informed of events by his slave Sosias, as maintained by some scholars,[15] he reacted with a violent rage – *orge* – which was out of keeping with his character (163ff.). He summoned Glykera, humiliated her by cutting her hair, and left home. When the play opens, he is staying somewhere in town (at an inn or in a friend's house), together with Sosias his slave, getting drunk in company with his friends (174-7).

We know nothing of the part of the play which preceded Agnoia's prologue, apart from the fact that Polemon and Glykera took part in it (127-30, 158). It has been surmised that the play opened with Polemon's return at dawn from some battle, and his meeting with Sosias who informed him of what had happened the previous day between Glykera and Moschion, whereupon he reacted as related by Agnoia.[16] Another hypothesis is that it was Polemon who appeared first in a monologue, in which he reported the events of the previous evening and gave vent to his outraged emotions.[17] Upon his exit in Sosias' company, Glykera emerged from within the house, bewailing her violent treatment by Polemon and announcing her intention to seek refuge with Myrrhine. This, indeed, is precisely what she sets out doing later on in the first act, immediately after the prologue. Another possible reconstruction extends the exposition to include other protagonists, notably Moschion and Pataikos, who subsequently appears as one of Polemon's drinking mates, and may be the friend with whom he stays.[18]

Whatever the precise nature of the exposition,[19] it was mainly concerned with Polemon's angry outburst. Indeed, it is Polemon's action in cutting Glykera's hair (which may well have taken place on the stage)[20] on which we should concentrate. Engineered by Agnoia in order to reunite Pataikos' family, this action demonstrates the ambivalent nature of divine influence in the play. As Agnoia herself claims:

All of this was set on fire
on account of what's to follow — that he should be driven
into a rage — *I* led him to it, not because he is such
by nature, but in order that the rest may begin to be revealed —
as well as that they may find their blood-relatives.
So, if any of you reacted in disgust to this [the stage event, N.Z.]
and thought it a disgrace, let him now change his mind.
Evil, even as it occurs, turns to good
through divine intervention.

(162-70)

Agnoia's reference to the indignant reaction of the audience (possibly to a scene which had just taken place before their very eyes) would have had its full dramatic effect only in the context of the protagonist's deviation from a long-accepted code of social behaviour. By making Agnoia draw attention to this deviation, Menander is here exhorting the audience to liberate themselves from the shackles of stock reactions and stock characterization, thus forcing them to ponder the unusual nature of the divinely motivated human drama which will be unfolded before them.

Agnoia's explanation of the nature and function of Polemon's act widens the gap between the audience's awareness and that of the *dramatis personae*. The audience's fuller knowledge of events enables them to distinguish between the negative quality of the act and its positive consequences. Thus the characters in the play adhere to the conventional concept of Polemon's act, while the audience are capable of seeing it in a new and wider perspective, that of human-divine relations and the gap between appearance and reality.

Following Agnoia's speech, the audience await with interest the positive consequences which are supposed to follow from Polemon's negative act. The manner in which the initial *kakon*, evil, is turned into *agathon*, good, to use Agnoia's own words (169), further demonstrates Menander's artistic ability in depicting the relation between the divine and the human plot in his plays.

Immediately after the prologue, Sosias, Polemon's slave, makes his appearance on the pretext of having been sent to fetch his master's civilian cloak, but his true purpose is to keep an eye on what is going on in Polemon's house. There is a reference at the very beginning of the monologue to Polemon's violent behaviour:

> Our swaggering soldier of a moment ago, our war-hero, the one who won't let women keep their hair, is lying down in tears.
>
> (172-4 Hunter)

Doris, Glykera's maidservant, who is at that moment on her way to Myrrhine's neighbouring house in order to ask her to give temporary shelter to her mistress, cannot refrain from expressing her negative view of her mistress's lover:

> Miserable
> the woman who takes a soldier for a lover. They're
> all thugs; you can't trust them an inch. Oh my mistress,
> how unfairly you are being treated!
>
> (185-8)

These two initial references to Polemon's act form part of a whole range of direct and indirect literary devices by means of which Menander draws attention to the implications of this act for both Polemon himself and the rest of the *dramatis personae*, thus underscoring the dramatic and thematic value of the relationship between the divine prologue-speaker and the plot. Let us review these devices briefly, in order to illustrate an important feature of Menander's dramatic technique in *Perikeiromene*.

At the end of Act I, Myrrhine's slave Daos makes it clear that his mistress has decided to grant temporary shelter to Glykera (262ff.). Since this arrangement is already a *fait accompli* at the beginning of the second act, it may reasonably be surmised that Glykera moved into Myrrhine's house immediately upon the latter's agreement, i.e. within the gap of about 70 verses following Doris' monologue (191ff.).[21] Thus, it is possible for Menander to open the next act with a dialogue between Daos and Moschion, in which the latter is misled into believing that Glykera's stay with Myrrhine was arranged by Daos himself to accommodate his master's desire. Moschion's passion for Glykera, reflected so vividly in his contradictory reactions to Daos' proposal to arrange a love affair between his master and Polemon's ex-mistress, serves to offset Polemon's state of depression. Polemon's emotional state is revealed by his slave Sosias, who reappears immediately after Daos and Moschion have re-entered Myrrhine's house, bearing Polemon's military cloak and sword (354ff.).

Again, Sosias' present task, to return these objects to Polemon's house, is but a camouflage for his real duty – to ascertain the state of affairs in his master's house. But, in contrast with his attitude during his first mission, one is struck by the strong note of pity in his discussion of his master's condition:

> ... did I not feel so very sorry for him.
> I've never seen my master so unhappy, even
> in a dream – this I know. Oh What a bitter homecoming!
>
> (358-60)[22]

Should we see in this expression of sympathy an indication of the decreasing significance of the theme of Polemon's violent *orge* in the play? The rest of the plot, as reflected in the remains of the play, precludes any such suggestion. Shocked to discover that his mistress has moved to her neighbour's house, Sosias threatens to put Myrrhine's house under blockade. Doris tries to convince him that Glykera's stay with Myrrhine has nothing to do with Moschion, and only her fear of Polemon – yet another reminder of his act (400ff.) – has driven her to seek refuge there, but to no avail. In the gap that follows (60 lines, approximately), Sosias apparently informs Polemon of Glykera's flight. Having heard his report, Polemon puts Myrrhine's house under siege with the aid of some of his friends, probably soldiers, his slave Sosias, and a flute-girl named Habrotonon. The text begins again in the middle of an argument between Polemon and Pataikos, his old friend. Pataikos clearly objects to the blockade. Line 467 implies that at some point during the missing section Pataikos has been to Myrrhine's house, apparently to mend the quarrel between his friend and Glykera. He has been prevented from carrying out his undertaking by the commencement of the siege, and he leaves Myrrhine's house to beg Polemon to lift it.[23]

His initiative arouses Sosias' fury. Sosias accuses Pataikos of having been bribed to betray Polemon's 'army' to the 'enemy', i.e. Myrrhine's household (467-8), and, turning to Polemon, he declares:

> You are running things badly. He will attempt a cease-fire,
> when he could have taken the house by force.
>
> (478-9)

Sosias' *orge* is the comic counterpart of Polemon's initial state of mind, and it stands in striking contrast to Polemon's ultimate – albeit reluctant – acquiescence in Pataikos' request.

While the setting of the blockade by Polemon was merely another expression of the continuing influence on Polemon of the divinely initiated *orge*, the argument which follows (486-504) introduces the human reasons, logical and legal, for its lifting.[24] Pataikos points out that Polemon's desire to treat Glykera as his wife has no legal foundation, and that she is perfectly free to leave him whenever she chooses (489ff.). He does not hesitate to relate Polemon's present violent behaviour to his past violence (492ff.), thus focusing Polemon's attention on the nature of his relationship with Glykera in general. He reminds him that the course of *bia*, violence, he is choosing to follow will have judicial consequences, and stresses the damage which may befall Polemon if he continues to act in this manner (500ff.). The only way open to Polemon to recover Glykera is persuasion (498f.).

Slowly and reluctantly, Polemon allows himself to be convinced. He beseeches Pataikos to act as a go-between and to talk to Glykera on his behalf (507ff.). Pataikos agrees, and thereby another possible act of *orge* is circumvented, while the *orge* itself makes way for an act of persuasion. Menander's treatment of Polemon's *orge* fits in completely with the general truth expressed by one of his characters in an unknown play:

> There's no remedy, so it seems, for rage
> other than a serious word from a friend.
>
> (fr. 518K.-T.)

It may be an exaggeration to claim that Pataikos' intervention here and the thwarting of another act of violence on Polemon's part are directly initiated by Agnoia's influence, but undoubtedly we have here a turning-point in the play in which the initial *kakon* is rendered *agathon*. It is that very course of violence which Polemon intends to follow that causes Pataikos to intervene and try to divert Polemon to another, more positive, type of action. Again, it is this intervention of Pataikos that enables him to rediscover his daughter during their conversation at the opening of the fourth act, of which we possess a considerable part. Moreover, in this present act, the audience are presented with firm proof that *orge* is *not* an integral part of Polemon's character, as is shown in particular by his ready support for the peaceful course of action proposed by Pataikos (511-13).

In the fourth act, where father and daughter recognize one another, the positive consequences of Polemon's initial negative act are all the more obvious. Glykera, hurt and offended by the stain on her honour caused by Polemon's extreme action against her, proudly refuses to forgive Polemon (708ff.). She *insists* on proving to Pataikos her free descent (742ff.).[25] At her order, Doris brings out the box which contains Glykera's swaddling clothes (755ff.). Pataikos, who apparently had already glanced at the box while inspecting Glykera's wardrobe at Polemon's request during the previous act (516ff.), now recognizes the figures embroidered on them as his wife's handiwork (758ff.). After a short investigation, Pataikos identifies Glykera as his lost daughter (824). It turns out that his son's tokens are no longer in Glykera's possession, yet they have somehow come into the hands of Moschion, who has been eavesdropping on their conversation from its early stages (815ff.). Now, as he stealthily listens to Glykera's reply to her father concerning the tokens, he identifies them as his own. He emerges from hiding, reveals himself to his sister and father, and the family is reunited.[26]

It was clearly the brutality of Polemon's act, as a result of which Glykera's honour was stained, that made the latter disclose her secret box to Pataikos, thus bringing about the *anagnorisis* between her and her father. The process by which the initial *kakon* has resulted in *agathon* is now completed, and Agnoia's aim has been achieved.

Following the *anagnorisis* in the fourth act, the protagonists move from a state of Agnoia — ignorance — to one of knowledge. Therefore there is no more room in the fifth act, of which only a small section has come down to us, for further elaboration of the theme of Polemon's *orge*. We learn that Polemon has been informed, either by Sosias or by Doris, of Glykera's kinship with Moschion (985ff.). Doris is sent by Polemon to Glykera in a further attempt at mediation (982f.). The latter has meanwhile been persuaded, probably by Pataikos, to make up her quarrel with her lover (1006ff.). When Doris returns with the good news, Polemon hurries home to make an offering to the gods. To Pataikos and Glykera, whom he later meets as they emerge from Myrrhine's house, he describes it as a thankgiving sacrifice for Glykera's good fortune which has helped her to find her lost family (1010ff.). Pataikos betrothes Glykera to Polemon.

In fact, from the point of view of the formal plot, it would have been enough if we had Polemon's promise that he would never repeat his behaviour (1018ff.). The play could have been concluded at this point. But Menander, who is seeking a two-dimensional representation of his characters, chooses to put into Pataikos'(?) mouth a statement which strongly reminds the audience of Agnoia's remarks at the end of her speech:

> For now your acting like a drunken man has become
> a source of blessing for us.
> > (1021-2; cf. 164-6 quoted above, p. 151)

Disregarding the irony of Pataikos' situation, who is expressing unawares the ideas of the goddess, we have here for the first time the coalescence of the human and divine points of view. The dramatic circle opened with Agnoia's revelation is closed here, emphasizing the ambivalent function of the *orge* element in the plot. Clearly, Agnoia's plans have been carried out as one would expect and in the manner she intended.

The two plays we have been discussing represent, each in its own way, a pattern of human-divine plot relationship which does not entail the intervention of the divine prologue-speaker in the later dramatic developments. The divine prologue contents himself with setting in motion a chain of events which finally leads to the specific situation he had aimed at. His human agents react according to his expectations, and nowhere do they endanger the fulfilment of his plan. In this respect, these plays may be considered quite ordinary from the point of view of plot development, although the elaboration by Menander of the divine and human relationships in them indicates, as we have already seen, an artistic and skilfully imaginative approach. *Dyskolos* represents a different type of divine-plot relationship, in which the divine prologue's intervention is required during the course of the play as well, in order to prevent the plot diverging from the course of events he desires.[27]

The play opens with a prologue put into the mouth of the god Pan, who expounds the background to the plot, set in the Deme of Phyle. Sostratos, a young and wealthy townsman, comes to the neighbourhood to hunt, and *under Pan's influence* falls in love with the daughter of the farmer Knemon. Pan's purpose in this unusual match is to reward the chaste and gentle daughter for her respectful attitude towards him and towards his companions, the Nymphs, an attitude which stands in sharp contrast to her father's indifference towards them:

> By being meticulously nice
> and reverent to my companions the Nymphs
> she's persuaded us to take some care
> of her. There's a young man whose father's exceedingly
> wealthy and cultivates an estate here worth
> many talents. The son is a city-dweller,
> but he went on a hunting expedition with a sporting friend
> and accidentally arrived in here.
> And I've made him possessed by a divinely inspired love.
>
> (36-44)

Knemon is a misanthrope, totally absorbed in hard labour and in endless quarrels with his neigbours. His irascibility has ruined his marriage: his wife has left him and moved over to live with Gorgias, her son from an earlier marriage, who earns his living by tilling his small lot, inherited from his father, with the help of his slave, Daos. The daughter lives with Knemon, together with an old maidservant, Simiche.

The first act opens when Sostratos makes his appearance accompanied by Chaireas, the parasite. The two discuss Sostratos' sudden falling in love with an unknown girl (50-4). Menander's object in introducing this discussion at the outset of his plot is twofold:

(1) it enlivens the background details of the divine plan as a preparation for the human drama which is about to ensue from it;

(2) it focuses the audience's attention on this plan and on the initial step which the divine prologue speaker has taken towards its realization. The way in which Menander has chosen to carry out his object is remarkable in its conciseness, and is entirely different from the elaborate dramatic means which we have seen him using to achieve similar effects in *Aspis* and in *Perikeiromene*. The difference in technique may be linked to the difference in the position of the divine prologue; for while in *Aspis* and in *Perikeiromene*, the delayed

position of the prologue enables the dramatization and elaboration to the utmost degree of those expository details which are worthy in Menander's mind of special emphasis, in *Dyskolos* the position of the prologue at the very beginning of the play has rendered superfluous and even undesirable, both from the structural and from the purely dramatic point of view, any attempt to over-dramatize.

From the subsequent discussion between Sostratos and Chaireas, it emerges that the emotion which Pan has implanted in Sostratos is one which excites in him impatience and unnecessary over-activity.[28] This psychological condition has already found its expression in two of Sostratos' actions preceding his entrance on to the stage: his summoning of Chaireas even before the consequences of Pyrrhias' (his slave's) mission to the girl's father are known,[29] and the use of a family slave as a go-between when the issue is marriage with a free-born girl (55ff.). The latter act, as Sostratos himself is forced to admit, is out of keeping with the accepted social norms:

> Yes, I did wrong. Such jobs
> are not for slaves, perhaps. When you're in love,
> though, it's not easy to make out what's best.
>
> (75-7 Arnott)[30]

The protagonists assume that Sostratos' over-activity is attributable to *Eros*, and it has no significance for them apart from its immediate emotional implications; but the audience, being aware of the real source of Sostratos' emotions, are able to perceive here a tangible example of Pan – here functioning as Eros – influencing Sostratos. The audience, unlike the *dramatis personae*, are able to distinguish between Sostratos as a lover and Sostratos as Pan's agent, whereby the way is paved for their objective appreciation of the hero's actions, both on the human level, and – what is more relevant to our discussion – within the framework of the divine prologue speaker's general plan. As we shall presently see, this objective appreciation is the key to understanding the continuity of Pan's involvement in the plot.

By the end of the conversation between these two characters, the difficulties involved in the accomplishment of Pan's plan emerge in sharp detail.

Pyrrhias rushes on to the stage shouting. From his confused

report, it turns out that he has totally failed in his task, for Knemon had chased him away from his premises before he had managed to deliver his message, hurling clods of earth at him (81ff.). Chaireas is frightened, and hurriedly takes off making various excuses (125ff.). Knemon's own ill-tempered entry dismays even Sostratos, and excludes any possibility of a dialogue between the two (145ff.). After Knemon's departure, Sostratos decides to turn for help to Getas, his father's slave. But an abrupt encounter with Knemon's daughter, on her way to draw water from the spring in the nearby Nymphs' cave, somewhat delays his exit (189ff.).[31] Despite himself, Daos becomes an eye-witness to this meeting, and he hurries off to report what he has seen to his master, Gorgias (218ff.).[32]

The succession of events in Act I makes it plain that Knemon is quite unapproachable, and therefore any attempt to influence him directly should be avoided. First Pyrrhias, then Chaireas, and finally Sostratos prove themselves incapable of handling the misanthrope; but precisely at the moment when the fulfilment of Pan's plan seems to be in danger, Sostratos shows himself to be truly *entheastikos echon*, 'divinely inspired', to use Pan's own words in the prologue (44): not only does he refuse to give up hope of marrying his beloved, but he also decides to consult Getas immediately, claiming that

> I don't approve of delay in
> this matter. Much can happen in
> one day.
>
> (186-8)

Sostratos' decision stands in sharp contrast to Chaireas' earlier advice, approved by Pyrrhias, to defer things for a more auspicious occasion (126ff.), or at least till the morrow (131ff.). Indeed, Sostratos has revealed his dominant characteristic already in Act I: the recurrent obstacles increase the lover's passion instead of cooling it (cf. 383). Over-active, impatient, incredibly optimistic (cf. 570ff.), Sostratos *might* give the impression of being the ideal means of achieving Pan's aim. And yet, on examining his movements in the first act, it becomes increasingly apparent that, far from being conducive to the fulfilment of Pan's plan, the line of action chosen by Sostratos could in effect seriously undermine it. His first step – sending Pyrrhias as a go-between to the girl's father – has proved to be a mistake, as a result of which two possible allies, Pyrrhias and Chaireas, have deserted the battle. Sostratos himself was little more than a coward when he was facing Knemon. He is now thinking of promoting an intrigue against Knemon, presumably to be contrived by Getas; but both Pan and the audience can see that such an intrigue is likely to fail, since the whole succession of events in Act I has shown that this kind of approach can have no effect on Knemon.

It thus appears that Pan will have to introduce yet another method in order to resolve the complications of the plot. The nature of this method is made known to the audience only towards the end of the second act, whilst it is not until Knemon's fall into the well in his yard at the beginning of the fourth act and his subsequent rescue by Sostratos and Gorgias that the implications of its use for the dramatic action are fully established. But before proceeding to discuss this method, and modern views on it, let us glance briefly at the succession of events in the three acts in question.

The second act opens with the entry of Daos and Gorgias, discussing the meeting just described. Gorgias has hardly finished rebuking Daos for failing to interfere while his step-sister's honour was hanging in the balance, when Daos notices the approaching Sostratos (255ff.). From his monologue it appears that his search for Getas had come to nothing, for his mother had sent the latter to hire a cook for the sacrificial meal in honour of one of the gods (259ff.).[33] As a last resort, he decides to turn to Knemon personally (266ff.). His meeting with Gorgias prevents him from carrying out his plan. Gorgias explains to Sostratos, who has convinced him of the purity of his intentions towards his sister, that Knemon's character renders marriage with his daughter virtually impossible (323ff.). Sostratos, however, does not lose heart, and even manages to prevail upon Gorgias to come to his aid. Daos suggests to Sostratos that he should put on a common peasant's dress and share their work with them, for thus he may perhaps meet Knemon and even make a favourable impression upon him (364ff.). All three return to Gorgias' farm, Sostratos disguised as a peasant, a mattock in his hand and a jerkin on his shoulders.[34]

Getas and Sikon, the cook, now make their appearance on their way to prepare the sacrificial meal. Their dialogue reveals the reason for the meal: Sostratos' mother has dreamed *that Pan has tied her son's feet, presented him with a peasant's jerkin, and sent him off to work a nearby field* (409-17).

At the beginning of the third act, Knemon is about to set out for his daily work. Hearing the tumult of the guests at the sacrificial meal, he shuts himself up at home (454f.). Sostratos' envisaged meeting with him is thereby rendered impossible.[35] In the following scenes, Knemon is made the object of repeated harassment by Getas and Sikon, each attempting in vain to borrow a cauldron from him (456ff.).[36]

Sostratos now makes his appearance on his way back from his work in the field (522ff.). Having reported his failure to meet Knemon, he encounters Getas, who informs him of the sacrificial meal (554ff.). Sostratos immediately conceives the idea of inviting Gorgias to the solemn event in order to further the business of his marriage (560ff.). He has hardly left the stage upon this errand, when Simiche rushes in with woeful screams (574ff.). It turns out that in her attempt to retrieve a bucket she has dropped into the well, she has also dropped a mattock which she was trying to use to reach the bucket. Knemon, in his rage, threatens her, and descends into the well (588ff.). Sostratos returns, accompanied by Gorgias, both ignorant of what has transpired (611ff.).

The fourth act opens with Simiche bemoaning Knemon's fall into the well. Sikon, whom she is addressing, responds with total indifference (620ff.). In her despair, the old woman calls out Gorgias' name (635). He runs on to the stage, with Sostratos in tow, and they cooperate in the rescue of Knemon (666ff.). The misanthrope is now wheeled on to the stage by his daughter and Gorgias (690ff.). He explains his past conduct and general outlook, admits to having been mistaken, and adopts Gorgias as his son, appointing him guardian over both his property and his daughter (710ff.). Gorgias immediately proposes Sostratos as a bridegroom for Knemon's daughter and obtains his consent (748ff.).[37]

Three main objections have been raised against the theory of Pan's intervention in the course of events just described:[38]

(1) No miraculous event is evident in the play: the dramatic developments are the natural result of human motivation, whereas Knemon's fall into the well may be regarded as a pure case of *tyche* – chance.

The fallibility of an argument such as this has been amply

demonstrated by Ludwig, whose comments on this subject, although referring to another play, are worth quoting in full:

> The implied assumption that 'naturally' and 'divinely' motivated actions are mutually exclusive seems to me to be a fundamental error. The fact that everything takes its natural course, that action develops through individual decisions and through the unexpected concurrence of independent events is often taken as proof for a god's non-intervention in the play. Apparently 'supernatural' miracles are asked for. Can only a god who breaks though natural processes claim to be acknowledged as such? Anyone who thinks this completely misunderstands the perceptions popular among Menander's contemporaries. The 'divine' revealed itself in and through events, not against and in contradiction to them.[39]

(2) In his prologue, Pan had said nothing about punishing Knemon, nor had he set out to explain the nature of the play's *peripeteia*, of which this punishment forms part. Hence the *peripeteia*, ranging from Sostratos' mother's dream to Knemon's fall into the well, can hardly be credited to Pan.

In fact, nothing compels us to believe that Knemon's fall into the well was intended as a *punishment* by Pan. Rather, it is a means to an end, enabling Pan to achieve his aim – namely, the rewarding of Knemon's daughter for her piety by marrying her off to a rich young man, an aim impossible to attain were it not for the well incident.[40] Indeed, if this were to be regarded as Knemon's punishment, this could only be in the realms of 'poetic justice', which goes far beyond Pan's own interest as presented by him in the prologue. Moreover, nowhere in the surviving New Comedy prologues does the divine speaker reveal the different stages of the *peripeteia*, or announce his future influence on events in detail. The information he presents to the audience is limited to the facts preceding the dramatic action – usually unknown to the characters on stage – and to a soothing assurance of a happy ending under his guidance.[41] Having revealed his final aim and initiated its realization, he vaguely outlines the future line of action and lets matters take their natural course.

(3) Sostratos' intrigue is comic, even farcical, so that we should not take any of the references to Pan's influence in the play seriously.

Such an objection would seem to ignore the fact that, being a comedy, *Dyskolos* can only be expected to treat its characters and their experiences in a manner appropriate to the nature and purpose of the poetic genre to which it belongs. Indeed, once we accept Pan's role in the play as a *dramatic necessity*, we are no longer bothered by the comic character of his influence in the play, as reflected in Sostratos' intrigue; for Pan, like all the humans on the stage, is subject to the rules of comedy. Hence his smiling figure in the prologue;[42] hence the comic manner in which he achieves his aim, making the tender Sostratos take up a mattock on the one hand, and Knemon the misanthrope fall into the well on the other; and hence the dramatic irony effected by the delayed report of Sostratos' mother's dream. One is also reminded of the fact that Pan is not one of the great Olympians, but a minor god who fits easily into the world of comedy or that of Satyric drama.

Bearing these criticisms in mind, let us now focus our attention on the consequences for the dramatic action of Sostratos' mother's dream, especially in relation to Sostratos' attempts to meet Knemon. This will help us examine the nature of Pan's influence on the play's action. It is important to establish from the start that the dream has been sent by Pan. Indeed, dreams being a common method of divine communication with human beings in Greek literary tradition and belief, one is justified in attributing this dream to Pan, even though it is not specifically stated in the play that he was responsible for it. It is therefore clear from the above synopsis that Pan, by sending that dream to Sostratos' mother, has in effect frustrated Sostratos in his attempts to communicate with Knemon, thus preventing his own human agent from carrying out his mission in his own way. It is as a result of this dream that Getas, who was to plan and execute Sostratos' first intrigue, is sent to hire a cook to prepare the sacrificial meal in Pan's honour. He is thus removed from the scene at the very moment when he is most needed. Similarly, Knemon, in his attempt to avoid meeting with the sacrificial party, decides to stay at home, and thus Sostratos' planned meeting with him in the fields is precluded. In other words, the god deliberately keeps Sostratos apart from Knemon, rendering yet another line of action necessary, and allowing the dream to have its effect on the misanthrope. Knemon's fall into the well in consequence of his staying at home, is evidently the result of that dream, and represents, from the point of view of pure drama, its most important effect. What on the surface appears to be a parody of intrigue[43] is, in fact, a carefully premeditated plan on the part of the divine speaker. The unique charm of *Dyskolos* lies in its reflecting *two* different streams of thought and action, the divine and the human, both centring on Knemon's static figure – an apparently objective obstacle to the promised marriage, yet a source of interest for a character-study. As a result of Knemon's isolation from Sostratos, an essential condition both for the credibility of his misanthropic character and the realization of Pan's plan, the play appears to have what Schäfer rightly termed a 'Doppelhandlung',[44] but despite his severe judgement of its structure, the plot of *Dyskolos* as a whole, from the point of view of the *divine* drama, seems to follow a unified pattern. Sostratos' meeting with Gorgias as a preparation for the eventual solution to the complications of the plot, and Knemon's fall into the well in consequence of Pan's intervention – each being determined by the sacrifice which follows the dream – are two different aspects of a single dramatic event, namely, the dream sent to Sostratos' mother. Similarly, the divine intervention which separates Sostratos' line of action from that of Knemon in Act II reunites them in Act IV through that very sacrifice.[45] This underlying concept of dramatic unity gains its strongest emphasis in the final act where *all* the characters end up in Pan's shrine.

In the exposition, the objective obstacle to achieving Pan's aim is defined and any doubt concerning human ability to handle it is removed. Pan ought to divert his impatient agent from the wrong course of action – intrigue – to a better one. Thus Sostratos, originally a principal agent of Pan, becomes secondary. The gap between appearance and reality generates a high degree of dramatic irony which culminates in Sostratos' representation of the accomplishment of the marriage plan in one day as a single-handed achievement (860-5).

Unaware of his 'reduced' position, Sostratos retains the same characteristic – driving impatience – during most of the play. From the point where the dream is first mentioned by Getas, the audience become aware of a fascinating interaction between Pan and his impatient agent. For the divinely inspired Sostratos strives incessantly to meet Knemon, while Pan wisely frustrates this plan again and again through the agency of the dream and the sacrificial meal consequent upon it. However, the moment Sostratos meets Gorgias, his impatience is gradually transformed into a constructive factor: instead of Chaireas, the *praktikos*, 'man of action' (56), Sostratos believes he has found Gorgias, the *chresimos*, 'useful man', 'a source of durable profit' (320). This is why he is not persuaded by Gorgias to give up any hope of marrying the latter's step-sister, but declares unequivocally:

> Yes, I can see you *haven't* been in love. What you say on the subject certainly suggests lack of experience. You tell me to give up. But that's no longer in my hands, it's in the god's hands.
> (345-7 Miller with alterations)

The god in whose power Sostratos represents himself as being is Eros, but the audience, aware of the real source of Sostratos' emotions, know that this god is in fact Pan. By putting into Sostratos' mouth this ambivalent statement, Menander is reminding the audience that Sostratos is actually *Pan's agent*, and that his persistence in following his desire, far from being an ordinary emotional experience, is in fact a stage in the realization of Pan's will. This persistence is demonstrated once more in the play, quite strikingly, when Sostratos, having failed to meet Knemon in the fields, returns to the scene, still impatient to achieve his aim, but this time without a definite plan (543-5).

On encountering Getas, whom he was so keen to consult at the end of the first act, Sostratos not only avoids any suggestion of contriving intrigues with him, but maintains a complete silence with regard to his new love.[46] Instead, he conceives the idea of inviting Gorgias to the sacrificial meal, the details of which he has just heard from Getas. Menander lends significance to this critical point in the play by making Sostratos himself drag Pan into the picture with the following comment:

> It'll be all right today, Getas – I'll play the prophet on that myself, Pan, though I also pray as I always do when I pass you – and I'll be generous!
> (570-3 Miller)[47]

Later in the play, at the end of Act III, we find Sostratos impatiently pushing the reluctant Gorgias forward (611ff.). Sostratos has gone to fetch him, and they are thus able to arrive in time to rescue Knemon at the beginning of the next act. The fact that during the rescue operation Sostratos becomes secondary to Gorgias (670ff.) is revealing. It demonstrates the extent to which Menander was conscious of the need to retain the credibility of both divine and human aspects of the plot. As Kamerbeek puts it:

A romantic poet would have assigned the handsome role of saviour to the young lover; but it is not thus that Menander understands his art and life: by giving this part to Gorgias, he has Knemon saved by the only person who could reap the latter's gratitude, the only person who was entirely disinterested, the one who also, for his noble character and courage, merits this handsome role.[48]

It is interesting to note to what extent Pan, while seeming to undermine his agent's mission by engineering his failure to communicate with Knemon, is nevertheless actually consolidating his schemes, having woven a careful plan which in the end turns to Sostratos' advantage. Thus his digging the field, as a result of which his face has become sunburnt (535), contributes as much to his favourable impression on Knemon as does his share in the rescue (752-5). Moreover, both the digging and the rescue episodes serve to build up the fruitful relationship between Sostratos and Gorgias, preparing Gorgias for the role of mediator between Sostratos' line of action and that of Knemon.[49]

The moment Pan's aim has been achieved, the lover ceases to feel that he is divinely inspired and becomes somewhat rational and sober, even to the extent of finding himself able to exhibit a certain amount of patience. The transformation of Sostratos, the irrational, impatient lover, into a young man once more aware of social conventions and knowing precisely 'what's best' (cf. 76-7) is clearly outlined by Menander at the end of the fourth act when Kallippides, Sostratos' father, arrives on the scene. Seeing that Kallippides is dying of hunger, Sostratos advises Gorgias to postpone any talk of marriage until after the sacrificial meal, claiming that 'then he'll be more indulgent' (778-9 Arnott). At this point, Sostratos' short alliance with Pan has clearly come to an end, and the rest of the play is demonstrably dominated by human considerations alone.

Similar patterns of divine-human plot relationship – divine intervention in the later dramatic developments to prevent the plot diverging from the initial plan – are to be found in Euripides' *Ion*, the Plautine *Aulularia* (possibly an adaptation from Menander) and conceivably also in *Cistellaria*.[50] The analogy between these plays and *Dyskolos* helps to underline an important aspect of Menander's dramatic technique, also pointing to its conceivably Euripidean origin.

We have noted that the divine element in Menander's plays, quite apart from its contribution to the exposition, has an important thematic and dramatic function. This function varies from play to play, but the underlying dramaturgical concept remains the same: the attempt to vary the ordinary everyday story by introducing 'something else' outside the normal framework of human events. This 'something' is a divine dimension, which may stand in harmony or in disharmony with the world of the protagonists, but is always apprehended as being linked to a deeper and more comprehensive point of view. Within this framework, the private incident receives its proper place in relation to this other dimension. The critical and objective awareness of this dual dimension which was required from Menander's audience led them to perceive in the everyday experiences unfolding on the stage a world view far more rich and significant than what they were offered in conventional plays which lack this additional dimension. Above all, this awareness enables us to redeem the plot and the protagonists from that one-dimensionality which ordinarily characterizes many plays dealing with everyday life. Indeed, it is the gap between appearance and reality which Menander is seeking to emphasize in his plays by means of their divine prologues, thus prompting his audience to free themselves from conventional situations and characters imposed on them by the genre concerned.

It must be stressed that Menander is *not* a religious playwright, nor would any of his divine-prologued comedies which have survived the centuries wholly or in part have lent itself to the exclusively moralistic, exclusively religious interpretation which some scholars have attempted to impose on them[51] – although a special emphasis on divine-human relationships, based in varying degrees on moral considerations, must necessarily be taken into account when analysing them.

What is notable about Menander's treatment of his dual pattern is the powerful illusion of reality maintained both on the human and the divine level. This is clearly one of the poet's main objectives: no miraculous event, no unnatural phenomenon, can be claimed to occur in the Menandrian plays we have discussed. Rather, the divine action is presented in terms as compatible as possible with ordinary human experience. Thus, in *Dyskolos*, it is through making Sostratos fall in love with Knemon's daughter, combined with his mother's dream, that Pan seeks to achieve his aim. Similarly, in *Aspis*, Kleostratos' mistaken identity and Smikrines' inborn greed are exploited by Tyche in order to inflict punishment on the old man; and in *Perikeiromene*, Polemon is driven by Agnoia to commit a violent act of jealousy against his mistress Glykera, thus setting in motion a chain of events which finally leads to the latter's rediscovery of her lost father and to the reunion of her family.[52] Indeed, it is precisely this tendency towards a purely realistic, purely intimate representation of divine workings,[53] so widely different from Aristophanes' almost surrealistic approach to the matter,[54] which is most revealing of Menander's artistic preferences as a playwright.

Epilogue

Menander is the best-documented representative of a comic genre which flourished in the third century BC and exercised much influence – through the medium of his Latin adapters, especially Plautus and Terence – on the formation of Western drama as a mode of expression which is realistic and romantic at the same time. In recent years, we have come to depend less and less on the evidence of our ancient sources as to his talent for a credible and realistic depiction of character, and the substantial differences between him and his Latin adapters are emerging with increasing clarity as more and more papyri of his plays are discovered.

These differences, some of which have been discussed in the course of the previous chapters, present us with an important criterion for assessing Menander's unique position in the comic tradition of late antiquity. Above all, they make us recognize the basic fact that what could be defined as Menander's dramatic art had no successors among the authors of that kind of Roman comedy known as *palliata*. Take, for example, that controlled mixture of dramatic economy simultaneously with a humane emphasis on the characters and their experiences which is so typical of Menander; or that combination between lively humour – *vis comica* at its best, to use the famous definition given by Julius Caesar to Menander's artistic superiority over Terence (Suet. *Vita Terenti*, 7) – and the expressions of emotion which touch us to the quick in their direct simplicity; or the coexistence between divine and human drama, both realistically conceived and executed, and both constituting an integral part of an overall dual plot. To all these features we find no adequate parallels in the adaptations of Menandrian comedies made by Plautus and Terence.

This is only to be expected; for these adaptations by Plautus and Terence were never aimed at reconstructing for the Roman audience the dramatic experience derived by the Greek audience from watching Menander, but rather at presenting a new version, including some innovations (although not necessarily revolutionary ones), which would reflect the independent achievement of the *Roman* adapter within the tradition of his Greek predecessor. Hence the exaggerated farcical tone of *Aulularia* and *Bacchides*; the uncontrolled sentimentality of *Cistellaria*; the extreme didacticism on the one hand and the complete moral laxity on the other hand, of *Stichus*. Terence – to refer only to those changes he introduced into his adaptations on his own evidence and that of Donatus – repeatedly breaks the original Menandrian pattern by turning monologues into dialogues and *vice versa*; by introducing scenes from the works of other Greek playwrights, or by combining elements from two Menandrian plays in one of his own comedies. The omission, commonly assumed by scholars, of the divine prologue from Terence's adaptations of Menander did deprive them of the two-dimensional character so typical of the original plots, but at the same time it added to them a new dimension of tension and surprise which one never encounters in Menander's comedies.

All these and many other differences are incorporated in a continuous dramatic presentation marked – especially in the case of Plautus – by a strong lyrical and musical constituent and relying on an impressive intermingling of Greek and Roman elements. This places Roman comedy in some of its aspects in a dramatic category quite unlike that of Menandrian comedy. The detection, however incomplete, of this creative tension between original and adaptation is a direct result of the rediscovery of Menandrian comedy in recent years.

Notes

I. Convention and Variation

1. Post 1913: 115ff.; Cairns 1972: 98ff.

2. For the use of the term 'convention' in the theatrical context, see Bain 1987: 1ff. For the early Roman poets' attitude to generic composition, see Leo 1912: 88ff.

3. Post 1913: 114-15.

4. Transl. Brown 1990*a*: 246. On this passage, see *ibid.*: 251-3; also 255-8 on its limited value for the study of Menander. See also below, Ch. II n. 71.

5. Euseb. *Praep. ev.* x 3.12 (465d) = K.-T., *Testimonia* 51. This title was probably not the one which Aristophanes of Byzantium himself gave to his work: Nesselrath 1990: 182 n. 98.

6. Euseb. *Praep. ev.* x 3.12 (465d) = K.T., *Testimonia* 51.

7. Porphyr. *ap.* Euseb. *Praep. ev.* x 3.13 (465d). The above evidence concerning the conventional nature of the works of Menander could help us see in the correct perspective the following famous anecdote from Plutarch, *Mor.* 347F (= K.-T., *Testimonia* 11): 'The story is also told that one of Menander's intimate friends said to him, "The Festival is nearly here, Menander, and you haven't composed your comedy, have you?" Menander answered, "Indeed, I have composed the comedy. The plot's worked out – I have just to make up the verses to go with it." ' What we have here is not, as so many scholars tend to believe, evidence of the supreme importance Menander attaches to plot-construction, but, more likely, a delightful example of a playwright who is capable of making the most of the opportunities offered by the particular generic framework within which he works.

8. For parallel expressions in Roman comedy, see Gomme-Sandbach 1973: n. *ad Dysk*. 46.

9. See also *Mis.* 465-6; *Sam.* 736-7; Vogt 1959: 192; Gomme-Sandbach 1973: n. *ad Dysk*. 968-9; Katsouris 1976: 243-56. For Menander's conventional way of introducing the chorus on its entrance, see below, pp. 72ff.

10. See, however, Handley 1965*a*: n. *ad* 401ff.

11. Useful discussions of Menander's creativity within generic composition are found in: Gomme 1937: 252ff., 261ff.; Post 1913; Goldberg 1980: 13ff.

12. On the Menandrian technique of repetition in the framework of the individual play, see below, pp. 83-7.

13. See below, pp. 22f., 69, 97.

14. Holzberg 1974: 16ff.

15. See below, pp. 98ff.

16. Cf. Plaut. *Poen.* 1294ff.

17. See below, p. 150. On the basis of the analogy to *Dyskolos* and *Misoumenos*, I tend to agree with Gomme-Sandbach 1973: 467-8, that it was Sosias who spotted Glykera and Moschion embracing, and reported this to Polemon.

18. See below, p. 150ff.

19. For a detailed summary of this monologue, see below, pp. 114f.

20. See also below, pp. 124ff.

21. For further examples of Menander's technique of parallel composition, see Görler 1961: 299-307; Williams 1961: 221ff.; Arnott 1964*b*: 232ff.

22. See below, pp. 84ff.

23. See below, pp. 83f.

24. Handley 1965*a*: n. *ad* 198ff.

25. See e.g. Marx 1959: nn. *ad* 414ff. *passim*.

26. See below, pp. 69, 96-8.

27. Pomeroy 1975: 72, 'Because fetching water involved social mingling, gossip at the fountain, and possible flirtations, slave girls were usually sent on this errand.'

28. For the realistic effect of Daos' criticism, see below, p. 97; on the ironic aspect of the scene, see below, pp. 73f.

29. Gomme-Sandbach 1973: n. *ad* 202.

30. The date of Diphilos' play is not known: see Webster 1970: 154. Handley 1965*a*: n. *ad* 198ff., believes it is later than *Dyskolos*. In fact, we have no proof that Diphilos' play might not have been earlier than that of Menander. Be that as it may, we have before us two versions of the same formula, and it is only reasonable to suppose that these were not the only ones in New Comedy. Handley 1965*a*: n. *ad* 189: 'Possibly the figure of the lamenting girl carrying her pot to get water is intended to recall the situation of the Euripidean Electra' (*El.* 54ff., 112ff.). Note Menander's economical treatment of the scene at the door as opposed to Plautus' lavish treatment of it. On Menander's economy see below, pp. 59ff.

31. Webster 1960: 169ff.; *idem* 1974: 57ff.

32. Webster, *ibid.*; Post 1913: 131f.

33. See Webster's reconstruction of the scene, 1974: 186.

34. *Ibid.*

35. Contrast the situation in Act IV of *Perikeiromene*. Below, p. 155.

36. 1974: 186. Cf. Plaut. *Poen.* 1099ff.

37. See e.g. *Perik.* 780ff.; Plaut. *Cist.* II 3, 745ff.; Ter. *And.* V 4; *Heaut.* IV 1.

38. Lloyd-Jones 1966: 146 (= 1990: 66).

39. See below, pp. 57f.

40. Cf. the technique applied to the recognition scene in *Perikeiromene*: below, pp. 51f.

41. With the possible exception of *Sik.* 280ff., where the text resumes after a gap of about 20 verses and, from 291 onwards, we have but scanty remains of the scene. See however below, pp. 60f.

42. For a detailed summary of the situation, see below, p. 155. See also below, pp. 51f.

43. The divine dimension of the situation, however, should also be taken into account: see below, pp.. 150ff., 154ff.

44. See below, pp. 51f., 57f.

45. See below, pp. 51f.

46. Solmsen 1932: 1ff. (= 1968: 141ff. = Schwinge 1968: 326ff.).

47. Euripides' play *Ion* is an impressive exception in this sense: neither the divine scheme (of Apollo) nor the human scheme (Creusa's) is implemented according to plan. See below, pp. 166f. with n. 50.

48. For a detailed summary of the intrigue in *Aspis*, see below, pp. 147ff.

49. See below, pp. 156ff., 159ff.

50. Zagagi 1979: 39ff. See below, pp. 47f., 164ff.

51. Quoted above, pp. 16f.

52. Several Plautine comedies, above all *Miles Gloriosus* (see esp. 767ff., 902ff., 1161ff.), are marked by a strong tendency to prepare the audience for the intrigue about to be unfolded before it. This tendency is used, quite unconvincingly, by Hough 1939: 422-35 as a criterion for dating these plays to the so-called early and middle periods of Plautus' career.

53. Herein lies the essential difference between the Menandrian intrigues and, for example, the intrigue of Orestes and Pylades together with Electra in Euripides' *Orestes* (1031-245); although it grew out of a situation of despair, its *components* did not stem directly from what was happening on the stage at the time. Those Plautine intrigues, which could be described as allowing for improvisation (for example, *Pseud.* 384ff., 394ff., 574ff., 667ff., 697ff.) stem from fundamentally artificial situations and do not give the impression of natural occurrences – unlike the Menandrian intrigues to be discussed below. For the element of improvisation in Plautine comedy in general, see Slater 1985.

54. At some point before Sostratos exits from the stage at 392 (perhaps here), he must remove his cloak and don a peasant's jerkin (cf. the dream of Sostratos' mother, 415f.). But see Handley's comment 1965*a* on *Dysk.* 370.

55. Cf. Gomme-Sandbach 1973: n. *ad* 329-30. An intrigue involving Thrasonides' pretence of suicide in Act IV of *Misoumenos* (403ff.) has been postulated by Maehler 1992: 62 (*P. Oxy.* 3967).

56. Arnott 1968: 15. See in general Körte 1937; Burck 1933: 417-31 (= 1966: 23-35); MacCary 1969: 277-94; *idem* 1970: 277-90; *idem* 1971: 303-25; *idem* 1972: 279-98. MacCary's somewhat dogmatic approach to Menandrian characters is criticized by Brown 1987: 181ff.

57. The type is as old as Lamachos in Aristophanes' *Acharnians*. On the comic soldier, see Wehrli 1936: 101-13; Webster 1970: 64f.; MacCary 1972: 279-98; Hofmann-Wartenberg 1973.

58. On the question of *Agnoia*'s involvement in the plot of *Perikeiromene*, see in detail below, pp. 149ff.

59. 1972: 284. Moschion's bragging finds its expression mainly in his behaviour in Act II. In *Sikyonios* too, we find character traits being transferred from the soldier-type (Stratophanes) to the young lover (Moschion): MacCary, 1972.

60. Thrasonides' special relationship with Krateia became exemplary: Arr. *Diss. Epicteti* IV 1.19; Diog. Laert. 7.130; Iren. *Haer.* 2.27.151.

61. Cf. Brown 1980: 5.

62. 1974: 163-4. Note that Webster's conjecture is based on the experience of Kleostratos in *Aspis*.

63. Choricius may not have read the play very carefully. Note the sympathetic way in which Getas relates to Thrasonides in the opening scene (A90-A93): 'What on earth can have gone wrong? It's not even as if you were particularly disagreeable – not enough to speak of. Of course, you don't get much pay as a soldier, that's a drawback. But your face is very refined' (Miller).

64. For Stratophanes, the lover-soldier in Menander's *Sikyonios*, see MacCary 1972: 286ff. To this list of Menandrian symphathetic soldiers, Kleostratos in *Aspis* must be added. MacCary 1972: 288f.

65. Young lovers noted for their initiative and activity in Menandrian comedy are Sostratos in *Dyskolos* and Chaerea in *Eunuchus*.

66. By contrast, the soldier in *Kolax* seems to have been a traditional braggart.

67. Revelation of Stratophanes' civic status is one of the major themes of the play *Sikyonios*.

68. Webster 1970: 63f. See in general Hauschild 1933; Gilula 1980: 142-65; Henry 1985; Brown 1990*a*: 241-66. Brown *ibid.*: 254 may be right in claiming that there may not have been such a one-sided 'traditional' portrayal of *hetairai*; but fourth-century evidence is too fragmentary to allow for any decisive conclusion on this point.

69. *Epitr*. 535, 538ff., 544ff., 551, 557ff., fr. 7K.-T.; *Sam*. 338ff., 348ff., 391ff., 507ff. (see below, pp. 127ff.); Ter. *Eun*. 67ff., 102ff., 197f., 352-4, 507ff., 926ff., 984ff., 1072ff. For the type of the *hetaira* presented by Menander in traditional terms, see e.g. Bacchis in *Heautontimoroumenos*; Men. *Thais*, fr. 185K.-T. (cf. Prop. IV. 5.43); Ovid. *Am*. I. 15.18. There is no real basis for Wiles' claim 1989: 39 that in Roman comedy 'the focus of the Greek material upon rape and marriage is replaced by a new focus upon prostitution'. Cf. Brown 1990a: 245-6.

70. For this motif, see Wehrli 1936: 36. The character which corresponds to Chrysis in *Samia* is the wife of Nikeratos.

71. 775-9. On Chaireas, see Gomme-Sandbach 1973: 131; Handley 1965a: n. *ad* 57ff. For the type of the parasite in Greek comedy, see Handley, *ibid.*; Nesselrath 1985: 15ff.

72. For further Menandrian examples of this technique, see MacCary 1972: 285-6. For Menander's individual treatment of cooks, see Theuerkauf 1960: 85ff.; Handley 1965a: n. *ad* 393; *idem* 1970: 8ff.; Gomme-Sandbach 1973: nn. *ad Dysk*. 398; *Sam*. 283, 285; but see Blume 1974: 99-101.

73. The siege scene in *Eunuchus* apparently does not originate with Menander's *Eunuchos*, but is taken from his own play *Kolax*: see the evidence of Terence in the prologue (30ff.) regarding the origin of the characters of Thraso the soldier and Gnatho the parasite, both of whom participate in the siege scene. Ludwig 1959: 20ff. believes that Terence's scene (in outline) must come from Menander's *Eunuchos*. On the motif we are discussing, see in general Wehrli 1936: 23, 31 n.1, 103f., 110f.

74. See below, p. 154.

75. What follows is an abridged, revised version of my paper 1988: 193ff. For the traditional background of this motif, see *ibid.*: 193 n. 1

76. See below, pp. 116ff.; cf. pp. 138ff.

77. See *Sam*. 428ff.; Ter. *Ad*. 899f.

78. *Art. cit.*: 208 n. 59. Referring to the controversy over the date of *Samia*, I tend to favour the later date. There is an obvious difference between *Cistellaria* and *Samia* in the treatment of the exile-situation, which indicates clearly the higher artistic standards of the latter, although the fragmentary state of the exile-scene in *Cistellaria* must surely be taken into account. For bibliography, see *art. cit.*: 208 n. 60.

79. *Art. cit.*: 197ff.

80. Euripides' *Herakles Mainomenos*. *Art. cit.*: 206 with n. 51.

81. The same technique – rapid reversal of mood and situation combined with the element of madness – appears, though on a much smaller scale and without involving a parody of a tragedy, in *Cist*. 284ff.

82. *Art. cit.*: 208 n. 58.

83. *Art. cit.*: 197-9.

84. *Art. cit.*: 202f.

85. See below, pp. 87ff., 105f., 118f., 120, 125, 138.

86. For role reversal in Aristophanes, see e.g. *Frogs* (master and slave); *Lysistrata* (man and woman; husband and wife); *Clouds* (father and son). Plautus' plays *Asinaria* and *Persa* are wholly based on the device of motif-reversal. See also the conclusion of the plays *Epidicus* and *Pseudolus* (master-slave relations).

87. Neumann 1958: 105ff. (with regard to women). In *Menaechmi*, the question of the quality of the morals of the brothers Menaechmus is treated as irrelevant, since this is a comedy of errors revolving around the identical twins.

88. If, indeed, the play had a prologue in the original, as is assumed by certain scholars (e.g. Leo 1912: 196-8), it is reasonable to suppose that it included information on the identity of the soldier. But this does not necessarily imply that the treatment of the *character* of the soldier in the *body* of the play was different in the Greek original from its treatment by Plautus.

89. For this traditional pattern of behaviour of the comic lover, see [Men.] *Pap. Antinoop.* 15.4; Plaut. *Merc.* 3-5; Sisti 1986: n. *ad* A1.

90. *aph'hesperas* Austin. Gronewald's <*kato t'ano*> at the beginning of l. 8: 1989: 35 is highly speculative.

91. See in general Copley 1956.

92. See Aristoph. *Eccl.* 960ff.; *Lys.* 845ff.; Plaut. *Curc.* 87ff., 145ff.; *Truc.* 758ff.; *Men.* 696ff.; *Merc.* 408ff.; *Asin.* 127ff.

93. Turner 1979*b*: 109 (= 1984: 245); Bornmann 1980: 157. In *Mis.* 381-413 (*P. Oxy.* 3967) which seem to be the end of a long monologue of Thrasonides, the jilted hero 'may again be waiting outside his own house for a sign of a change of heart from Krateia': Maehler 1992: 61.

94. Cf. A37. Krateia's legal status in the play is not clear. In A38, the expression *peritheis eleutherian* does not necessarily imply Krateia's complete release by Thrasonides after he had bought her – as Turner understood it in his translation 1979*a* 'I gave her her freedom'; *idem* 1979*b*: 116ff. (= 1984: 250ff.); cf. Bornmann 1980: 158f. This, of course, is not the technical term for manumission. It is far more likely that the meaning of the expression here is 'I treated her as a free woman', the manumission itself being delayed to a later part of the play – when Krateia's father is discovered. See Getas' comment in 315. Brown 1980: 6; cf. Barigazzi 1985: 120, 122f. Borgogno 1988: 94-7, however, may be right in suggesting that Krateia's manumission is conceived of by Menander as a bipartite legal procedure, following everyday practice.

95. Cf. Turner 1979*b*: 108f. (= 1984: 244f.).

96. Turner 1979*b*: 110f. (= 1984: 246f.).

97. Motif-reversal, more modified in character, may be found in the relations between Moschion and Demeas in Acts IV and V of *Samia*. See below, pp. 130ff.; Ch. V n. 134. For this feature in the Latin adaptations of Menander, see Plaut. *Bacch.* 763-5, 772 (Chrysalus longs to see Nicobulus in his anger and, in contrast to the constant fear of the slaves of their masters, presents his master's rage as a condition for the *success* of his intrigue); 795ff. (Chrysalus is *glad* of the chance that he may be caught and put in chains by his master). See Blume 1974: 23 n. 41.

98. Barsby 1986: n. *ad loc.*

99. Cf. Ter. *Hec.* 756ff., 775-6, 834-6.

100. For further examples of this technique in Roman comedy, see Plaut. *Truc.* 482ff.; *Trin.* 16-17; *Merc.* 3-8; *Pers.* 465-6; *Pseud.* 566-70, 1239-42; *Cas.* 860-1; *Capt.* 54-8, 778-9 (instead of the typical *servus currens*, a running slave, we have here the non-typical running *parasite*; cf. however, *Curc.* 280ff.), 1029-34; Ter. *Hec.* 274ff., 866-8. The *parabasis* of Old Comedy is traditionally exploited by the comic playwrights for self-praise.

101. Cf. Plaut. *Truc.* 826ff.; *Aul.* 750ff., 789ff.; Men. *Sam.* 67ff.

102. See above, pp. 24f.

103. Cf. Plaut. *Aul.* 691ff.

104. *Sam.* 301ff., 421, 440ff.; *Asp.* 164ff.; *Dysk.* 206ff., 427ff., 456ff., 546ff., 874; *Epitr.* 430f.; Plaut. *Bacch.* 179ff., 526ff.; Ter. *And.* 228ff., 684f.; *Heaut.* 175ff., 842ff., 879ff.; *Ad.* 787f. For the exploitation of this convention by the Roman comic playwrights, see also Plaut. *Cas.* 144ff., 309ff., 780ff.; *Men.* 110ff., 466ff.; *Merc.*

962f.; *Mil.* 156ff.; *Most.* 1064ff.; *Pers.* 85ff.; *Poen.* 615ff.; *Pseud.* 133ff.; *Rud.* 331f.; *Trin.* 39ff.; *Truc.* 95ff., 711ff.; Ter. *Hec.* 243ff., 623ff.

II. Artistic Principles

1. See below, pp. 94ff., 167f.
2. See e.g. Goldberg 1980: 25: 'The double plot, either nascent or developed, found in such Terentian plays as *The Andrian Girl* and *The Brothers* remains without parallel in extant Menander. We find instead situations, such as Demeas' disrupted relationship with Chrysis and Moschion's reunion with his father and sister in the *Perikeiromene*, that enrich the action of the play without being developed in their own right. Disparate situations serve only to move the main action to its close, and it will prove helpful to speak of multiple situations but only a single plot in each play.' Also pp. 56f., 106f., 107; Norwood 1932: 147 went as far as to suggest that: 'This duality-method is the centre, the focus of Terentian art and the Terentian spirit ... So far as can be learned, it is entirely his own – another, and the most impressive, proof of his originality not merely in play-conception but in play-construction also. For he actually recasts his "original" in order to secure this dualism'; Duckworth 1971: 184 speaks of 'the "duality-method" which is the outstanding feature of Terentian plot-construction'; cf. also Levin 1967: 301-5; Goldberg 1986: 123ff. But see Holzberg 1974: 20ff., 30, 34, 39; also Duckworth 1971: 188-90. On the issue of the double action in Terence, see most recently Gilula 1991: 81-93. Terence's exploitation of the double plot pattern was much praised in antiquity: see Donat. *ad And.* 301; *Phorm. Praef.* I.9; Euanthius, *De fabula* 9.
3. For a detailed study of the divided dramatic structure of *Dyskolos*, see the profound analysis of Schäfer 1965: 45ff., 75ff.; Zagagi 1979: 39ff.; Arnott 1989: 30ff. Schäfer's analysis is criticized by Kraus 1968: 338f.; Anderson 1970: 199ff.; and most recently by Brown 1992: 8ff. See below, n. 5.
4. Even when this need has arisen, the link between the misanthrope and his would-be son-in-law remains loose in the extreme: see below, pp. 105f., 109; also below, pp. 159ff.
5. See Zagagi 1979: 39ff. I have not been convinced by Brown's attempt 1992: 8-20 to present the construction of *Dyskolos*, Acts I-IV as flawless. Brown's view, however, *ibid.*: 8 'that Menander has overcome the difficulties (such as they are) with considerable success, and above all that he has exploited these apparent difficulties, and turned them to positive advantage, by using them as opportunities to create comic effects' is in full conformity with my own analysis of the play in 1979: 39ff.; 1990: 78ff. (= Ch. VI, pp. 156ff.) as well as with my discussion of it in Chapters IV and V of this book.
6. See below, pp. 162ff.; also Zagagi 1979, *passim*. Cf. the way in which in *Samia* everyone wants the marriage to take place and yet it keeps being delayed.
7. See below, pp. 147f.
8. For the difficulties involved in establishing the part played here by Kleinias, and the nature of his relation to Krateia (his sister?), see Gomme-Sandbach 1973: 440-1.
9. A third, minor plot-line involving a love affair between Theron, a parasite, and a *hetaira* named Malthake, may be discerned in the remaining fragments of the play: 145, fr. 9 Sandbach (= 377K.-T.); Lloyd-Jones 1966: 155, 156 (= 1990: 74, 75); Webster 1974: 183, 187.
10. Syros or Syriskos? At line 270 the charcoal-burner is referred to as Syriskos. The evidence of the Mytilene mosaics (*BCH* LXXXVI (1962) 875) suggests, however, that his name was Syros, although applying it to the wrong character, namely Daos.

Since Syros is a common name for the slave type in New Comedy, it seems preferable to assume that it was made diminutive of familiarity at line 270. On the question of the charcoal-burner's name, see Gomme-Sandbach 1973: 303, n. *ad Epitr.* 270.

11. See below, pp. 138ff.; also above, pp. 35ff.

12. Donat. *ad* 301, 977.

13. *Eun.* 30-3.

14. I.e. Plautus' *Bacchides*, and possibly *Aulularia*; Terence's *Heautontimoroumenos* and *Adelphoe*. Above, n. 2.

15. Quint. *Inst. or.* x.i.69, stresses the strong link between Menander and Euripides: 'Menander, as he often testifies in his works, had a profound admiration for Euripides, and imitated him, although in a different type of work' (transl. H.E. Butler, Loeb). For a detailed study of the Euripidean multiple plot see in general, Burnett 1971. An analogy between the double plot of Euripides' *Hekabe* and *Andromache* and that of Plautus' *Poenulus* and *Rudens* has been established by Friedrich 1953: 30-45, 47-60. For a critical evaluation of Friedrich's theory as applied to New Comedy in general, see Katsouris 1975: 5-10.

16. Katsouris, *op. cit.* offers a useful collection of examples from Menander and other New Comedy playwrights, even though it is largely predetermined by the author's own subjective approach to this issue. See recent discussion by Hunter 1985: 114ff. On the question of the relation between the two genres and on Menander's own attitude to tragedy in particular, see Lanowski 1965: 245-53; Hurst 1990: 93ff.

17. The tragic background of this scene has been the subject of much discussion: Legrand 1917: 270-1; Maas 1913: 361f. (= *Kl. Schr.* 78-80); Andrewes 1924: 5-6; Sandbach 1970: 126ff.; Gomme-Sandbach 1973: 519-25; Lloyd-Jones 1974: 212f. (= 1990: 28ff.); Bain 1987: 116 n. 2; Fitton 1977: 10; Poole 1978: 60; Goldberg 1980: 53f., 60-1.

18. Gomme-Sandbach 1973: n. *ad* 779ff. Since the translations supplied here do not attempt to reflect the original metre, the Greekless reader will not notice how closely Menander is following in this passage the versification of tragedy.

19. See Lloyd-Jones 1974: 212 (= 1990: 28-9) against the rendering of the line in Gomme-Sandbach 1973 by 'what now is still existing of my family?'

20. I follow here Lloyd-Jones' reading *[pal]ai* in *art. cit.*: 213 (= 1990: 29-30). Sandbach, *OCT* 1990: 345 writes *pal[a]i* (*sic!*) and mistakenly attributes this reading to Rea.

21. On this passage, see Blundell 1980: 68; Bain 1983*b*: n. *ad loc.* Blume 1974: 118ff. takes this speech too seriously.

22. There is indeed a big difference between the *Perikeiromene* passage and the *Aspis* passage. In the former, the use of tragedy lends a solemn, but in the latter a comic, note to the scene. For further discussion of the *Aspis* scene, see below, p. 148.

23. Gomme-Sandbach 1973: 303. For the dramatic significance of Syros' reference to the myth of Neleus and Pelias (treated by Sophocles in his play *Tyro*), see Goldberg 1980: 66, 70.

24. Following Sandbach. Körte attributes these lines to Sophrone – on which see Gomme-Sandbach 1973: n. *ad* 1120ff.

25. Mythological *exempla* involving the myth of Zeus and Danaë are quite common in Greek literature: see Austin 1970: n. *ad* 590ff.; Asclep. *A.P.* v. 64. I find it difficult to accept Offermann's suggestion 1978: 152 that the ultimate meaning of the golden rain is (for Nikeratos' family) the marriage of Plangon to the son of their rich neighbour.

26. See Austin 1970: n. *ad* 598 against Gomme-Sandbach's interpretation 1973: n. *ad loc.* 'if he thought well of ', 'gave honour to Danaë', followed by Bain 1983*b* and Miller 1987.

27. Katsouris 1975: 131ff., 178; and most recently West 1991: 17ff.

28. See below, p. 125.

29. Handley 1965*b*: 47ff.; *idem* 1970: 22f.; Kassel 1965: 8f.; Lloyd-Jones 1966: 140f. (= 1990: 61f.); *idem* 1971: 192 (= 1990: 22); Sandbach 1970: 129; Gomme-Sandbach 1973 *ad loc.*; Arnott 1972*a*: 74f.; *idem* 1979*b*: XLIf.; Poole 1978: 61f.; Goldberg 1980: 22f. For the popularity of the Euripidean scene among the Athenian public, see Fraenkel 1912: 12; also 34ff.

30. On this speech, see Handley 1965*a*: n. *ad* 708-47.

31. See however Handley 1965*a*: n. *ad* 758.

32. On the legal implications of this scene, see below, pp. 106ff. For further examples of tragic and mythological exploitation in Menander, see *Dysk.* 153ff. (Zagagi 1980: 29f., 42 n. 90); 683; *Sam.* 495ff. (Zagagi 1980: 30f., 40 n. 86, 42 n. 90, 53); *Kolax*, 124; frr. 88K.-T.; 198K.-T.; 250K.-T.; 288K.-T.; 718K.-T.; Plaut. *Bacch.* fr. xv (Zagagi 1980: 39, 40, 42, 63), 155ff., 241f., 275, 665f., 810f., 925ff. (Zagagi 1980: 16 n. 10, 29, 40, 42, 61ff.); Reinhardt 1974: 57ff. and *passim*; Barsby 1986: Index, *s.v.* Mythological allusion, Greek.

33. Goldberg 1980: 22ff. esp. 29ff. (*Aspis*); Hunter 1985: 53ff.

34. Hunter 1985: 54.

35. Goldberg 1980: 33f. See below, pp. 143ff.

36. See below, p. 154; also above, pp. 34f.

37. For instance, the cook in the above-mentioned scene in *Samia* is wholly within the tradition of the *bomolochos*, clown, of Old Comedy. Cf. Moschion's eavesdropping on the conversation of Glykera and Pataikos in *Perik.* 779ff.

38. Transl. D.A. Russell and M. Winterbottom, *Ancient Literary Criticism* (Oxford, 1972), p. 531.

39. See below, pp. 129ff.

40. See below, pp. 148f. with n. 13.

41. Note the farcical ending of Plautus' *Stichus* and Terence's *Adelphoe*, *Eunuchus* and *Heautontimoroumenos*: all of them adaptations of Menandrian comedies. On these endings, see Brown's recent discussion 1990*b*: 39ff.

42. It is at the end – after the *lysis*, denouement, – that the atmosphere of the *komos* takes over: Süss 1910: 450ff.; cf. Lloyd-Jones 1973: 283 (= 1990: 92).

43. Gomme-Sandbach 1973: n. *ad. loc.*

44. See below, Ch. v, n. 21.

45. For the form and content of this scene cf. *Dysk.* 751ff. Knemon's wish to ignore Sostratos is best attributed to his misanthropy, as revealed in earlier stages of the play.

46. See below, pp. 124ff.

47. See above, n. 37.

48. Gomme-Sandbach 1973: 441.

49. It is difficult to see how *beltion* could stand with the plural following in Sandbach's *OCT*. Sir Hugh Lloyd-Jones has kindly suggested to me the following reading: *hapaxap[an ti t]es*, which I adopted as against Sandbach's *hapaxap[anta t]es*. The reading is in any case very uncertain: see ed. pr. and its plate.

50. It is typical also that this new entrance comes at the end of an act: see below, pp. 77f.

51. See below, pp. 85, 92, 139f.

52. See Theuerkauf 1960: 77ff.

53. See below, p. 166.

54. See above, Ch. I n. 30.

55. See below, pp. 109, 166.

56. For this character trait of Moschion, see Mette 1969: 432-9.

57. See below, pp. 126f.

58. Cf. Sandbach 1970: 121.

59. See below, p. 127. Most pertinent to the present discussion are Arnott's comments 1964a: 112-13 on Sostratos' entrance monologue in Act II of *Dyskolos* (259ff.). 'Dramatically, Menander shows himself effortlessly juggling with a dozen balls in the air at once' (*ibid.*: 112).

60. See e.g. Plaut. *Bacch.* 520ff., 530ff. (cf. *Dis Ex.* 47ff.; below, n. 75); *Cas.* 64-6, 1012ff.; *Cist.* 774ff.; *Merc.* 1005ff.; *Pseud.* 387ff.; Ter. *And.* 980f.; *Hec.* 873ff.

61. Consider also *Perik.* 267ff. As I have pointed out elsewhere, 'It is usual to speak of Menander in terms of an economical playwright who – in sharp contrast to Plautus – shows no interest in elaborating the element of *geloion* in his plays beyond what is dramatically relevant. But note the analogy between Menander's comic technique in the opening scene of Act II of the *Perikeiromene* and that of Plautus in *Asinaria*, 649ff. and *Mercator*, 907-9' (Zagagi 1988: 205ff.); 'A "Plautinisches" in Menander? ...' (Handley-Hurst 1990: 158).

62. Almost all the material to be discussed below is absent from that part of Schmude's recent study (1988) which considers the relevant Greek material. See my review of Schmude's book 1991: 13ff. esp. 15.

63. For the sake of contrast, compare the plot of *Dyskolos* with that of *Rudens*, Plautus' adaptation of a play by Diphilos. In the latter play, young Plesidippus arrives in a new environment, but no attempt is made by Diphilos/Plautus to develop the relationship between him and the other characters to any significant extent. The plot centres on the conventional element of the *anagnorisis*, hardly leaving any room for character-study, whether in social terms or otherwise.

64. A comparable example is the situation of Hegio in the Plautine *Poenulus*. What is unique about *Dyskolos* is its presentation of a new network of relationships between young people (Sostratos, Gorgias): in all the comedies extant in their Latin versions, the young heroes are either related by family ties, have been friends from childhood, or are suitors for the hand of the same girl.

65. See below, pp. 107f. Most pertinent to the present discussion of *Dyskolos* is also the face-to-face confrontation between Sostratos and his father in Act V, following which the latter consents to the marriage of his daughter with Gorgias.

66. For the divine dimension of this chain of events, see below, pp. 154ff.

67. See below, pp. 109, 112.

68. See also above, pp. 48f. (with reference to *Perikeiromene*).

69. For these conventions and their influence on New Comedy, see Ferguson 1911: 77ff.; also Fantham 1975: 44-74.

70. See above, pp. 22f.; below, pp. 97ff.

71. See below, pp. 95ff., 101f.

72. See above, pp. 22f.; below, pp. 73f., 97.

73. See below, Ch. V nn. 8, 9.

74. Transl. Brown 1990a: 245-6. A useful discussion of this passage from Plutarch is found in Gilula 1987: 511-16. But see Brown *ibid.*: 251-3.

75. Plautus, for instance, faced in *Bacch.* 520ff. with the need of bridging the break between Acts II and III of the Greek original (*Dis Exapaton* 47ff.), omitted the father-son conversations before and after the choral interlude. As Barsby 1986: 142 rightly observed, '... in doing so he has speeded up the action but has rejected the opportunity to explore the father-son relationship'. Similarly Terence, seeking to avoid the lengthy narrative speeches of Menander's *Andria* and *Eunuchos* (see

Donat. *ad And*. 14; *idem ad Eun*. 539), replaced these speeches by dialogues involving the original Menandrian protagonists together with protatic figures presumably of Terence's own invention. However, Terence's use of his protatic figures, being artificial and limited in the extreme, has contributed little, if anything, to the further dramatization of the human situation provided in the originals. On the other hand, it disrupts unnecessarily the straightforward revelation by the protagonists of their personal feelings and thoughts. For the possibility of Plautus having substituted a farcical dialogue-scene between Alcesimarchus and his slave in *Cist*. 231-49 for the emotional monologue of the young lover of Menander's *Synaristosai*, see Zagagi 1981: 312-17. For Terence's introduction of characters and plot-lines from other Menandrian plays into the particular model, see above, Ch. I n. 73; p. 50 with nn. 12, 13. A convenient summary of Terentian changes is given by Lowe 1983: 428-31. On the entire question, see e.g. Gaiser 1972: 1027-113.

76. E.g. Webster 1960: 222; Blanchard 1970: 38-51; *idem* 1983 on which see Lowe 1986: 309-10; Primmer 1984 with Lowe's review, 1985: 396-7. See Holzberg's judicious approach to the matter, 1974: 1-5, 114ff. (with further bibliography).

77. *Op. cit*. 16ff.

78. Brown 1990*b*: 39ff.

79. Holzberg 1974: 121ff.

80. Brown 1990*b*: 46f. 'It is thus clear that there was no regular Menandrian pattern for the endings of the plays, for the construction of the fifth act, or for its relationship to the preceding acts. In these circumstances, who can say what would or what would not have been possible for Menander, particularly on the basis of such a small sample?' (*ibid*.: 48).

III. The Chorus and Related Problems

1. On the comic chorus in the fourth century, see in general Maidment 1935: 1-24; Hunter 1979: 23-38; Silk 1980: 147-51; and most recently Rothwell 1992: 209-25.

2. Gomme-Sandbach 1973: n. *ad* 230.

3. Cf. the chorus of fishermen in Plautus' *Rudens*, 290ff. and that of the *advocati* of Plautus' *Poenulus*, 504ff. Hunter 1979: 37f.; cf. Rothwell 1992: 220. On the possible Plautine origin of these choruses, see now Lowe 1990: 274-97.

4. See Alexis, fr. 112K.-A.; Antiphanes, fr. 91K.-A.

5. In *P. Köln* 243a, a fragment of a comedy that seems to happen in Ephesus, the introduction of the chorus has been conjecturally restored by Lloyd-Jones, *Kölner Papyri*, Vol. VI (= *Papyrologia Colonensia*, Vol. VII, 1987) 58. See also Brown 1980: 6 (on *P. Oxy*. O 19, fr. C = *Mis*. A103f. [Sandbach *OCT* 1990: 354]).

6. The context of the entrance of the chorus at the end of Act I in *Epitrepontes*, *Perikeiromene*, *Samia* and *Fab. Incerta* iv Mette is too fragmentary for any valid evaluation to be made of the dramatic effect obtained by the appearance of the chorus at these points. Nor is the evidence of Plaut. *Bacch*. 106 (see Leo 1911: 292ff.) very helpful in determining the dramatic function of the first appearance of the chorus in Plautus' original, Menander's *Dis Exapaton*.

7. See below, pp. 156ff.

8. Gomme-Sandbach 1973: 301, following Gomme 1936: 64. For other possible reasons for Menander's refraining from having the chorus participate in the plot, see *ibid*. It is important to note how restricted is the participation of the *advocati* and the fishermen in the action of Plautus' *Poenulus* and *Rudens* respectively. Lowe 1990: 275-7 has a convenient summary of the main differences between the choruses of Plautus and Menander. A modest level of interaction between actors and chorus has been postulated for fourth-century comedy other than Menander by Rothwell 1992: 218ff., following Hunter 1979: 33ff.

9. Holzberg 1974: 121, 133ff.

10. See in general Arnott 1975a: 140ff.; *idem* 1975b: 22; *idem* 1979b: XLIIIf.

11. On Menander's complex treatment of 'act' and 'scene', see Handley 1987: 299-312; also Lloyd-Jones 1987b: 313-21.

12. See Handley 1970: 1-42 esp. 11ff.; *idem* 1987: 299ff. with later references. For *Dis Exapaton* (= Plautus' *Bacchides*), see Clark 1976: 92f.

13. See below, pp. 90, 109f.

14. By contrast in *Aspis*, the entrance of the cook and his helper at the end of Act I (216ff.), does not serve in promoting the plot, but only in reminding the audience of the marriage which did not materialize. See Gomme-Sandbach 1973: n. *ad* 216-49.

15. Cf. also the first entrance of Getas and Sikon at the end of Act II, in *Dysk.* 393ff. Elsewhere, however, I have pointed out the difficulties involved in any attempt at interpreting Menandrian act-division: 'To what extent was Menander conscious of the need for act-division as such in his comedy? His noticeable tendency toward introducing new characters as well as new strands of action at the end of the act would seem to suggest that rather than thinking in terms of a drama divided into five, self-consistent parts, Menander had been engaged in the process of creating – by means of choral interludes – mechanical, possibly obligatory interruptions in a dramatic sequence' (Handley-Hurst 1990: 149).

16. See Holzberg 1974: 118.

17. The first part of Nikeratos' concluding speech, 416-17, takes us back to the final scene of Act I, 96ff. See above, pp. 65f.; Holzberg 1974: 38.

18. See Gomme-Sandbach 1973: n. *ad* 550.

19. Demeas' concluding speech at the end of Act IV (614-15) winds up the part of the play in which the major plot complication reaches its resolution, but does not, as might have been expected, link this act with the following act. Cf. Brown 1990b: 47.

20. See below, p. 152.

21. See, in general, Webster 1974: 72f.

22. Cf. the short time-span required by Getas to bring his master Thrasonides from his home nearby to the house of Kleinias in *Mis.* 237-59 with the much longer time required for Parmenon to go to the market in *Samia* – a journey which covers the time-gap between Acts II and III (189ff.). Generally, a journey to the market and back takes place in the framework of two acts, not one.

23. Gomme 1936: 67. But see Gomme-Sandbach 1973: 479; Frost 1988: 91.

24. A similar effect is attained by the gap between Acts I and II in *Dyskolos*: at the end of the first act, Sostratos sets out for his father's country house to bring back his slave Getas (181ff.). In Act II, he comes back on stage without him (259ff.). Nevertheless, there is some progress in the plot in terms of the information given Gorgias by his slave Daos – during the interval between the two acts – as indicated by their conversation at the start of the second act (233ff.).

25. See Sandbach in Gomme-Sandbach 1973: 325-6 following van Leeuwen 1919: note on *Epitr.* 244 by his numbering; also *idem* 1986: 156-8. Against this view see Arnott 1977: 17-18; *idem* 1979a: 358 n. 20; and recently 1987: 19-31; 1988b: 26. Arnott believes *Heautontimoroumenos* to be the only certain example in any comedy associated with Menander of a departure from the set time framework of a single day.

26. Gomme-Sandbach 1973: 326 suggest examples from Plautus' *Captivi*, Terence's *Heautontimoroumenos* and *P. IFAO* 337 published by Boyaval 1970: 5-7.

27. See in general Arnott 1979a: 343-52.

28. See Lowe 1985: 397; *idem* 1990: 275 n. 4 (against Primmer 1984: 16-20, 53-65).

29. Handley 1968: 13f.; *idem* 1970: 17f.; Barsby 1986: n. *ad Bacch.* 105-8. See in general *idem*, Index, s.v. act-divisions.

IV. Technical Variety in the Use of Motifs

1. For tragedy, see Taplin 1978: 123ff., 127ff. For Old Comedy, see e.g. Aristoph. *Clouds*, 1214ff.; *Birds*, 1373ff.; *Plutos*, 823ff.; *Ecclesiazusai*, 877ff. For New Comedy, Hunter 1985: 56.

2. For further discussion of the dramatic implications of this repeated chain of events, see below, p. 148.

3. See below, pp. 119ff., 129ff.

4. 1985: 56.

5. See below, pp. 134ff.; also above, pp. 61f.

6. See below, p. 140.

7. See above, pp. 22f.

8. Arnott 1979b: 286 (n. *ad* 629-33). But see Gomme-Sandbach 1973: n. *ad* 628-9.

9. See Arnott 1979b: 288 n. 1.

10. Several of the Latin adaptations of Menander, e.g. Plautus' *Bacchides* and *Stichus* and Terence's *Adelphoe*, betray the same preoccupation with repetition and parallelism, and this may be taken as evidence for their reflecting the original. For *Stichus*, see Arnott 1972b: 68ff.; *idem* 1979b: XXXIX, n. 1; for *Bacchides*, see Clark 1976: 85-96; for *Adelphoe*, see Damen 1990: 85-106.

11. See in general Ireland 1983: 45ff.

12. On Menander's play on the audience's expectations in this play, see Friedrich 1953: 153ff.; Marti 1959: 34 n. 2.

13. It is interesting to note that Syros' promise to meet Onesimos again the next day (415) is not fulfilled either. The text, however, is too fragmentary for any definitive conclusions to be reached on this issue.

14. The same technique is to be found in Act III of *Samia*: cf. the cook's report in 361-6 of Demeas' behaviour with Demeas' own subsequent appearance.

15. See below, pp. 118f.

16. See below, Ch. VI nn. 5, 9. *epikleros*, 'an heiress', one to whom the *kleros*, the family estate, attaches and so passes to her future husband.

17. Theuerkauf 1960: 77ff. criticizes the relevant passages in *Dyskolos* as definite flaws, having failed to recognize in them instances of premeditated false foreshadowing.

18. See below, pp. 105, 165.

19. Martin 1972: n. *ad* 183-4; cf. Arnott 1964a: 111.

20. See below, pp. 160, 163f.

21. See below, p. 111.

22. For further Menandrian examples, see below, pp. 91ff. The evidence concerning false foreshadowing in Roman comedy is gathered in Langen 1886: 89-232; Marti 1959. See also Harsh 1935: 93ff.; Duckworth 1971: 227.

23. Arnott 1973: 49ff. For Aeschylus, see Garvie 1978: 63-86; for Sophocles, see Friedrich 1953: 150ff.

24. See below, Ch. V n. 124.

25. The use here by Menander of repeated exits and entrances by one character for the purpose of disappointing the expectations of another – who remains constantly on stage – has its counterpart in Act II of *Perikeiromene*. In the latter play, Moschion is looking forward to Glykera appearing, but instead of Glykera, it is Daos who shows up over and over again. In discussing the relevant movements of the actors in *Samia* and *Perikeiromene* Frost 1988: 91ff., 114f. has failed to recognize this analogy.

26. Gomme-Sandbach 1973: n. *ad* 687-91.

27. On this, see Frost 1988: 2-3.

28. Frost 1988: 111-15 has a convenient summary of the exits and entrances of the characters in the above-discussed scenes from *Samia*.

V. Between Comedy and Life

1. Tarn 1952: 273. Tarn's contempt for Hellenistic literature in general and for Menander in particular, still so typical of many admirers of the Classical Period, is echoed in Peter Green's recent study of the Hellenistic age 1990: 65-79. The comedy of Menander is claimed to be a faithful representation of contemporary Athenian society by Körte 1937 and by Rostovzeff 1941: 166. More critical in his approach to the matter is Ferguson 1911: 66ff., esp. 72ff. See also Préaux 1957: 84-100.

2. On this, see Arnott 1959; *idem* 1962: 107-22. The Greeks had no knowledge of realistic scenery, nor did they expect to be presented in their dramas with a straightforward imitation of life. The Dionysiac stage being symbolic and un-changeable, the Athenian audience came to the theatre prepared to use its own imagination in order to bridge over the gap between poetic realities and stage conventions. What it saw and what it was invited to imagine were more often than not two different things. That it should let itself be deluded by a basically anti-illusionistic form of drama, and play an active role in constructing the poet's world of fantasy, was part of the convention. (On the exploitation by Menander of the audience's imagination for the production of his plays, see Webster 1962/3: 235-72; also *idem* 1956: 20-8.) Again, it must be stressed that while the Greeks had no term to correspond to our 'dramatic illusion', the notion itself was by no means alien to their way of thinking. One is reminded of the use of *apate, apatema*, 'deception', *apatan*, 'to deceive', in Gorg. fr. B 23 (II 305) Diels-Kranz, fr. B 11.10 (II 291) Diels-Kranz, and that of *exapatan*, 'to deceive thoroughly', in the sophistic treatise *Dissoi logoi*, fr. 90.3.10 (II 410-11) Diels-Kranz. But it is, above all, the attestation in numerous places of the Greeks' awareness of their own susceptibility to the illusionistic effect of their poetry that proves beyond doubt that dramatic illusion of the highest order formed part of their overall theatrical experience (e.g. Gorg. fr. B 11.9-10 (II 290-1) Diels-Kranz; Plat. *Ion*, 535B-E). Sifakis' objection to the existence in Greek drama of the notion of make-believe and illusion 1971: 7ff. is justly dismissed by Bain 1987: 3ff. On the question of illusion in ancient comedy, see Görler 1973: 41-57.

3. See below, pp. 160ff.

4. On the legendary and romantic elements in the plot of *Dyskolos*, see Theuerkauf 1960: 40f., 64f.; Fantham 1975: 53.

5. On the question of the way *Dyskolos* relates to the reality of Menander's times in general, see Zucker 1965: 7-42, 85-102, 115-46. On the legal backgound to the plot, see Paoli 1961: 53-62; Préaux 1960: 222-39.

6. Chaireas' statement is quoted by Noy 1990: 386 with n. 52, 389 n. 72 as the only evidence in New Comedy that shows how marriages were made in fourth-century Athens.

7. On Sostratos as an impatient and vigorous suitor, see Zagagi 1979: 39ff.

8. Lacey 1968: 158ff.; Dover 1974: 95ff., 209ff.; Pomeroy 1975: 58ff., 79ff.; also Post 1940: 420-59. But see Gomme 1925: 1-25 (= 1937: 89-115); and most recently Just 1989: ch. 6 'Freedom and Seclusion'; Cohen 1989: 3-15; *idem* 1990: 147-65; *idem* 1991a: 133-70; Brown 1993: 201-3. Below, n. 22.

9. See below, n. 57.

10. Meetings between youths and free-born girl citizens were extremely rare in New Comedy: see Burck 1933: 421f. (= 1966: 27).

11. See Handley 1965a: n. *ad* 205f.

12. Lacey 1968: 159. On the importance of honour and shame in Greek society, see Dover 1974: 226ff.; Lloyd-Jones 1987a: 1-28 (= 1990: 253-80).

13. Handley 1965a: nn. *ad* 271-87, 297f.; Gomme-Sandbach 1973: nn. *ad* 279, 297, 298.

14. Treu 1960: n. *ad* 292; Paoli 1952a: 265-9. On the Greeks' attitude to rape see Dover 1974: 147; Fantham 1975: 53-4; Cole 1984: 97-113; Just 1989: 68f. Below, nn. 57, 59. *Dysk*. 289-93 is quoted by Brown 1991: 533-4 in support of Harris' case 1990: 370-7 against uncritical acceptance of Lys. I.30-5 as evidence that the Athenians regarded seduction as a worse crime than rape.

15. Préaux 1960: 223-5. On *engyesis, engye*, see Wolff 1944: 51-3; Harrison 1968: 3-9; Bickerman 1975: 8ff.; Lacey 1968: 105-6; MacDowell 1978: 86.

16. Préaux 1960: 231; Men. *Perik*. 1013-15; *Sam*. 726-9; Bickerman 1975: 12 esp. n. 54. Gorgias' consent to his marriage to Sostratos' sister in Act V may have been given in the lacuna of the text before l. 842. There would then be no need for him to undertake formally to accept the terms of the *engyesis*: see Préaux *ibid*. (following the ed. pr. by V. Martin 1958). I am not convinced by the arguments given by Handley 1965a: n. *ad* 837-40 against the possibility of Kallippides and Gorgias entering into dialogue during that lacuna.

17. For example, Plautus' plays *Aulularia* (apparently an adaptation of a play by Menander) and *Trinummus* (an adaptation of Philemon's play *Thesauros*). In these two comedies, love plays no part in the decision of the intended bridegrooms to waive the dowry. Other Menandrian plays in which a wealthy man weds a poor girl are *Adelphoe* (Terence's adaptation of a play of the same name by Menander) and *Samia*.

18. In fact Sostratos, like Megadorus and Lysiteles in *Aulularia* and *Trinummus* respectively, *insists* upon marrying a *poor* girl. Sostratos' generous gesture in renouncing a dowry is part of the romantic-comic convention of the play, whose plot is based on a sharp distinction between rich and poor. See below, pp. 102, 111f.

19. Harrison 1968: 48-9; MacDowell 1978: 87. On the importance of the dowry in Athenian weddings, see Wolff 1944: 53ff.; *idem* 1957: 133ff.; Harrison 1968: 45-60; Lacey 1968: 109-10.

20. Wolff 1944: 48-51.

21. On these obligations and on the legal status of the *kyrios* with respect to the woman under his patronage, see Harrison 1968: 108-15. On the authority of the father over his children, see Harrison 1968: 70-8; also Pomeroy 1975: 62ff.

22. The uniqueness of Knemon's daughter's social situation lies in the fact that her working in the fields is *not* a matter of economic necessity but of her father's free choice. On the question of Knemon's 'poverty', see below, p. 102. There can be little doubt that citizen women of poor families went out to work: Lacey 1968: 171; Dover 1974: 98: '... below a certain point in the social scale, in families which owned few or no slaves, it simply cannot have been practicable to segregate the women-folk. They would have to go on errands, work in the fields, or sell in the marketplace.' Recent scholarship tends to over-emphasize the economic role played by the women in ancient Athens: e.g. Cohen 1989: 9: 'Common sense (and a great deal of anthropological and social historical evidence) should suffice to suggest that in a society like that of classical Athens there would have been relatively few families which could dispense with the essential economic activities of the women – activities which necessarily involve going out of the house'; Pomeroy 1991: 266: 'Seclusion of free women was a luxury and an indicator of social and economic status.'

23. There is no solid ground for the assumption that the tendency in the play to deal with the disparity between rich and poor was meant to reflect the principles of the social reform of Demetrios of Phaleron. See Luria's excellent discussion in Zucker 1965: 23ff. A recent modern, and altogether unsuccessful, attempt to read *Dyskolos* as an essentially political comedy is provided by Wiles 1984: 170-80.

24. Gomme-Sandbach 1973: n. *ad* 327.

25. Lowe 1987: 131: 'Cnemon is by fourth-century standards a comparatively wealthy landowner, though clearly not in the same bracket as Callippides, whose estate of six talents or more would place him within the wealthier ranges of the speechwriters' clientele ... Cnemon, in fact, is a social, as well as a human, aberration: like Euclio in the *Aulularia*, a self-imposed exile from human society whose wealth is withheld from his family by his own decision. Thus the social barriers in the *Dyskolos* are less divisions of class *per se* than of wealth, demography, and lifestyle, in which the familiar town/country polarities are subjected to a complex system of subversions and mediations.'

26. Handley 1965*a*: n. *ad* 384-9.

27. Handley 1965*a*: n. *ad* 447-54.

28. Lacey 1968: 155f.

29. For instance, Schäfer 1965: 48ff., 80ff., 91ff.

30. Kamerbeek 1959: 126 (quoted below, p. 166); cf. Anderson 1970: 206-7.

31. *emmanos* (688) translated here by 'madly' is supplemented by Fraenkel.

32. Theuerkauf 1960: 53 n. 2 believes that in these lines there is a play with the motif of rape that so frequently arises in New Comedy.

33. It may be argued, however, that since Sostratos is not on his own with Knemon's daughter, his restraint is not at all surprising: he had not the same opportunity as Chaerea in Ter. *Eun.* 549-606!

34. Handley 1965*a*; Gomme-Sandbach 1973: nn. *ad* 714.

35. Lacey 1968: 117f. On the legal backgound to ll. 729ff., see in general Préaux 1960: 225ff.; Paoli 1961: 53ff. (= 1976: 559ff.); Handley 1965*a*: n. *ad* 729-39.

36. There is no solid ground for Préaux's assumption 1960: 225 that Gorgias' adoption by Knemon is used by Menander to highlight the selfishness of the misanthrope. Harrison 1968: 88: 'Even with a boy who was of age one might have expected that the principle of preserving *oikoi* might have dictated a rule allowing the father of an only son to veto that son's adoption, but there is no evidence for such a rule.'

37. Below, n. 47. 'A man who had a daughter could adopt a son, but in this case the adopted son had either to marry the daughter himself or give her in marriage to another man *with half her father's property as dowry* [my emphasis, N.Z.] ...' (MacDowell 1978: 100, following Paoli's interpretation of *Dysk.* 737-9, 763 [1961: 61-2 = 1976: 569-70]). But see Golden 1990: 230 n. 10.

38. Handley 1965*a*: n. *ad* 22; Gomme-Sandbach 1973: n. *ad Epitr.* 570-1; Harrison 1968: 40.

39. Harrison 1968: 40ff.; MacDowell 1978: 88.

40. On the question of Knemon's divorce from his wife, see Brown 1983: 417-18 (against the dogmatic approach of Karnezis 1977: 155ff.).

41. It has been disputed whether the consent of the groom's father was a strict legal requirement or merely a matter of domestic practicability: see Paoli 1952*a*: 265-9; *idem* 1952*b*: 267-75; Martina 1972/3: 871ff. (*ad Sam*. 50-3); Harrison 1968: 18; MacDowell 1978: 86.

42. *Perik*. 1013-15; *Sam*. 726-9; *Mis*. 444-6; fr. 682K.-T.; *Fab. Incert*. (*Fragmentum dubium*) 4-7. Also Ter. *And*. 950-1; Austin, *CGFPR* fr. 250, fr. 266.

43. On the institution of the Athenian *engyesis / engye*, see bibliography in n. 15.

44. Harrison 1968: 18; Martina 1972/3: 934.

45. See e.g. Theuerkauf 1960: 74f. A more thorough study of the question of Gorgias' marriage may be found in Schäfer 1965: 63ff. See also Holzberg 1974: 126ff.

46. On the Athenian institution of marriage, see Wolff 1944: 43ff.; Bickerman 1973: 1ff. Presumably most Athenians did not marry for love. Cf. Just 1989: 80: 'inasmuch as there might have been "love matches" in Athens it could be hazarded that they occurred within the confines of the extended family.' There is, however, an element of exaggeration in Walcot's claim 1987: 8 that Athens was 'a society which denied the validity of love as the basis for a happily married life'. See Jarcho 1983: 357-73 and most recently Brown 1993: 189-205. A balanced picture of husband-wife relationship in the classical period is offered by Lefkowitz 1983: 31-47 (= 1986: 61-79). For Sostratos as a romantic hero, see Rudd 1981: 144-5; Walcot 1987: 6; Brown 1993: 190f., 195f., 199.

47. Handley 1965*a*: n. *ad* 842-4 (following Finley 1951: 79, 266ff.); Schaps 1981: 99 (with special reference to the exaggeratedly large dowries in Menandrian comedy); *idem* 1985-8: 70-2 (with special reference to the dowry proposed by Knemon). See however Gomme-Sandbach 1973: nn. *ad Dysk*. 738; *Epitr*. 134ff.; Webster 1974: 25f.; Casson 1976: 53ff.; Golden 1990: 174-80.

48. Handley 1965*a*: n. *ad* 842-4.

49. Schäfer 1965: 66ff.; Holzberg 1974: 129f.

50. Note the enormous list of items the two wish to 'borrow' from Knemon (914ff.) – most of them luxuries which would have no place in a peasant's home; and their pretence that Knemon's house is full of servants whom they call to answer the door (911ff.). Schäfer 1965: 70.

51. A useful discussion of the relation between *Samia* and contemporary Athenian realities is found in Martina 1972/3: 853-940.

52. On the question of Nikeratos' poverty, see Keuls 1973: 9ff. See below, n. 72.

53. See below, pp.118, 122, 137.

54. On the significance of *Sam*. 35-50 for the study of the festival of *Adonia*, see Weill 1970: 591-3.

55. On the question of Chrysis' child, see Sandbach 1986: 158-60; Dedoussi 1988: 39-42; and most recently West 1991: 11f.

56. Martina 1972/3: 853-72.

57. Ferguson 1911: 78ff.; Martina 1972/3: 867 n. 2, 869 n. 1; Leo 1912: 159; Dover 1974: 209; Brown 1993: 196-8.

58. E.g. Menander's *Epitrepontes* (see esp. 1112ff.); Plautus' *Aulularia* and Terence's *Hecyra*.

59. See above, n. 14; Martina 1972/3: 868ff.; Paoli 1950: 123ff. (= 1976: 251-307); Cohen 1984: 147-65; *idem* 1990: 147-65 (extensively reproduced from his article in *G&R* 1989: 3-15); *idem* 1991*b*: 171-88. Moschion is defined as *moichos*, adulterer/seducer, by Nikeratos in 717.

60. This has been argued by Paoli, referred to at n. 41.

61. Harrison 1968: 70ff.; MacDowell 1978: 91.

62. See above, n. 12.

63. For New Comedy, see e.g. Taubenschlag 1926: 71-4; Préaux 1957: 93f.; Martina 1972/3: 884ff.; Ter. *Heaut.* 626ff. The extent to which infant exposure was practised in ancient Greece has been the subject of much scholarly discussion: see e.g. Glotz 1892: 930-9; Weiss 1921: 463-9; Hook 1920: 134-45; Cameron 1932: 105-14; Tarn 1952: 100-2; Pomeroy 1975: 46, 69-70, 140, 228; *eadem* 1983: 207-22; Engels 1980: 112-20; *idem* 1984: 386-93; Golden 1981: 316-31; *idem* 1990: 86-7, 94, 135, 173, 179; Harris 1982: 114-16; Patterson 1985: 103-23.

64. Martina 1972/3: 861-6; Jacques 1971: xxx; Dover 1974: 226-42.

65. See 145ff., 431ff., 623ff., 729.

66. The role of *Eros* in *Samia* is over-emphasized by Flury 1968: 16f. The centrality of the father-son relationship in the plot of *Samia* has long been recognized: see e.g. Treu 1969: 232; Mette 1969: 439; Jacques 1971: xLvif.; Lloyd-Jones 1972: 144 (= 1990: 52); Keuls 1973: 1ff. (overstressing the theme of adoptive versus natural parenthood); Holzberg 1974: 132; Blume 1974: 8; Grant 1986: 172-84. For further examples of Menander's extensive treatment of this motif, see Fantham 1971: 970-98.

67. For the Athenian law of adoption, see Harrison 1968: 82ff.; MacDowell 1978: 99ff. Keuls' attempt 1973: 13ff. to extend the theme of adoption to Chrysis' relations with Moschion's baby has no real basis in the play and is, moreover, incompatible with the Athenian law under consideration.

68. For the Athenian institution of *pallake*, see Harrison 1968: 13ff.; MacDowell 1978: 89f.; Wolff 1944: 65ff.

69. See below, p. 124.

70. See above, pp. 101f., 111f.; also n. 60.

71. Martina 1972/3: 876ff.

72. Any attempt to speculate about Demeas' reasons for supporting a nuptial link between his son and his poor neighbour's daughter is unfruitful in view of the fragmentary state of our text. But see Jacques 1971: xLf.; cf. Lloyd-Jones 1972: 130 (= 1990: 41f.): '... for all we know Demeas may have decided on a family alliance with his old friend simply because he admires his character and approves of his way of educating his daughter'; Gomme-Sandbach 1973: n. *ad* 114; Keuls 1973: 9ff. See also below, pp. 122, 137.

73. See above, pp. 96, 101, 103.

74. See above, pp. 111f.

75. A child is held to be *gnesios*, legitimate, only if its parents are Athenian citizens and were married by means of the *engyesis*/*engye* or *epidikasia*, the legal procedure for attaining the hand of an heiress (*epikleros*). Otherwise, the child would be regarded as a *nothos*, bastard, apparently lacking all claim to inheritance from his father, and most certainly without any such inheritance rights if there are also legitimate sons. He would not belong to the circle of citizens, and accordingly would be deprived of all political rights. On the law concerning *nothoi*, see Harrison 1968: 61ff.; MacDowell 1978: 99; Martina 1972/3: 876ff.

76. Sandbach 1986: 160: 'I find it significant that after Demeas has made it clear that he is warmly in favour of the marriage Moschion says not a word about the baby or of any desire to resume it.' Brown 1990a: 266 (end of n. 73): 'We may observe how cleverly Menander has constructed Act II to make this seem plausible; after Moschion has kept up an elaborate pretence about the baby in the first part of the Act, he cannot very easily reveal the truth the moment he discovers that pretence is no longer needed.' Dedoussi 1988: 42 emphasizes the dramatic necessity for

Moschion's silence about the baby. West 1991: 15 suggests that 'the timetable goes wrong, and that Demeas was not meant to encounter the baby until Moschion (whose meeting with his father appears to take him by surprise [127ff.]) had explained the situation'.

77. Gomme-Sandbach 1973: n. *ad* 141-2: ' "The good man is legitimate, the bad illegitimate as well as bad"; this is a *sententia* on legitimacy more striking than any that can be quoted as parallels.' Golden 1990: 173 and subsequent note.

78. Cf. Soph. fr. 87 Radt; Eur. frr. 141, 168, 377N^2; *El.* 551; *Hipp.* 309; *Andr.* 638; *Alexandros* 40 Snell. For Menander, see also frr. 612K.-T.; 213K.-T.

79. See above, pp. 111f.; also p. 90.

80. See above, n. 75.

81. See above, n. 75. Turner's *alloi* at the beginning of line 135 is problematic: see Kassel 1973: 8-9; Bain 1983*b*: n. *ad loc.* I accept Austin's conjecture of *all' e* (*CGFPR*, p. 185, *app. crit.* n. *ad loc.*) and translate with Bain: 'Do you *really* expect me to bring up a bastard son?' (instead of 'Do you expect me to bring up a bastard son for *someone else*?').

82. For these implications, see in detail nn. 14, 59; above, p. 119. West 1991: 14: 'The real grounds for anxiety surely lie in the reaction to be expected from Niceratus on discovering that in his absence his daughter had borne a child fathered by their rich young neighbour ... Moschion might well fear that Niceratus, who appears to be characterized as poor but proud, would choose to prosecute him for rape rather than commit his daughter's happiness to a young playboy.'

83. However, if Moschion declared himself in a missing part of his opening speech to be in love with Plangon (above, p. 116), perhaps the spectators would not give much thought to this fear of legal sanctions.

84. Cf. *Asp.* 291-3.

85. For the manner in which these formalities are reflected in the play, see Martina 1972/3: 910ff.

86. Bickerman 1975: 1ff.

87. In his essay on Menander, written before the partial discovery of Acts I and II of *Samia*, Gomme 1937: 270 makes an interesting distinction between this play and Terence's adaptation of Menander's *Andria* in connection with the point under consideration: 'The length of a day in a Greek play could be as elastic as that of the street which is the scene of it; and Demeas and Nikeratos in *Samia* had similarly made all arrangements for a wedding within the day. But there the decision is, probably, part of the preliminary story and we are therefore the more ready to accept it, and besides that all the principals are longing for it and the hurry is an essential part of the comedy. But in the *Andria*, the decision is part of the play, opposition to the marriage by one of the principals is the whole story, and, as well, *attention is drawn to the improbability* [my emphasis. N.Z.]: Pamphilus is given to the wedding day itself to hold out against it (155ff.) ... .'

88. See Martina 1972/3: 910ff.

89. It is a remarkable feature of New Comedy as opposed to Old Comedy that the play's action is always conceived in close relation to Athenian law and custom: Préaux 1960: 222ff.; Davies 1977/8: 113-14. Also Treu 1977: 24-5; *idem* 1981: 211-14.

90. See above, pp. 106ff.

91. See above, pp. 107ff.

92. Katsouris 1975: 131ff., 178; West 1991: 17ff. Above, p. 56.

93. See above, p. 108.

94. See below, n. 119.

95. See above, n. 71.

96. Groton 1987: 437-43 has a useful discussion of the role of the insanity/anger theme in this play.

97. It should be noted that this ambivalent presentation of the manner in which Demeas performs as head of *oikos* – a direct result of Menander's overall realistic approach to the drama – plays an important part in establishing the ironic aspect of Demeas' situation and, of course, goes far beyond the mere application of everyday norms to the play.

98. On the question of misogyny in the ancient Greek world, see Pomeroy 1975: 2ff., 48-52, 97, 103ff., 117; Lefkowitz 1986: 112ff.

99. The translation is based on Gomme-Sandbach 1973: nn. *ad* 339, 340-2. On the Greek social attitudes reflected in this passage, see Leo 1912: 159; Jacques 1971: xxx n. 1; 23 n. 1; Dover 1974: 103, 147.

100. Cf. Moschion's argumentation at the beginning of Act II. Above, pp. 119ff.

101. Lloyd-Jones 1972: 131, n. 18 (= 1990: 41 n. 18): 'According to Athenian notions a wife was for the procreation of legitimate children, a concubine for pleasure; that is why Demeas says that he has a mistress who has turned out to be a wife.' [Dem.] LIX 122.

102. See 35-6, 265, 353-4. In 405/4 BC, it was decided to allow the status of Athenian citizens to be granted to natives of Samos. There is no hint in the play, however, of any attempt by Menander to take advantage of this fact, and it should not be assumed that women of a professional past such as Chrysis would have had any grounds for expecting to be granted this status in Athens. Samos was famous for its prostitutes: Bain 1983*b*: n. *ad* 21.

103. *Perik.* 486ff.; cf. *Mis.* A40, 262f., 297ff., 305ff.

104. 381-3. Gomme-Sandbach 1973: n. *ad loc.*; Martina 1972/3: 894ff.; Paoli 1952*a*: 273ff.; Schaps 1979: 10ff. esp. 12; cf. Plaut. *Mil.* 1099-100, 1147-8, 1204-5. For recent discussion of the Menandrian passage, see Thomas 1990: 215-18. Thomas' attempt to argue against l. 381 having juridical connotations applicable to Chrysis' right to take back her own possessions on separation from Demeas is not convincing. Moreover, it fails to take sufficient account of the Athenian norms concerning a *pallake* or a *hetaira*.

105. Gomme-Sandbach 1973: n. *ad loc.*

106. I follow Austin 1969 in accepting the reading of C *hai kata se* which seems to me to be preferable in meaning to B's text *ou kata se* followed by Gomme-Sandbach 1973. See Austin 1970: n. *ad* 392; Gomme-Sandbach 1973: n. *ad* 392-3.

107. Note Demeas' address to the audience in 447 and 461. Cf. n. 109.

108. Note also Demeas' earlier remark: 'It's none of your business, it's mine and mine alone' (454-5 Miller).

109. Gomme-Sandbach 1973: n. *ad* 461.

110. As the course of events in this act unfolds, Nikeratos at no time gives any serious consideration to this request.

111. Taking Moschion's words to refer directly to Demeas' preceding prohibition 'Don't talk to me' (466), Bain 1983*b* (cf. Miller 1987) translates: 'I must, father.' But Demeas' subsequent reaction (467-8, translated below) clearly shows that the obligation in question is Demeas', not Moschion's. See subsequent note.

112. Bain's translation (cf. Miller 1987): '*You* must?' etc. seems to me to ignore the general sense of Demeas' line of argumentation.

113. 489ff.; cf. 705ff.

114. A continuation of a theme familiar to us from the prologue, 23ff.

115. Dover 1974: 180ff.; also Lloyd-Jones 1987*a*: 19 (= 1990: 271). Archil. fr. 23.14-15 West; Solon, fr. 13. 5-6 West.

116. See below, n. 119.

117. See above, p. 126.

118. For Nikeratos' hyperbolic mythological comparisons (495ff.), see Zagagi 1980: 30ff., 42 n. 90, 53.

119. For the Athenian father's right to *apokeryxis* – a formal repudiation of his son – see Harrison 1968: 75f.; MacDowell 1978: 91.

120. Chrysis is a free woman (577) and Demeas would not have the authority to sell her into slavery even if he wished to do so.

121. For *eischyne lektron*, here translated as 'sullied my couch', cf. Eur. *Hipp.* 944 (Theseus, referring to Hippolytos' presumed sexual offence against his wife Phaidra); for *hybrise*, here translated as 'wronged', see Lys. I.2.4: Eur. *Hipp.* 1073; Dover 1974: 54; Martina 1972/3: 903f.

122. Nikeratos' indignant reaction is couched in terms partly derived from tragedy: Gomme-Sandbach 1973: n. *ad* 507. 'One cannot say that it was impossible for an Athenian to resort to the language of tragedy if he had strong feelings to express. There may be some element of exaggeration here, but Menander may nevertheless still be "representing life" '(*ibid.*). For the significance of the Greek expression 'to be a man' (512), see Dover 1974: 102.

123. Cf. Nikeratos' own words, 493; Dover 1974: 253.

124. There is no real support for Gomme-Sandbach's claim 1973: n. *ad* 561 that 'It is Chrysis whom Nikeratos threatens to kill, not his own wife.' Sandbach's view only makes sense in the limited context of Nikeratos' statements in lines 558-61. But as soon as we hear Demeas' reaction to Nikeratos' threat of murder, it becomes evidently clear that the potential victim is none other than Nikeratos' own wife, referred to as *he gyne* by husband and neighbour alike (558, 561; cf. 200, 580). Note the emphatic position of *ten gynaika* at the beginning of Nikeratos' speech, matched by *tes gynaikos*, the opening words of Demeas' subsequent question. Indeed, Nikeratos' accusation at line 562: 'she's conscious of all that is going on', in itself a fair representation of his wife's passive participation in the plot as he conceives it, would be a serious anti-climax if used to qualify the major role attributed by him to Chrysis.

125. See above, pp. 107ff., esp. pp. 109ff.

126. Cf. 551-2.

127. See below, pp. 137f.

128. 1. See MacDowell 1978: 123-4 (on battery and deliberate wounding); also 130; Gomme-Sandbach 1973: n. *ad* 577: 'The law against *hybris*, roughly speaking assault, gave equal protection to men and women, to free and slave (Dem. XXI.47). But the penalty against a man convicted was for the court to settle, and it may be guessed that a woman might arouse more pity than a man and a free woman than a slave-woman.' 2. *Idem* 1973: n. *ad* 572-6: 'Nikeratos uses the formula *typteseis me;* which is effectively a warning against committing an assault, cf. *Dysk.* 168n. ... Since an assault might be resisted, but yet be the subject of a legal action, it was important to establish that the accused "began it".' 3. For *taut' ego martyromai* – a 'standard formula to call bystanders to witness wrongful treatment, above all an assault' (Gomme-Sandbach 1973: n. *ad* 572-6), see *ibid.*; Lacey 1968: 155f. (155: '... private citizens had to obtain witnesses when involved in situations which were likely to lead to action in the courts'). 4. For Nikeratos' attempt to summon witnesses by crying *io 'nthropoi,* 'Ho! people!', in line 580, see Bain 1981: 169-71; *idem* 1982: 42; also Davies 1982: 74. See in general Schulze 1918: 418-51 (= *Kl. Schr.* 160-89). On the entire passage, see Bain 1983*b*: nn. *ad* 575ff., 580.

129. See above, pp. 98f.

130. On this question, see the recent discussion by Brown 1990*b*: 43f.

131. For the technique of repetition employed here by Menander, see above, p.

92. Contrast Demeas' reaction with that of Nikeratos in 715ff.; below, p. 140; also above, p. 85.

132. See above, pp. 58f.

133. See above, pp. 35ff.

134. There is, however, an element of role-inversion in the father-son relationship as depicted by Menander in this scene. See esp. Moschion's comment in 724-5: 'If you'd done this at once, father, you wouldn't / have had the trouble of all that moralizing just now' (Bain). Grant 1986 extends the theme of reversal to the Moschion-Demeas relationship throughout the play – a line of interpretation with which I find it hard to agree.

135. Following Austin's supplement *<g'>i[sth' hoti* 1969: *app. crit.* n. *ad* 703.

136. See above, p. 137.

137. See above, pp. 109ff., 111f.

138. The engagement formula, which mentions the requirement to bear legitimate offspring, would certainly have raised a laugh among the audience when applied to a bride and a bridegroom who are already parents.

139. See Bain 1983*a*: 36.

140. Harrison 1968: 19; Martina 1972/3: 940; Gomme-Sandbach 1973: n. *ad* 727; cf. Plaut. *Truc.* 840-5.

VI. Divine Interventions and Human Agents

1. On the question of the relation between the divine prologue-speaker and the human plot in Menander, see esp. Ludwig 1970: 45-96; Holzberg 1974: 105ff. For *Dyskolos*, see below, n. 27.

2. The analogy between Aphrodite's and Dionysos' role in Euripides' *Hippolytos* and *Bacchai* respectively and that of Pan in Menander's *Dyskolos* has been over-emphasized by Photiades 1958: 108ff. See below, n. 51. For *Ion*, see Ludwig 1970: 78; below, pp. 166f. with n. 50. That Philemon consciously gave an Euripidean form (of the type found in *Hippolytos*) to his divine prologist, the goddess Tryphe, Extravagance, in his play *Thesauros*, the original of Plautus' *Trinummus*, is postulated by Hunter 1980: 225f.

3. For the religious and intellectual background of Menander's audience, see Tarn 1952: 325ff.; Murray 1935: 123ff.; Stewart 1977: 503ff.; Lloyd-Jones 1984: 65f. (= 1990: 243f.).

4. A useful discussion of Tyche's role in *Aspis* is to be found in Konet 1976: 90-2. See most recently Vogt-Spira 1992: 75ff.

5. On which see Schaps 1981: 25ff. See above, Ch. IV n. 16.

6. Literally: 'being ahead in years'. Gomme-Sandbach 1973: n. *ad* 142.

7. See Tarn 1952: 340; Murray 1935: 131-4; Wilamowitz-Moellendorff 1932: 298ff; Nilsson 1961: 200ff.; *idem* 1948: 86f.; Roscher, s.v. Tyche 1319ff; Lloyd-Jones 1983: 162, 229 n. 6. For the role of Tyche in New Comedy, see Hunter 1985: 141ff.; Vogt-Spira 1992: 1ff., 51ff.

8. Quoted by Polybius, XXIX 21 with reference to the defeat of Perseus, king of Macedon, by the Romans at Pydna in 168 BC. Trans. Murray 1935: 133 n. 2. For similar references to Tyche in Menander, see e.g. frr. 295K.-T., 348K.-T., 417K.-T., 463K.-T., 464K.-T., 468K.-T., 630K.-T., 632K.-T., 637K.-T., 788K.-.T. See in detail Vogt-Spira 1992: esp. 19ff., 37ff.

9. The plot of *Aspis* as a whole has been taken to express Menander's hostility to the institution of the epiklerate: MacDowell 1982: 51; cf. Karabelias 1970: 384ff.; Turner 1979*b*: 120 (= 1984: 254): '... it is hard to imagine that the institution of the epiclerate emerged in good standing from this derisory treatment.' But see Brown

1983: 412ff.; Fox 1985: 229f. Daos' ethnic observation is a commonplace in Greek thought: Gomme-Sandbach 1973: n. *ad* 206; Goldberg 1980: 35.

10. For the contrast between Love and Law, expressed in Chaireas' speech, see MacDowell 1982: 42ff.

11. See also Chaireas' statement in 370-3, which is reminiscent of Tyche's depiction (143-6) of Smikrines' future fate quoted above. On the notion of 'good Tyche' in Menander, see Vogt-Spira 1992: 42ff.

12. See the tragic quotations in 411, 416-18 (quoted above, p. 53), and Daos' own comments on the situation 400-3, 408-9.

13. Lloyd-Jones 1971: 189 (= 1990: 19); Webster 1974: 126f.

14. Gomme-Sandbach 1973: n. *ad* 150; 502.

15. Webster 1960: 5; *idem* 1974: 169; Gomme-Sandbach 1973: 467f.

16. See preceding note.

17. K.-T. 1955: xxixf.

18. Jensen 1929: xxxif.; Gomme-Sandbach 1973: 469. For further reconstructions, see bibliography in Gomme-Sandbach 1973: *ibid*.

19. See most recently Arnott 1988a: 11-15 with reference to the *Perikeiromene* picture published by V.M. Strocka, *Die Wandmalerei der Hanghauser in Ephesos* (*Forschungen in Ephesos* VII/1, Vienna, 1977) 48, 55f. and plate 66.

20. This is implied by Agnoia's reference to the repugnant response of the audience (quoted below) as well as by the participial title of the play – *Perikeiromene* – 'She who has her hair cut': Webster 1960: 5f.; Gomme-Sandbach 1973: 468. Such participial titles may allude to a particularly effective dramatic scene – in our case most probably part of the exposition – as in Menander's *Epitrepontes* (Act II) and *Synaristosai* (Plautus' *Cistellaria*, Act I, sc. 1); Diphilos' *Kleroumenoi* (Plautus' *Casina*, Act II, sc. 6) and *Synapothneskontes* (Terence's *Adelphoe*, Act II, sc. 1; see prol. 6-11). See, however, Gomme-Sandbach 1973: *ibid*.; Arnott 1988a: 13f.

21. See above, Ch. III n. 23. Since Sosias is still ignorant of these facts when he reappears in 354ff., he must have left Polemon's house *before* he could learn about them.

22. Note Menander's conscious use of the technique of repetition at the beginning of Sosias' monologue (354ff.): '*Another* expedition! I've got to bring back his travelling cloak and his sword so that I can spy on her and report back' (Hunter).

23. Gomme-Sandbach 1973: 500-1; Webster 1960: 10; *idem* 1974: 170.

24. Quoted above, pp. 34f.

25. On Menander's artistic criteria in shaping this *anagnorisis* scene, and its polyphonic nature, see above pp. 26, 51f.

26. Moschion's monologue 526ff. is broken by a long gap – about 160 verses – which covers the end of Act III and the beginning of Act IV. When he reappears after the gap, it turns out that he has already got wind of his kinship with Glykera. We shall possibly never know how this happened. Was it Myrrhine, who disclosed the secret to her adoptive(?) son in an attempt to prevent his entanglement in an incestuous love affair with his own sister (Gomme in Gomme-Sandbach 1973: 511-13)? Or was it perhaps Daos, who learned the truth by eavesdropping upon a conversation between Myrrhine and Glykera, referred to in 791-3 (Webster 1960: 13; *idem* 1974: 170)?

27. Opinions on Pan's role as speaker of the prologue in *Dyskolos* have oscillated between two extremes: Photiades' religious-moralistic approach 1958: 108-22 and Kraus' negation of Pan's own statements in 36ff., 1960: 18; *idem* 1968: 338. See e.g. Hooker 1958: 107; Turner 1959/60: 254f.; Cantarella 1959: 91ff.; Theuerkauf 1960: 18, 68-70; Treu 1960: 105f.; Pastorino 1960: 79ff.; Martin 1972: 193-6; Jacques

1976: xx, xxvIIf., 44 n. 1. A balanced view is taken by Handley 1965a: n. *ad* 37ff.; Schäfer 1965: 31ff., 68ff.; Gomme-Sandbach 1973: 134; Ludwig 1970: 84ff.; Holzberg 1974: 105-7. See most recently Hunter 1987: 296ff. (with reference to Mercury/Hermes' role in Plautus' *Amphitruo*). Also below, p. 167 with n. 51.

28. See above, Ch. v n. 7.

29. We have no parallel in New Comedy for such an over-activity on the lover's part: a lover, impatient and worried at the beginning of the play would normally summon *either* a friend *or* a slave. (The opening scene of the Plautine *Curculio*, referred to by Schäfer 1965: 45, is irrelevant to the situation in *Dyskolos*, since Palinurus' role is nowhere defined in terms of active participation in Phaedromus' love affair.) Theuerkauf 1960: 51f.

30. See above, p. 96.

31. Quoted above, pp. 22f. On the social implications of this encounter and Menander's originality in shaping it, see above, pp. 22, 69, 73f., 97.

32. See above, p. 98.

33. An unfulfilled motif: see above, p. 89; below, pp. 163f.

34. On the improvisatory nature of this intrigue see above, pp. 27f. On Menander's realism in presenting the confrontation between Gorgias and Daos and between Gorgias and Sostratos, see above, pp. 98ff.

35. An unfulfilled motif: see above, p. 90; below, pp. 163f.

36. On these confrontations between Knemon and his human environment, see above, pp. 103f. On the technique of repetition employed here by Menander, see above, p. 85.

37. See above, pp. 109f.

38. See n. 27 *passim*. The modern views to be discussed below show the influence of Leo's treatment of New Comedy prologues as a purely expository device: 1912: 188ff.

39. 1970: 79 (my translation).

40. Sikon the cook erroneously attributes to Pan the desire for revenge against Knemon, to whom he is really completely indifferent: 639-45. See below, n. 42; also ll. 875-8.

41. See e.g. Men. *Asp.* 97ff. (admittedly Tyche predicts a few more facts concerning Smikrines' reaction to events and subsequent frustration, 138ff.); *Perik.* 121ff., 162ff; *Sik.* 2ff.; Plaut. *Aul.* 6ff., 25ff.; *Cist.* 154ff. (Ludwig 1970: 68f. postulates the substitution by Plautus of Auxilium's military statement at 197ff. for the traditional promise of a happy ending; cf. Leo 1912: 213); Eur. *Ion*, 67ff. For the Menandrian prologues, see in general del Corno 1970: 99-108; Dworacki 1973: 33-47; Holzberg 1974: 16ff. The exploitation by New Comedy playwrights of overdetailed divine prologues is criticized in P. Argent. 53 (= Austin, *CGFPR*, fr. 252); above, p. 45.

42. See 10-13: Knemon's indifference to Pan is light-heartedly acknowledged by the latter. Contrast Aphrodite's and Dionysos' persistent rage at human neglect of them in Euripides' *Hippolytos* and *Bacchai* respectively.

43. Schäfer 1965: 83ff.

44. 1965: 75ff.; cf. Zagagi 1979: 39ff.; above, pp. 46ff.

45. Schäfer 1965: pp. 85ff.

46. An unfulfilled motif: above, p. 89; also p. 64.

47. A similar technique is employed by Menander in 311-13.

48. 1959: 126 (my translation).

49. See above, p. 110.

50. Ludwig 1961: 44-71 esp. 53ff., 247ff.; *idem* 1970: 66ff., 71ff. In discussing divine intervention in *Dyskolos*, Ludwig 1970: 84ff. failed to recognize the pattern under consideration. The analogy between Euripides' *Ion* and Menander's *Dyskolos* is further discussed by Brown 1992: 20. On the question of the relation between *Dyskolos* and *Aulularia*, see e.g. Theuerkauf 1960: 46ff.; Schäfer 1965: 96ff.; Hunter 1981: 41ff.; and most recently Arnott 1988c: 182f.; *idem* 1989: 27ff.

51. The *Dyskolos* criticism in particular has been marked by the religious-moralistic approach: see e.g. Photiades 1958: 108-22; Hooker 1958: 105-7; Martin 1972: 193-6; Post 1960: 152-61; Stoessl 1960: 204-9; Vicenzi 1962: 421ff.; Keuls 1969: 209-20. Cf. Pastorino's criticism of Photiades' approach, 1960: 79-82, 94ff.; and Ludwig's 1970: 88ff.; also Hunter 1987: 296ff.

52. Fortenbaugh 1974: 430-43 has some interesting comments on the compatibility of the role of Agnoia with Polemon's own agency and moral responsibility.

53. Menander's realistic treatment of divine workings fits well with the Greeks' complex view of the matter, for which see Lloyd-Jones 1983: 162.

54. As well as from that of Diphilos as reflected in the Plautine *Rudens*. Note the artificial manner in which the aim of the divine prologue-speaker, the star Arcturus, is achieved in this play (67-9): 'Then it was that I, beholding the maiden borne away, / came to her rescue, and also came with ruin to the pimp. / I raised a blustering gale and waked the waters of the deep' (Nixon).

Bibliography

Anderson, M., 1970: 'Knemon's *Hamartia*', *G&R* 17: 199-217.
Andrewes, M., 1924: 'Euripides and Menander', *CQ* 18: 1-10.
Arnott, P.D., 1959: *An Introduction to the Greek Theatre* (London; repr. 1963).
—— 1962: *Greek Scenic Conventions in the Fifth Century B.C.* (Oxford).
Arnott, W.G., 1964a: 'The Confrontation of Sostratos and Gorgias', *Phoenix* 18: 110-23.
—— 1964b: 'A Note on the Parallels Between Menander's *Dyskolos* and Plautus' *Aulularia*', *Phoenix* 18: 232-7.
—— 1968: 'Menander, qui vitae ostendit vitam ...', *G&R* 15: 1-17.
—— 1972a: 'From Aristophanes to Menander', *G&R* 19: 65-80.
—— 1972b: 'Targets, Techniques, and Tradition in Plautus' Stichus', *BICS* 19: 54-79.
—— 1973: 'Euripides and the Unexpected', *G&R* 20: 49-64.
—— 1975a: 'The Modernity of Menander', *G&R* 22: 140-55.
—— 1975b: *Menander, Plautus, Terence, G&R, New Surveys in the Classics*, no. 9 (Oxford).
—— 1977: 'Four Notes on Menander's Epitrepontes', *ZPE* 24: 16-20.
—— 1979a: 'Time, Plot and Character in Menander', *Papers of the Liverpool Latin Seminar II, ARCA, Classical and Medieval Texts, Papers and Monographs* 3: 343-60.
—— 1979b: (ed.) *Menander* vol. I (Loeb Classical Library, Cambridge, Massachusetts & London).
—— 1987: 'The Time-Scale of Menander's Epitrepontes', *ZPE* 70: 19-31.
—— 1988a: 'New Evidence for the Opening of Menander's Perikeiromene?', *ZPE* 71: 11-15.
—— 1988b: 'An Addendum to "The Time-Scale of Menander's Epitrepontes"', *ZPE* 72: 26.
—— 1988c: 'The Greek Original of Plautus' Aulularia', *WS* 101: 181-91.
—— 1989: 'A Study in Relationships: Alexis' *Lebes*, Menander's *Dyskolos*, Plautus' *Aulularia*', *QUCC* 33: 27-38.
Austin, C., 1969: (ed.) *Menandri Aspis et Samia* I, Textus (cum apparatu critico) et indices (*Kleine Texte für Vorlesungen und Übungen* 188a; Berlin).
—— 1970: *Menandri Aspis et Samia* II, Subsidia interpretationis (*Kleine Texte für Vorlesungen und Übungen* 188b; Berlin).
—— 1973: (ed.) *Comicorum Graecorum Fragmenta in Papyris Reperta* (Berlin & New York).
Bain, D.M., 1981: 'Menander, Samia 580 and "Not- und Hilfsrufe" in Ptolemaic Egypt', *ZPE* 44: 169-71.
—— 1982: 'Another Menandrean Summoning of Witnesses', *ZPE* 49: 42.
—— 1983a: 'Nikeratos' "will" (Menander, Samia 727-8)', *ZPE* 51: 36.
—— 1983b: (ed.) *Menander: Samia* (edited with translation and notes; Aris & Phillips).

—— 1987: *Actors and Audience: A Study of Asides and Related Conventions in Greek Drama* (2nd edn, Oxford).

Barigazzi, A., 1985: 'Menandro: L'inizio del Misumenos', *Prometheus* 11: 97-125.

Barsby, J.A., 1986: (ed.) *Plautus: Bacchides* (edited with translation and commentary; Aris & Phillips).

Bickerman, E.J., 1975: 'La conception du mariage à Athènes', *BIDR* 78: 1-28.

Blanchard, A., 1970: 'Recherches sur la composition des comédies de Ménandre', *REG* 83: 38-51.

—— 1983: *Essai sur la composition des comédies de Ménandre* (Paris).

Blume, H.-D., 1974: *Menanders 'Samia': Eine Interpretation* (*Impulse der Forschung* 15; Darmstadt).

Blundell, J., 1980: *Menander and the Monologue* (*Hypomnemata* 59; Göttingen).

Borgogno, A., 1988: 'Sul nuovissimo *Misumenos* di Menandro', *QUCC* 30: 87-97.

Bornmann, F., 1980: 'Il prologo del *Misoumenos* di Menandro', *A&R* 25: 149-62.

Boyaval, B., 1970: 'Quelques papyrus grecs', *ZPE* 6: 1-33.

Brothers, A.J., 1988: (ed.) *Terence: The Self-Tormentor* (edited with translation and commentary; Aris & Phillips).

Brown, McC. P.G., 1980: Rev. of Turner 1979*a* in *CR* 30: 3-6.

—— 1983: 'Menander's Dramatic Technique and the Law of Athens', *CQ* 33: 412-20.

—— 1987: 'Masks, Names and Characters in New Comedy', *Hermes* 115: 181-202.

—— 1990*a*: 'Plots and Prostitutes in Greek New Comedy', *Papers of the Leeds International Latin Seminar* 6: 241-66.

—— 1990*b*: 'The Bodmer Codex of Menander and the Endings of Terence's *Eunuchus* and Other Roman Comedies' in Handley-Hurst 1990: 37-61.

—— 1991: 'Athenian Attitudes to Rape and Seduction: the Evidence of Menander, *Dyskolos* 289-93', *CQ* 41: 533-4.

—— 1992: 'The Construction of Menander's Dyskolos, Acts I-IV', *ZPE* 94: 8-20.

—— 1993: 'Love and Marriage in Greek New Comedy', *CQ* 43: 189-205.

Burck, E., 1933: 'Die Kunst Menanders und ihre Bedeutung für die Entwicklung der Komödie', *NJW* 9: 417-31 = 1966: 23-35.

—— 1966: *Vom Menschenbild in der römischen Literatur*, in *Ausgewählte Schriften*, ed. E. Lefèvre (Heidelberg).

Burnett, A.P., 1971: *Catastrophe Survived: Euripides' Plays of Mixed Reversal* (Oxford).

Cairns, F., 1972: *Generic Composition in Greek and Roman Poetry* (Edinburgh).

Cameron, A., 1932: 'The Exposure of Children and Greek Ethics', *CR* 46: 105-14.

Cantarella, R., 1959: 'Il nuovo Menandro', *RIL* 93: 77-114.

Casson, L., 1976: 'The Athenian Upper Class and New Comedy', *TAPhA* 106: 29-59.

Clark, J.R., 1976: 'Structure and Symmetry in the *Bacchides* of Plautus', *TAPhA* 106: 85-96.

Cohen, D., 1984: 'The Athenian Law of Adultery', *RIDA* 31: 147-65.

—— 1989: 'Seclusion, Separation, and the Status of Women in Classical Athens', *G&R* 36: 3-15.

—— 1990: 'The Social Context of Adultery at Athens' in P. Cartledge, P. Millet & S. Todd (eds), *Nomos: Essays in Athenian Law, Politics and Society*, 147-65 (Cambridge).

—— 1991*a*: *Law, Sexuality and Society: The Enforcement of Morals in Classical Athens* (Cambridge).

—— 1991*b*: 'Sexuality, Violence, and the Athenian Law of *Hubris*', *G&R* 38: 171-88.

Cole, S.G., 1984: 'Greek Sanctions Against Sexual Assault', *CPh* 79: 97-113.

Copley, F.O., 1956: *Exclusus Amator: A Study in Latin Love Elegy* (Baltimore).

Corno, D. del, 1970: 'Prologhi Menandrei', *Acme* 23: 99-108.

Damen, M.L., 1990: 'Structure and Symmetry in Terence's Adelphoe', *ICS* 15: 85-106.

Davies, J.K., 1977/8: 'Athenian Citizenship: the Descent Group and the Alternatives', *CJ* 73: 105-21.

Davies, M., 1982: 'Aristophanes Clouds 1321ff. as a "Notruf"', *ZPE* 48: 74.

Dedoussi, C., 1988: 'The Future of Plangon's Child in Menander's Samia', *LCM* 13: 39-42.

Dover, K.J., 1974: *Greek Popular Morality in the Time of Plato and Aristotle* (Oxford).

Duckworth, G.E., 1971: *The Nature of Roman Comedy: A Study in Popular Entertainment* (5th edn, Princeton; repr. London 1994).

Dworacki, S., 1973: 'The Prologues in the Comedies of Menander', *Eos* 61: 33-47.

Engels, D., 1980: 'The Problem of Female Infanticide in the Greco-Roman World', *CPh* 75: 112-20.

—— 1984: 'The Use of Historical Demography in Ancient History', *CQ* 34: 386-93.

Fantham, E., 1971: '*Hautontimorumenos* and *Adelphoe*: a Study of Fatherhood in Terence and Menander', *Latomus* 30: 970-98.

—— 1975: 'Sex, Status, and Survival in Hellenistic Athens: a Study of Women in New Comedy', *Phoenix* 29: 44-74.

Ferguson, W.S., 1911: *Hellenistic Athens: An Historical Essay* (London).

Finley, M.I., 1951: *Studies in Land and Credit in Ancient Athens* (New Brunswick).

Fitton, J.W., 1977: 'Menander and Euripides, Theme and Treatment', *Pegasus* 20: 9-15.

Flury, P., 1968: *Liebe und Liebessprache bei Menander, Plautus und Terenz* (Heidelberg).

Fortenbaugh, W.W., 1974: 'Menander's *Perikeiromene*: Misfortune, Vehemence, and Polemon', *Phoenix* 28: 430-43.

Fox, R.L., 1985: 'Aspects of Inheritance in the Greek World' in P. Cartledge & F.D. Harvey (eds), *Crux: Essays Presented to G.E.M. de Ste Croix on His 75th Birthday*, 208-32 (Exeter).

Fraenkel, Ed., 1912: *De media et nova comoedia quaestiones selectae* (Diss. Göttingen).

—— 1922: *Plautinisches im Plautus* (Berlin).

Friedrich, W.H., 1953: *Euripides und Diphilos* (Zetemata 5; München).

Frost, K.B., 1988: *Exits and Entrances in Menander* (Oxford).

Gaiser, K., 1972: 'Zur Eigenart der römischen Komödie: Plautus und Terenz gegenüber ihren griechischen Vorbildern' in *Aufstieg und Niedergang der römischen Welt* I 2, 1027-1113 (Berlin).

Garvie, A.F., 1978: 'Aeschylus' Simple Plots', in *Dionysiaca: Nine Studies in Greek Poetry by Former Pupils Presented to Sir Denys Page on his Seventieth Birthday*, 63-86 (Cambridge and London).

Gilula, D., 1980: 'The Concept of the *bona meretrix*: a Study of Terence's Courtesans', *RFIC* 108: 142-65.

—— 1987: 'Menander's Comedies Best With Dessert and Wine (Plut. *Mor.* 712e)' [should be 712C, N.Z.], *Athenaeum* 65: 511-16.

—— 1991: 'Plots Are Not Stories: the So-called "Duality Method" of Terence' in H. Scolnicov & P. Holland (eds), *Reading Plays: Interpretation & Reception*, 81-39 (Cambridge).

Glotz, G., 1892: *Daremberg-Saglio*, vol. II 1 s.v. *Expositio* 930-9.

Goldberg, S.M., 1980: *The Making of Menander's Comedy* (London).

—— 1986: *Understanding Terence* (Princeton).

Golden, M., 1981: 'Demography and the Exposure of Girls at Athens', *Phoenix* 35: 316-31.
—— 1990: *Children and Childhood in Classical Athens* (Baltimore & London).
Gomme, A.W., 1925: 'The Position of Women in Athens in the Fifth and the Fourth Centuries BC', *CPh* 20: 1-25 = 1937: 89-115.
—— 1936: 'Notes on Menander', *CQ* 30: 64-72.
—— 1937: *Essays in Greek History and Literature* (Oxford).
—— & Sandbach, F.H., 1973: *Menander: A Commentary* (Oxford).
Görler, W., 1961: 'Menander, *Dysk.* 233-381 und Terenz, *Eun.* 817-922', *Philologus* 105: 299-307.
—— 1973: 'Über die Illusion in der antiken Komödie', *A&A* 18: 41-57.
Grant, J.N., 1986: 'The Father-Son Relationship and the Ending of Menander's *Samia*', *Phoenix* 40: 172-84.
Green, P., 1990: *Alexander to Actium: The Hellenistic Age* (London).
Gronewald, M., 1989: 'Zum Misumenos-Prolog', *ZPE* 78: 35-9.
Groton, A.H., 1987: 'Anger in Menander's *Samia*', *AJP* 108: 437-43.
Handley, E.W., 1965a: *The Dyskolos of Menander* (London).
—— 1965b: 'Notes on the *Sikyonios* of Menander', *BICS* 12: 38-62.
—— 1968: *Menander and Plautus: A Study in Comparison* (London).
—— 1970: 'The Conventions of the Comic Stage and their Exploitation by Menander', *Entretiens Fondation Hardt* XVI, *Ménandre*: 1-26.
—— 1987: 'Acts and Scenes in the Comedy of Menander', *Dioniso* 57: 299-312.
—— & Hurst, A., 1990: (eds) *Relire Ménandre* (*Recherches et Rencontres* 2; Genève).
Harris, E.M., 1990: 'Did the Athenians Regard Seduction as a Worse Crime than Rape?', *CQ* 40: 370-7.
Harris, W.V., 1982: 'The Theoretical Possibility of Extensive Infanticide in the Graeco-Roman World', *CQ* 32: 114-16.
Harrison, A.R.W., 1968: *The Law of Athens*, vol. I (Oxford).
Harsh, P.W., 1935: *Studies in Dramatic 'Preparation' in Roman Comedy* (Diss. Chicago).
Hauschild, H., 1933: *Die Gestalt der Hetäre in der griechischen Komödie* (Diss. Leipzig).
Henry, M.M., 1985: *Menander's Courtesans and the Greek Comic Tradition* (*Studien zur klassischen Philologie* 20, Frankfurt am Main, Bern & New York).
Hofmann, W. & Wartenberg, G., 1973: *Der Bramarbas in der antiken Komödie* (Berlin).
Holzberg, N., 1974: *Menander: Untersuchungen zur dramatischen Technik* (Nürnberg).
Hook, La Rue van, 1920: 'The Exposure of Infants at Athens', *TAPhA* 51: 134-45.
Hooker, G.T.W., 1958: 'The New Menander', *G&R* 5: 105-7.
Hough, J.H., 1939: 'The Understanding of Intrigue: a Study in Plautine Chronology', *AJP* 60: 422-35.
Hunter, R.L., 1979: 'The Comic Chorus in the Fourth Century', *ZPE* 36: 23-38.
—— 1980: 'Philemon, Plautus and the Trinummus', *MH* 37: 216-30.
—— 1981: 'The "Aulularia" of Plautus and its Greek Original', *PCPS* 207: 37-49.
—— 1985: *The New Comedy of Greece and Rome* (Cambridge).
—— 1987: 'Middle Comedy and the *Amphitruo* of Plautus', *Dioniso* 57: 281-98.
Hurst, A., 1990: 'Ménandre et la tragédie' in Handley-Hurst 1990: 93-122.
Ireland, S., 1983: 'Menander and the Comedy of Disappointment', *LCM* 8.3: 45-7.
Jacques, J.-M., 1971: *Ménandre*, tome I¹: *La Samienne* (Coll. Budé; Paris).
—— 1976: *Ménandre*, tome I²: *Le Dyscolos* (2nd edn, Coll. Budé; Paris).
Jarcho, V., 1983: 'Pflicht und Genuss in den ehelichen Beziehungen der alten

Athener (nach Euripides und Menander)', *Actes du VIIe Congrès de la FIEC*, vol. II: 357-73 (Budapest).

Jensen, C., 1929: (ed.) *Menandri reliquiae in papyris et membranis servatae* (Berlin).

Just, R., 1989: *Women in Athenian Law and Life* (London & New York).

Kamerbeek, J.C., 1959: 'Premières reconnaissances à travers *le Dyscolos* de Ménandre', *Mnemosyne* 12: 113-28.

Karabelias, E., 1970: 'Une nouvelle source pour l'étude du droit attique: Le "Bouclier" de Ménandre (P. Bodmer XXVI)', *RD* 48: 357-89.

Karnezis, J.E., 1977: 'Altération des institutions attiques dans le Dyscolos de Ménandre', *Athena* 76: 155-65 (sum. in French).

Kassel, R., 1965: 'Menanders Sikyonier', *Eranos* 63: 1-21 = *Kleine Schriften* 1991: 273-90.

—— 1973: 'Neuer und alter Menander', *ZPE* 12: 1-13 = *Kleine Schriften* 1991: 291-302.

—— & Austin, C., 1983– : (eds) *Poetae Comici Graeci* (Berlin & New York).

Katsouris, A., 1975: *Tragic Patterns in Menander* (*Hellenic Society for Humanistic Studies, International Centre for Classical Research*, 2nd ser.: *Studies and Researches*, 28; Athens).

—— 1976: 'The Formulaic End of the Menandrean Plays', *Dodone* 5: 243-56.

Keuls, E., 1969: 'Mystery Elements in Menander's *Dyscolos*', *TAPhA* 100: 209-20.

—— 1973: 'The Samia of Menander: an Interpretation of its Plot and Theme', *ZPE* 10: 1-20.

Konet, R.J., 1976: 'The Role of *Tuche* in Menander's *Aspis*', *CB* 52: 90-2.

Körte, A., 1937: *Die Menschen Menanders* (*Berichte über die Verhandlungen der sächsischen Akademie der Wissenschaften zu Leipzig, phil.-hist. Klasse* 89).

—— 1955: *Menandri quae supersunt, pars prior* (3rd edn, rev. by A. Thierfelder, Leipzig).

—— 1959: *Menandri quae supersunt, pars altera* (2nd edn, rev. by A. Thierfelder, Leipzig).

Kraus, W., 1960: *Menanders Dyskolos* (Wien).

—— 1968: Rev. of Schäfer 1965 in *Gnomon* 40: 337-46.

Lacey, W.K., 1968: *The Family in Classical Greece* (London).

Langen, P., 1886: *Plautinische Studien* (Berlin).

Lanowski, J., 1965: '*Kene Tragoidia* (Menander on Tragedy)', *Eos* 55: 245-53.

Leeuwen, J. van, 1919: (ed.) *Menandri Fabularum Reliquiae* (3rd edn, Leiden).

Lefkowitz, M.R., 1983: 'Wives and Husbands', *G&R* 30: 31-47 = 1986: 61-79.

—— 1986: *Women in Greek Myth* (Baltimore).

Legrand, Ph.E., 1917: *The New Greek Comedy. Komoedia Nea* (Engl. transl. J. Loeb with an introduction by J.W. White, London & New York; repr. Greenwood, 1970).

Leo, F., 1911: '*Chorou* bei Plautus', *Hermes* 46: 292-5.

—— 1912: *Plautinische Forschungen* (2nd edn, Berlin; repr. Darmstadt, 1966).

Levin, R., 1967: 'The Double Plots of Terence', *CJ* 62: 301-5.

Lloyd-Jones, H., 1966: 'Menander's *Sikyonios*', *GRBS* 7: 131-57 = 1990: 53-76.

—— 1971: 'Menander's Aspis', *GRBS* 12: 175-95 = 1990: 7-25.

—— 1972: 'Menander's *Samia* in the Light of the New Evidence', *YCS* 22: 119-44 = 1990: 31-52.

—— 1973: 'Terentian Technique in the *Adelphi* and the *Eunuchus*', *CQ* 23: 279-84 = 1990: 87-93.

—— 1974: 'Notes on Menander's *Perikeiromene*', *ZPE* 15: 209-13 = 1990: 26-30.

—— 1983: *The Justice of Zeus* (2nd edn, California; 1st edn 1971).

—— 1984: 'A Hellenistic Miscellany', *SIFC* 2: 52-72 = 1990: 231-49.
—— 1987*a*: 'Ehre und Schande in der griechischen Kultur', *A&A* 33: 1-28 = 1990: 253-80 (English).
—— 1987*b*: 'The Structure of Menander's Comedies', *Dioniso* 57: 313-21.
—— 1990: *The Academic Papers of Sir Hugh Lloyd-Jones* II: *Greek Comedy, Hellenistic Literature, Greek Religion, and Miscellanea (Oxford)*.
Lowe, J.C.B., 1983: 'The *Eunuchus*: Terence and Menander', *CQ* 33: 428-44.
—— 1985: Rev. of Primmer 1984 in *CR* 35: 396-7.
—— 1986: Rev. of Blanchard 1983 in *CR* 36: 309-10.
—— 1990: 'Plautus' Choruses', *RhM* 133: 274-97.
Lowe, N.J., 1987: 'Tragic Space and Comic Timing in Menander's *Dyskolos*', *BICS* 34: 126-38.
Ludwig, W., 1959: 'Von Terenz zu Menander', *Philologus* 103: 1-38.
—— 1961: 'Aulularia-Problem', *Philologus* 105: 44-71, 247-61.
—— 1970: 'Die plautinische Cistellaria und das Verhältnis von Gott und Handlung bei Menander', *Entretiens Fondation Hardt* XVI, *Ménandre*: 43-96.
Luria, S., 1965: 'Menander kein Peripatetiker und kein Feind der Demokratie' in Zucker 1965: 23-31.
Maas, P., 1913: 'Zu Menander', *RhM* 68: 361-2 = *Kleine Schriften* 78-80.
MacCary, W.T., 1969: 'Menander's Slaves: their Names, Roles and Masks', *TAPhA* 100: 277-94.
—— 1970: 'Menander's Characters: their Names, Roles and Masks', *TAPhA* 101: 277-90.
—— 1971: 'Menander's Old Men', *TAPhA* 102: 303-25.
—— 1972: 'Menander's Soldiers: their Names, Roles, and Masks', *AJP* 93: 279-98.
MacDowell, D.M., 1978: *The Law in Classical Athens (Aspects of Greek and Roman Life*; London).
—— 1982: 'Love Versus the Law: an Essay on Menander's *Aspis*', *G&R* 29: 42-52.
Maehler, M., 1992: 'Menander, *Misoumenos* 381-403, 404*-418*', *Oxy. Pap.*, vol. 59, no. 3967: 59-70.
Maidment, K.J., 1935: 'The Later Comic Chorus', *CQ*: 1-24.
Marti, H., 1959: *Untersuchungen zur dramatischen Technik bei Plautus und Terenz* (Diss. Winterthur).
Martin, J., 1972: *Ménandre: L'Atrabilaire* (édition, introduction et commentaire; 2nd edn, Coll. Érasme 2; Paris).
Martina, A., 1972/3: 'Aspetti sociali e giuridici nella *Samia* di Menandro', *AAT* 107: 853-940.
Marx, F., 1959: *Plautus: Rudens* (Text und Kommentar; Amsterdam).
Mette, H.J., 1969: 'Moschion *ho kosmios*', *Hermes* 97: 432-9.
Miller, N., 1987: *Menander: Plays and Fragments* (Penguin).
Murray, G., 1935: *Five Stages of Greek Religion* (London).
Nesselrath, H.G., 1985: *Lukians Parasitendialog: Untersuchungen und Kommentar (Untersuchungen zur antiken Literatur und Geschichte* 22; Berlin & New York).
—— 1990: *Die attische Mittlere Komödie: Ihre Stellung in der antiken Literaturkritik und Literaturgeschichte (Untersuchungen zur antiken Literatur und Geschichte* 36; Berlin & New York).
Neumann, M., 1958: *Die poetische Gerechtigkeit in der neuen Komödie* (Diss. Mainz).
Nilsson, M.P., 1948: *Greek Piety* (Engl. transl. H.J. Rose; Oxford).
—— 1961: *Geschichte der griechischen Religion*, vol. II (rev. München).
Nixon, P., 1916-38: *Plautus* (Loeb Classical Library) 5 vols.

Norwood, G., 1932: *Plautus and Terence* (New York).

Noy, D., 1990: 'Matchmakers and Marriage-Markets in Antiquity', *EMC* 34, n.s. 9: 375-400.

Offermann, H., 1978: 'Goldregen über Nikeratos' Haus (zu Menander Samia 589ff.)', *Philologus* 122: 150-3.

Paoli, U.E., 1950: 'Il reato di adulterio (MOIXEIA) in diritto attico', *SDHI* 16: 123ff. = 1976: 251-307.

—— 1952a: 'Note critiche e giuridiche al testo di Menandro', *Aegyptus* 32: 265-85.

—— 1952b: 'L'assentiment paternel au mariage du fils dans le droit attique', *Archives d'histoire du droit oriental et revue internationale du droit de l'antiquité* I: 267-75.

—— 1961: 'Note giuridiche sul *Dyskolos* di Menandro', *MH* 18: 53-62 = 1976: 559-70.

—— 1976: *Altri studi di diritto greco e romano* (Milano).

Pastorino, A., 1960: 'Aspetti religiosi del "Dyscolos" di Menandro' in *Menandrea: Miscellanea philologica*, 79-106 (Genova).

Patterson, C., 1985: ' "Not Worth the Rearing": the Causes of Infant Exposure in Ancient Greece', *TAPhA* 115: 103-23.

Photiades, P.J., 1958: 'Pan's Prologue to the Dyskolos of Menander', *G&R* 5: 108-22.

Pomeroy, S.B., 1975: *Goddesses, Whores, Wives, and Slaves: Women in Classical Antiquity* (New York).

—— 1983: 'Infanticide in Hellenistic Greece' in A. Cameron & A. Kuhrt (eds), *Images of Women in Antiquity*, 207-22 (London).

—— 1991: 'The Study of Women in Antiquity: Past, Present, and Future', *AJP* 112: 263-8.

Poole, M., 1978: 'Menander's Comic Use of Euripides' Tragedies', *CB* 54: 56-62.

Post, C.R., 1913: 'The Dramatic Art of Menander', *HSCP* 24: 111-45.

Post, L.A., 1940: 'Women's Place in Menander's Athens', *TAPhA* 71: 420-59.

—— 1960: 'Virtue Promoted in Menander's Dyskolos', *TAPhA* 91: 152-61.

Préaux, C., 1957: 'Ménandre et la société athénienne', *CE* 32: 84-100.

—— 1960: 'Les fonctions du droit dans la comédie nouvelle. A propos du Dyscolos de Ménandre', *CE* 35: 222-39.

Primmer, A., 1984: *Handlungsgliederung in Nea und Palliata: Dis Exapaton und Bacchides (Öst. Akad. d. Wiss. philos.-hist. Kl. Sitzungsb.* 441 Bd.; Wien).

Reinhardt, U., 1974: *Mythologische Beispiele in der neuen Komödie (Menander, Plautus, Terenz)*, Teil I (Diss. Mainz).

Roscher, W.H., *Ausführliches Lexikon der griechischen und römischen Mythologie* (Leipzig, 1884-1937; repr. Hildesheim, 1965), vol. V s.v. *Tyche* 1309-80.

Rostovzeff, M., 1941: *Social and Economic History of the Hellenistic World* (Oxford).

Rothwell, K.S., Jr., 1992: 'The Continuity of the Chorus in Fourth-Century Attic Comedy', *GRBS* 33: 209-25.

Rudd, N., 1981: 'Romantic Love in Classical Times?', *Ramus* 10: 140-58.

Sandbach, F.H., 1970: 'Menander's Manipulation of Language for Dramatic Purposes', *Entretiens Fondation Hardt* XVI, *Ménandre*: 111-36.

—— 1986: 'Two Notes on Menander (Epitrepontes and Samia)', *LCM* 11.9: 156-60.

—— 1990: *Menandri reliquiae selectae* (2nd edn, Oxford; 1st edn 1972).

Schäfer, A., 1965: *Menanders Dyskolos: Untersuchungen zur dramatischen Technik (Beiträge zur klassischen Philologie* 14; Meisenheim).

Schaps, D.M., 1981: *Economic Rights of Women in Ancient Greece* (2nd edn Edinburgh).

—— 1985-8: 'Comic Inflation in the Marketplace', *SCI* 8-9: 66-73.

Schmude, M.P., 1988: *Reden-Sachstreit-Zänkereien: Untersuchungen zu Form und Funktion verbaler Auseinandersetzungen in den Komödien des Plautus und*

Terenz (Palingenesia. Monographien und Texte zur klassischen Altertums-
wissenschaft 25; Stuttgart).

Schulze, W., 1918: 'Beiträge zur Wort- und Sittengeschichte II', SPAW: 418-51 =
Kleine Schriften 160-89.

Schwinge, E.R., 1968: (ed.) Euripides (Wege der Forschung 89; Darmstadt).

Sifakis, G.M., 1971: Parabasis and Animal Choruses: A Contribution to the History
of Attic Comedy (London).

Silk, M., 1980: 'Aristophanes as a Lyric Poet', YCS 26: 99-151.

Sisti, F., 1986: Menandro: Misumenos (edizione critica, traduzione e commento;
Genova).

Slater, N.W., 1985: Plautus in Performance: The Theatre of the Mind (Princeton).

Solmsen, F., 1932: 'Zur Gestaltung des Intrigenmotivs in den Tragödien des
Sophocles und Euripides', Philologus 87: 1-17 = 1968: 141-57 = Schwinge 1968:
326-44.

—— 1968: Kleine Schriften I (Hildesheim).

Stewart, Z., 1977: 'La religione' in R. Bianchi Bandinelli (ed.), La società ellenistica:
economia, diritto, religione (Storia e civiltà dei greci 8, 503-616; Milano).

Stoessl, F., 1960: 'Der Dyskolos des Menander', Gymnasium 67: 204-9.

Süss, W., 1910: 'Zwei Bemerkungen zur Technik der Komödie', RhM 65: 441-60.

Taplin, O., 1978: Greek Tragedy in Action (Oxford).

Tarn, W.W., 1952: Hellenistic Civilisation (3rd edn, rev. with the help of G.T.
Griffith; London).

Taubenschlag, R., 1926: 'Das attische Recht in der Komödie Menanders "Epitrepontes"', Zeitschr. d. Savigny-Stiftung für Rechtsgeschichte, röm. Abt. 46: 68-82.

Theuerkauf, A., 1960: Menanders Dyskolos als Bühnenspiel und Dichtung (Göttingen).

Thomas, R.F., 1990: 'Menander, Samia 380-3', ZPE 83: 215-18.

Treu, K., 1977: 'Aspekte Menanders: Die Polis – die Götter – das Spiel', Kairos 19:
22-34.

—— 1981: 'Menanders Menschen als Polisbürger', Philologus 125: 211-14.

Treu, M., 1960: (ed.) Menander: Dyskolos (griechisch und deutsch mit textkritis-
chem Apparat und Erläuterungen herausgegeben; München).

—— 1969: 'Humane Handlungsmotive in der Samia Menanders', RhM 112: 230-54.

Turner, E.G., 1959/60: 'New Plays of Menander', BRL 42: 241-58.

—— 1979a: The Lost Beginning of Menander, Misoumenos (London, British Acad-
emy) = PBA 63 (1977): 315-31.

—— 1979b: 'Menander and the New Society of his Time', CE 54: 106-26 = Actes du
VIIe Congrès de la Fédération Internationale des Associations d'Études clas-
siques, vol. I, 1984: 243-59 (Budapest).

Vicenzi, O., 1962: 'Der Dyskolos des Menander: Versuch einer Strukturanalyse',
Gymnasium 69: 406-26.

Vogt, E., 1959: 'Ein stereotyper Dramenschluss der Nea', RhM 102: 192.

Vogt-Spira, G., 1992: Dramaturgie des Zufalls: Tyche und Handeln in der Komödie
Menanders (Zetemata 88; München).

Walcot, P., 1987: 'Romantic Love and True Love: Greek Attitudes to Marriage',
Ancient Society 18: 5-33.

Webster, T.B.L., 1956: Greek Theatre Production (London).

—— 1960: Studies in Menander (2nd edn, Manchester).

—— 1962/3: 'Menander: Production and Imagination', BRL 45: 235-72.

—— 1970: Studies in Later Greek Comedy (2nd edn, Manchester).

—— 1974: An Introduction to Menander (Manchester).

Wehrli, F., 1936: Motivstudien zur griechischen Komödie (Zürich & Leipzig).

Weill, N., 1970: 'La fête d'Adonis dans la *Samienne* de Ménandre', *BCH* 94: 591-3.
Weiss, E., 1921: *RE* vol. XI.1, s.v. *Kinderaussetzung* 463-71.
West, St., 1991: 'Notes on the Samia', *ZPE* 88: 11-23.
Wilamowitz-Moellendorff, U. von, 1932: *Der Glaube der Hellenen*, vol. II (Berlin).
Wiles, D., 1984: 'Menander's *Dyskolos* and Demetrios of Phaleron's Dilemma: a Study of the Play in its Historical Context – the Trial of Phokion, the Ideals of a Moderate Oligarch, and the Rancour of the Disfranchized', *G&R* 31: 170-80.
—— 1989: 'Marriage and Prostitution in Classical New Comedy', *Themes in Drama* 11: *Women in Theatre*: 31-48. (Cambridge).
Williams, Th., 1961: 'On Antinoopolis Papyrus 55: Fragments of New Comedy', *RhM* 105: 193-225.
Wolff, H.J., 1944: 'Marriage Law and Family Organization in Ancient Athens: a Study on the Interpretation of Public and Private Law in the Greek City', *Traditio* II: 43-93.
—— 1957: *RE* vol. XXIII.1, s.v. *proix* 133-70.
Zagagi, N., 1979: 'Sostratos as a Comic, Over-active and Impatient Lover: On Menander's Dramatic Art in his Play Dyskolos', *ZPE* 36: 39-48.
—— 1980: *Tradition and Originality in Plautus: Studies of the Amatory Motifs in Plautine Comedy* (*Hypomnemata* 62; Göttingen).
—— 1981: 'Plautus, *Cist*. 231-49: Dialogue-Scene Substituted by Plautus for New Comedy Monologue?', *CJ* 76: 312-17.
—— 1988: '*Exilium amoris* in New Comedy', *Hermes* 116: 193-209.
—— 1990: 'Divine Interventions and Human Agents in Menander' in Handley-Hurst 1990: 63-91.
—— 1991: Rev. of Schmude 1988 in *Gnomon* 63: 13-16.
Zucker, F., 1965: (ed.) *Menanders Dyskolos als Zeugnis seiner Epoche* (Berlin).

A well-arranged list of editions of the main texts of Menander and of bibliographies devoted to him before and after 1958 will be found in the Loeb edition (Arnott 1979*b*): xlvii-lii.

Index of Passages Discussed

See also under individual play titles and names of ancient authors in the Subject Index. Reference to notes is not made where a discussion can be found through the main text. Numbers in **bold** type refer to the pages of this book.

* indicates where textual questions are treated.

Subject Index